CADOGAN

Rome Naples
Sorrento

Cadogan Guides
West End House, 11 Hills Place, London W1R 1AH
becky.kendall@morrispub.co.uk

The Globe Pequot Press
6 Business Park Road, PO Box 833, Old Saybrook,
Connecticut 06475–0833

Copyright © Dana Facaros and Michael Pauls 1999
Updated by Kicca Tommasi and Jon Eldan
Illustrations © Horatio Monteverde 1996

Book and cover design by Animage

Cover photographs © Kicca Tommasi

Maps © Cadogan Guides, drawn by Map Creation Ltd

Editorial Director: Vicki Ingle
Series Editor: Linda McQueen

Editor: Kate Paice
Proofreading: Linda McQueen
Indexing: Isobel McLean
Production: Book Production Services

A catalogue record for this book is available from the British Library
ISBN 1-86011-960-3

Printed and bound in Great Britain by Cambridge University Press

About the Authors

Dana Facaros and Michael Pauls have now written over 30 Cadogan Guides. For three years they and their two children Jackson and Lily lived in a tiny Umbrian hilltop village, then an equally remote French village in the Lot. They now live in Ireland.

About the Updaters

Jon Eldan studied history and baked bread in Berkeley, California before travelling to Europe in 1994, where he met Carla Lionello (a pastry chef from Venice) in a restaurant kitchen. They live in Rome and travel together.

Kicca Tommasi thinks her country is the best in the world. With typical Italian consistency, she has chosen to live in London where her time is jostled between design, photography and Argentinian tango.

Acknowledgements

A big thank you from the authors to Jon and Kicca for their updating and Kate for her editing.

Please help us to keep this guide up to date

We have done our best to ensure that the information in this guide is correct at the time of going to press. But places and facilities are constantly changing, and standards and prices in hotels and restaurants fluctuate. We would be delighted to receive any comments concerning existing entries or omissions, as well as suggestions for new features. Authors of the most helpful letters may be offered a copy of the Cadogan Guide of their choice.

Contents

Rome

Naples

Vesuvius and the Ancient Cities

Maps and Plans

Introduction

In the time of the Caesars, this area was the nerve centre of an empire. Not only Rome itself, but also the sublime coast around the bay of Naples, the favourite resort of the movers and shakers, a glittery place of volcanic spas, lavish villas and gardens and a climate sweeter than Rome's. It was the equivalent of a California lying just a short hop south of Washington and New York, a unique combination of power and wealth in a setting of astonishing natural beauty.

But in AD 79 the eruption of Vesuvius put paid to the flourishing commerce and agriculture of Pompeii, Herculaneum and surroundings, and exacerbated the economic decline of the south. Then Rome itself staggered and fell, and dragged everything down with it, though never as completely as is popularly supposed. It muddled through the Dark Ages, with its popes and gangster nobility, while Naples and Sorrento emerged as feudal dukedoms. Amalfi blossomed early in the 9th century as one the first of Italy's medieval maritime republics; and there then came a strange interlude of Normans and Angevins and Spaniards, before Naples became the seat of its own kingdom of southern Italy, while the popes became the temporal rulers of much of Central Italy. The Papal-Spanish-Neapolitan alliance would bedevil Italy and Europe for three centuries, reviving the Inquisition while impoverishing their respective states, but leaving Rome and Naples a legacy of lavish baroque churches, palaces, gardens and *piazze* that are among their chief glories today.

The combination of marbled grandeur and gilded frippery, romantic ruins, picturesque decadence and sensual pleasures made Rome and Naples the highlights of the 18th-century Grand Tour. The excavations of ancient treasures, most spectacularly the digs at Pompeii, begun in 1748, were a perennial source of interest, especially in the days when newly unearthed statues went to the highest bidders. Many foreigners fell under the spell of the *dolce vita* and never left—Sorrento became a cosy British expat colony, Capri attracted the wealthy and the crackpot, Rome the pious and poetic, while Naples provided a stage for the antics of Lord and Lady Hamilton.

Today, the same sirens sing, and Naples, although in the throes of a facelift, can still come up with pockets of picturesque decadence and total anarchy if that's what you're looking for. At the time of writing Rome is bracing itself for the Jubilee of 2000 and an expected 25 million pilgrims, offering the chance to combine piety with self-indulgence. Together, Rome and Naples offer a perfect balanced diet for an Italian holiday: a look at splendid Roman (and even some ancient Greek) ruins, museums of ancient art and baroque painting, along with a gorgeous stretch of Mediterranean coastline, a tour of the big volcano, and the best pizza in the world.

Guide to the Guide

Whether you want to soak up the atmosphere of an exciting city break, to delve into the wealth of remains from Italy's astonishing past or simply to relax in the perfect holiday atmosphere, Rome, Naples and the area round Sorrento are ideal bases for your travels.

The **Travel** and **Practical A–Z** sections will help you get to and around Italy and choose the right sort of place to stay. The **History and Art** and **Snapshots** chapters give you historical, cultural and social background to Rome, Naples and the area around the Bay.

The glorious cities of **Rome** and **Naples** have a chapter apiece, with specific backgrounds on history and art, and all the sights you might choose to visit. The next chapter covers the ancient sites in the volcanic area around Naples, among them **Cumae**, **Herculaneum** and **Pompeii**, with full historical and artistic details. The guide moves on to the rest of the bay: the charming resort town of **Sorrento**, the historic pleasure island of **Capri** and the stunning Amalfi Drive, from **Positano** to once-great **Amalfi** and charming **Salerno**. Each chapter has a practical guide to where to stay and eating out, shopping, nightlife and activities.

Finally, there is a section of historic and artistic **terms**, and a full **language** chapter with pronunciation advice, useful phrases and a detailed menu reader; as well as a list of suggestions for **further reading**.

Travel

By Air

From the UK and Ireland

Rome has an excellent choice of year-round flights. You can fly to **Naples** from London, and Manchester or Glasgow in the summer; only a few carriers fly there, so tickets can be more expensive and availability limited. Try **Alitalia**, London (flights to Naples via Milan and Rome from around £200), ℡ (020) 7602 7111, Dublin, ℡ (01) 844 6035; **British Airways** (direct flights to Naples), ℡ (0345) 222 111; **KLM** (Stansted to Rome from £155 plus tax), ℡ (0870) 5 074 074; **Aer Lingus**, Dublin, ℡ (01) 705 3333, or Belfast, ℡ (0645) 737 747. Scheduled services are usually more expensive than charters, and cheaper if you fly over a Saturday night. **Go**, ℡ (0845) 605 4321, a branch of BA, is a low-cost airline with cheap twice-daily flights between Stansted and Rome (14 times a week from around £120 return).

London is a great centre for discounted flights, and you should find a good deal. An off-peak return to Naples can cost as little as £155; contact an ABTA-registered agent, who won't leave you stranded. **APEX** or **SuperAPEX** fares can be excellent value; you have to book seven days ahead and stay a Saturday night, and they are usually unchangeable and non-refundable. **British Airways** have scheduled APEX fares to Naples, with two direct services daily from Gatwick, flying out and returning mid-week, currently around £250 in high season.

charter flights

Many inexpensive charter flights are available in summer. Look at the small ads in the travel pages, or in the classified sections of the weekend newspapers (in London, get *Time Out* or other listings magazines, and the *Evening Standard*). Or try a specialist agent (use an ABTA-registered one); they offer good student and youth rates. The main problems with cheaper flights tend to be inconvenient or unreliable flight schedules, and booking restrictions. Take good travel insurance. Peak seasons are Christmas, Easter and summer, when there are generally at least a couple of flights a day from London (book well ahead).

discount agencies and youth fares

Italflights, 125 High Holborn, London WC1V 6QA, ℡ (020) 7405 6771.

Italia Nel Mondo, 6 Palace Street, London SW1E 5HY, ℡ (020) 7828 9171.

Italy Sky Shuttle, 227 Shepherd's Bush Road, London W6 7NL, ℡ (020) 8748 1333.

Italy Sky Bus, 37 Harley Street, London W1N 1DB, ℡ (020) 7631 3444.

Trailfinders, 194 Kensington High Street, London W8 6BD, ℡ (020) 7938 3232.

Budget Travel, 134 Lower Baggot Street, Dublin 2, ℡ (01) 661 1866.

United Travel, Stillorgan Bowl, Stillorgan, County Dublin, ℡ (01) 288 4346/7.

Besides saving 25 per cent on regular flights, young people under 26 have the choice of flying on special discount charters.

Campus Travel, 52 Grosvenor Gardens, London SW1, or 174 Kensington High Street, London W8, ℡ (020) 7730 3402; also branches at most UK universities, including Bristol, ℡ (0117) 929 2494; Manchester, ℡ (0161) 833 2046; Edinburgh, ℡ (0131) 668 3303; or see the website at *www.campustravel.co.uk.*

STA, 74 and 86 Old Brompton Road, London SW7, or 117 Euston Road, London NW1, ✆ (0171) 937 9921; other branches include Bristol, ✆ (0117) 929 4399; Leeds, ✆ (0113) 244 9212; Manchester, ✆ (0161) 834 0668.

USIT, Aston Quay, Dublin 2, ✆ (01) 679 8833; Cork, ✆ (021) 270 900; Galway, ✆ (091) 565 177; Limerick, ✆ (061) 415 064; Belfast, ✆ (01232) 324 073.

Europe Student Travel, 6 Campden Street, London W8, ✆ (020) 7727 7647 (catering to non-students as well).

Some of the best bargains of all are posted on the **Internet**. Try *www.lastminute.com* (flights to Edinburgh from £50 return) or *www.travelocity.com*.

From Mainland Europe

Air travel between Italy and other parts of Europe can be pricey: it's worth checking overland options unless you're in a great hurry. Shop around, and consider travelling with a less prestigious carrier. Some airlines (**Alitalia, Qantas, Air France**, etc.) offer excellent rates on the European legs of intercontinental flights; Italy is an important touchdown for many longhaul services to the Middle or Far East. (These may have inconvenient departure times and booking restrictions.) Amsterdam, Paris and Athens are good centres for finding cheap flights.

From the USA and Canada

The main Italian gateways for direct flights from North America are Rome and Milan, from where you can travel on southwards by air or by train; Alitalia (US ✆ (800) 223 5730, Canada ✆ (800) 563 5954) has the most options. Or it might be worth taking a cheap flight to London and flying on from there. **Delta**, ✆ (800) 241 414. **TWA**, ✆ (800) 892 4141. **British Airways**, ✆ (800) 247 9297, fly from a number of cities. **Air Canada**, ✆ (800) 555 1212, and **KLM**, ✆ (800) 361 5330, operate from Toronto and Montreal.

charters, discounts and special deals

From North America standard scheduled flights on well-known airlines are expensive but reliable and convenient: older travellers or families may prefer to pay extra for such a long journey (9–15 hours' flying time). Resilient, flexible and/or youthful travellers may wish to shop around for budget deals on consolidated charters, stand-bys or even courier flights (you can usually only take hand luggage with you on these). Check the *Yellow Pages* for courier companies. For discounted flights, try the small ads in newspaper travel pages (e.g. *New York Times, Chicago Tribune, Toronto Globe & Mail*). Numerous travel clubs and agencies also specialize in discount fares, but may require an annual membership fee.

Airhitch, 2472 Broadway Suite 200, New York, NY 10025, ✆ (212) 864 2000.

Council Travel, 205 E 42nd Street, New York, NY 10017, ✆ (800) 743 1823.

Last Minute Travel Club, 132 Brookline Avenue, Boston, MA 02215, ✆ (800) 527 8646.

Now Voyager, 74 Varick Street, Suite 307, New York, NY 10013, ✆ (212) 431 1616; for courier flights.

STA Travel, 48 East 11th Street, New York, NY 10003, ✆ (212) 627 3111; or toll-free, ✆ (800) 777 0112.

Travel Cuts, 187 College Street, Toronto, Ontario M5T 1P7, ✆ (416) 979 2406; Canada's largest student travel specialists; branches in most provinces.

Rail travel is scarcely cheaper than flying unless you take advantage of student or youth fares. You can travel by train and ferry from London to **Rome** in 24 hours for around £210 second-class return plus £10 for a couchette. Or you can take a Eurostar to Paris and a high-speed train to Italy, which takes about 12 hours, but costs around £550. From London to **Naples** takes about 31 hours. Naples is a major rail hub and many services from the northern cities terminate here, rather than in Rome. There are hourly trains from Rome to Naples (journey time about 2½ hours), and you can get a train from the airport without going into the city.

Interail (UK) or **Eurail** passes (USA/Canada) give unlimited travel for under-26s throughout Europe for one or two months. Various other cheap youth fares (BIJ tickets etc.) are also available; organize these before you leave home. If you will only be travelling within Italy, one of the special Italian tourist passes may be a better bet (*see* 'Getting Around'): fares on FS (*Ferrovie dello Stato*), the Italian state railway, are among the lowest in Europe. You can pick up the Italian rail timetable (two volumes) at any station in Italy for about L4,500 each.

Rail Europe Travel Centre, (UK) 179 Piccadilly, London W1, ✆ (08705) 848 848; (USA) 226–30 Westchester Ave, White Plains, NY 10604, ✆ (914) 682 2999, or ✆ (800) 438 7245.

Eurostar, EPS House, Waterloo Station, London SE1, ✆ (0345) 881 881.

International Rail Centre, London Victoria Station, adjacent to Platform 2.

Eurotrain, 52 Grosvenor Gardens, London SW1, ✆ (020) 7730 8518.

Wasteels Travel, (UK) London Victoria Station, by Platform 2, ✆ (020) 7834 7066; (USA) 5728 Major Boulevard, Suite 308, Orlando, FL 32819, ✆ (407) 351 2537.

Accommodation Line Ltd, 11–12 Hanover Square, London W1, sell a pocket-sized Italian rail timetable (£6 plus 50p postage).

It may also be worth consulting **CIT** (the Italian state-run travel agency) before travelling. **UK**: Marco Polo House, 3–5 Lansdowne Road, Croydon, Surrey, CR9 1LL, ✆ (020) 8686 0677. **USA**: 15 West 44th Street, Fifth Floor, New York, NY 10036, ✆ (800) 248 7245. **Canada**: 1450 City Councillors Street, Suite 750, Montreal H3A 2E6, ✆ (514) 845 4310.

By Road

by bus and coach

Regular services run to many northern Italian cities but terminate at Rome, so you will have to change there. The journey is long and excruciatingly uncomfortable, and the small savings on price make it a masochistic choice in comparison with a discounted air fare, or even rail travel. **Eurolines**, London Victoria Coach Station, ✆ (0990) 808 080, are booked in the UK through National Express (return ticket London–Rome £125, London–Naples £141). Within Italy, you can obtain information on long-distance bus services from any CIT office.

by car

Italy is the best part of 24 hours' drive from the UK, even on fast toll roads. The most scenic and hassle-free route is via the Alps, but expect to pay around £14 (30SFr) for motorway use. In winter the passes may be closed and you will have to use the expensive tunnels (one-way tolls from about L37,000 for a small car). Avoid some driving by putting your car on the train: **Express Sleeper Cars** run to Milan from Paris or Boulogne (infrequently in winter). The **Italian Auto Club** (ACI), ✆ 06 44 77, offers reasonably priced breakdown assistance.

To bring a GB-registered car into Italy, you need a **vehicle registration document, full driving licence** and **insurance papers** (these must be carried at all times when driving). Non-EU citizens should preferably have an **international driving licence** which has an Italian translation incorporated. Your vehicle should display a nationality plate indicating its country of registration. Before travelling, check everything is in perfect order; minor infringements like worn tyres or burnt-out sidelights can cost you dear. A **red triangular hazard sign** is obligatory; also recommended are a spare set of bulbs, a first-aid kit and a fire extinguisher. Spare parts for non-Italian cars can be difficult to find, especially Japanese models. Before crossing the Italian border, remember to fill up; *benzina* is still expensive in Italy.

For more information on driving in Italy contact the **AA**, ✆ (0990) 500 600, or **RAC**, ✆ (0800) 550 550 in the UK, and **AAA**, ✆ (407) 444 4000, in the USA.

By Ferry

A whirl of ferries and hydrofoils connects Naples with resorts further down the coast and the islands in the Bay. **Siremar** and **Tirrenia** are the main long-distance ferry companies operating from Naples (also *see* p.111).

Entry Formalities

EU nationals with a valid passport can stay in Italy for as long as they like. Citizens of the **US, Canada, Australia** and **New Zealand** need only a valid passport to stay up to three months, unless they get a visa in advance from an Italian embassy or consulate:

UK, 38 Eaton Place, London SW1, ✆ (020) 7235 9371; 32 Melville Street, Edinburgh EH3 7HA, ✆ (0131) 226 3631; 111 Piccadilly, Manchester M1 2HY, ✆ (0161) 236 9024.

Ireland, 63–65 Northumberland Road, Dublin 4, ✆ (01) 660 744; 7 Richmond Park, Belfast BT9 5EF, ✆ (01232) 668 854.

USA, 690 Park Avenue, New York, NY, ✆ (212) 737 9100; 12400 Wilshire Boulevard, Suite 300, Los Angeles CA, ✆ (213) 820 0622.

Canada, 136 Beverley Street, Toronto, ✆ (416) 977 1566.

Australia, Level 45, The Gateway Building, Macquarie Place, Circular Quay, Sydney 2000, NSW, ✆ (02) 247 8442.

New Zealand, 34 Grant Road, Thorndon, Wellington, ✆ (04) 7473 5339.

EU nationals over 17 can import limitless goods for personal use. Non-EU nationals must pass through Italian Customs. You can bring in 200 cigarettes or 100 cigars, a litre of hard drink or three bottles of wine, a couple of cameras, a movie camera, 10 rolls of film for each, a tape-recorder, radio, sports equipment for personal use, and one TV (though you'll have to pay for a licence for it at Customs). Pets must be accompanied by a bilingual Certificate of Health from your local Veterinary Inspector. You can take these items home without hassle, except of course a British pet. US citizens may bring back $400 worth of merchandise—keep receipts.

There are no limits to how much money you bring into Italy: legally you may not export more than L20,000 000 in Italian banknotes, though officials rarely check.

A selection of specialist companies are listed below. Not all of them are necesssarily ABTA-bonded; we recommend you check before booking.

in the UK

Cresta Holidays, Holiday House, Victoria Street, Altrincham, Cheshire WA14 1ET, ✆ (0161) 927 7000. Package holidays and tours.

Magic of Italy, 227 Shepherd's Bush Road, London W6 7AS, ✆ (020) 8748 2661. Stylish city breaks in luxury hotels, self-catering villas and converted farmhouses.

Abercrombie & Kent, Sloane Square House, Holbein Place, London SW1W 8NS, ✆ (020) 7730 9600. City breaks.

Brompton Travel, Brompton House, 64 Richmond Road, Kingston-upon-Thames, Surrey KT2 5EH, ✆ (020) 8549 3334. Tailor-made trips, city breaks and specialized opera tours; also package holidays etc.

Citalia, Marco Polo House, 3–5 Lansdowne Road, Croydon CR9 1LL, ✆ (020) 8686 5533. Opera tours etc.

Kirker, 3 New Concordia Wharf, Mill Street, London SE1 2BB, ✆ (020) 7231 3333. Cty breaks and tailor-made tours; can arrange internal rail travel and any length of stay.

Martin Randall Travel, 10 Barley Mow Passage, Chiswick, London W4 4PH, ✆ (020) 8742 3355. Tailor-made cultural tours for groups of up to 22 focusing on art, architecture, wines, gardens and music, with expert guides.

Andante Travels, The Old Telephone Exchange, Winterborne Dauntsey, Salisbury SP4 6EH, ✆ (01980) 610 555. Archaeological sites, art and architecture.

Camper & Nicholsons, 25 Bruton Street, London W1X 7DB, ✆ (020) 7491 2950. Specialist yacht charters for motor and sailing boats.

Italiatour, Unit 9, Whyteleafe Business Village, Whyteleafe Hill, Surrey CR3 0AT, ✆ (01883) 623 363. All-inclusive seven night package tours to Sorrento.

Prospect Music & Art, 36 Manchester Street, London W1M 5PE, ✆ (020) 7486 5705, ✉ (0171) 486 5868. Lavish week-long guided art, architecture, music and archaeology tours focusing on Rome (Ancient and Renaissance Rome) and the classical antiquities of Naples, Pompeii, Mount Vesuvius and Capri.

Travel for the Arts, 117 Regent's Park Road, London NW1 8UR, ✆ (020) 7483 4466. Mix of music and opera tours and tailor-made package tours.

Alternative Travel, 69–71 Banbury Road, Oxford OX2 6PE, ✆ (01865) 310399. Guided walking and cycling tours near Rome.

Arblaster & Clarke, 104 Church Road, Steep, Petersfield, Hants GU32 2PD, ✆ (01730) 893 344. Lavish wine and gourmet tours, staying in five-star hotels.

British Museum Tours, 46 Bloomsbury Street, London WC1B 3QQ, ✆ (020) 7323 8895. Specialist tours in art, architecture, history and archaeology led by curators from the museum. Three- and four-star hotels.

Gordon Overland, 76 Croft Road, Carlisle, Cumbria CA3 9AG, ✆ (01228) 526 795. Annual month-long Italian language, history, music and art workshops; mainly for retired people.

JMB, Rushwick, Worcester WR2 5SN, ✆ (01905) 425 628. Opera holidays in Rome.

First Choice, 2nd Floor, Astral Towers, Betts Way, Crawley, West Sussex, ✆ (0161) 745 7000. Wide range of good value package tours.

Special Tours, 81a Elizabeth Street, London SW1W 9PG, ✆ (020) 7730 2297. Escorted cultural tours run by small private travel company for National Art Collections Fund members.

Venice Simplon-Orient Express, Suite 200, Hudson's Place, Victoria Station, London SW1V 1JL, ✆ (020) 7928 6000. Luxury rail tours.

Wallace Arnold, Gelderd Road, Leeds LS12 6DH, ✆ (01132) 310 739. Coach tours.

in the USA/Canada

American Express Vacations, 300 Pinnacle Way, Norcross, GA 30093, ✆ (800) 241 1700. Prepacked or tailor-made tours.

Archaeological Tours Inc., Suite 904271, Madison Avenue, New York, NY 11116, ✆ (212) 986 3054. Rome and southern Italy.

Connaissance & Cie, 790 Madison Ave, New York, NY 10021, ✆ (212) 472 5772. Wine.

Dailey-Thorp Travel, 330 West 58th Street, New York, NY 10019, ✆ (212) 307 1555. Music and opera.

Italiatour, 666 5th Avenue, New York, NY 10103, ✆ (212) 765 2183. Fly-drive.

Esplanade Tours, 581 Boyston Street, Boston, MA 02116, ✆ (617) 266 7465. Art and architecture.

Maupintour, 1515 St Andrew's Drive, Lawrence, KS 66047, ✆ (785) 843 1211.

Olson Travelworld, 970 West 190th Street, Suite 425, Torrance, CA 90502, ✆ (310) 546 8400.

Stay and Visit Italy, 5506 Connecticut Avenue NW, Suite 28, Washington, DC 20015, ✆ (202) 237 5220/✆ (800) 411 3728, 📠 (202) 966 6972. Tours of Campania.

Getting Around

Italy has an excellent network of airports, railways and roads and you'll find getting around fairly easy—until one union or another goes on strike (to be fair they rarely do it during the high holiday season, but learn to recognize the word in Italian: *sciopero* (SHO-per-o), and do as the Romans do—quiver with resignation). There's always a day or two's notice, and strikes usually last only a day, just long enough to throw a spanner in the works if you have to catch a plane. Keep your ears open and watch for notices posted in the stations.

By Air

Air traffic within Italy is intense, with up to ten flights a day on popular routes. Domestic flights are handled by Alitalia, ATI (its internal arm) or Avianova. Air travel makes most sense between north and south. Shorter journeys are often just as quick (and much less expensive) by train or even bus if you include check-in and airport travelling times. Domestic flight costs are comparable to those in other European countries, and a complex system of discounts is available (some only at certain times of year). Each airport has a bus terminal in the city; ask about schedules as you purchase your ticket to avoid hefty taxi fares. Baggage allowances vary between airlines. Tickets can be bought at CIT offices and other large travel agencies.

By Sea

A complex network of ferries and hydrofoils links **Naples** with the islands in the bay and several further afield (Sardinia, Malta, Corsica, Sicily), and other resorts down the coast. In summer, up to six ferries and 20 hydrofoils run to Capri. Services for Capri and Sorrento depart from the Molo Beverello in Naples. Hydrofoils also serve the bay islands from Mergellina in the western suburb of Naples. Ferries are cheaper than the faster hydrofoils, and less affected by rough weather. The daily newspaper, *Il Mattino*, lists timetables.

In addition, there are ferries and hydrofoils daily from **Sorrento** to Capri. You can usually buy tickets when you turn up at the port; return tickets don't generally offer any savings.

By Rail

FS train information: ✆ 1478 888 088 (open 7am–9pm); *www.fs-on-line.com*.

Italy's national railway, the **FS** (*Ferrovie dello Stato*), is well-run, inexpensive and often a pleasure to ride. Possible unpleasantnesses, besides strikes, are delays, crowding (especially at weekends and in the summer), and crime on overnight trains, where someone rifles your bags as you sleep. Reserve a seat in advance (*fare una prenotazione*): the small fee can save hours standing in a corridor. On more expensive trains, and for sleepers and couchettes on overnight trains, **reservations** are mandatory. When buying tickets in advance, check the date is correct; tickets are only valid the day they're bought unless you specify otherwise.

It is easier to buy tickets at a travel agent in a city centre. Fares are strictly determined by the kilometres travelled. The system is computerized and runs smoothly, at least until you try to get reimbursed for an unused ticket (usually not worth it). Ask which platform (*binario*) your train arrives at; the boards in the stations are not always correct. Always stamp your ticket (*convalidare*) in the not-very-obvious yellow machines at the head of the platform before boarding the train. Failure to do so could result in a fine. If you get on a train without a ticket you can buy one from the conductor, with a 20 per cent penalty. You can also pay a conductor to move up to first class or get a couchette, if there are places available.

There is a fairly straightforward **hierarchy of trains**. At the bottom is the sometimes excruciatingly slow *Locale* (euphemistically known sometimes as an *Accelerato*) which often stops even with no station in sight. When you're checking the schedules, beware of taking the first train to your destination—if it's a *Locale*, it will be the last to arrive. A *Diretto* stops far less, an *Expresso* just at the main towns. *Intercity* trains whoosh between the big cities and rarely deign to stop. *Eurocity* trains link Italian cities with major European centres. Both of these services require a supplement—some 30 per cent more than a regular fare. The *ETR 500 pendolino* trains, similar to the French TGV, can travel at up to 186mph. Reservations are free, but must be made at least five hours before the trip; some trains have only first-class coaches. The super-swish, super-fast *Eurostars* make very few stops, have both first- and second-class carriages, and carry a supplement which includes an obligatory seat reservation.

The FS offers several **passes**. The 'Flexi Card' ('Freedom Pass' in the UK) allows unlimited travel for 4, 8 or 12 days within a month (L206,000, L287,000 or L368,000, plus seat reservations and supplements on Eurostars). The *Kilometrico* allows 3,000km of travel, made on a maximum of 20 journeys, and is valid for two months (second class L206,000, first class L338,000); it can be used by up to five people at once; supplements are payable on *Intercity* trains. Other discounts are available for day returns, families, senior citizens and under-26s.

Refreshments on routes of any great distance are provided by bar cars or trolleys; you can usually get sandwiches and coffee from vendors along the tracks at intermediary stops. Station bars often have a good variety of take-away travellers' fare; consider at least investing in a plastic bottle of mineral water, since there's no drinking water on the trains.

Most stations have a *deposito*, where you can leave your bags for hours or days for a small fee. Larger ones have **porters** (who charge L1,000–1,500 per piece) and some have luggage trolleys; major stations have an *albergo diurno* ('day hotel', for a shower, shave and haircut), information offices, currency exchanges open at weekends (not at great rates), hotel-finding and reservation services, kiosks with foreign papers, restaurants, etc. You can have a rental car awaiting you—Avis, Hertz, Aurotrans and Maggiore are the most widespread firms.

In **Rome**, most trains arrive and depart from **Termini Station** (Piazza dei Cinquecento), chaotic, but modern and efficiently run. The rail information booth is usually very crowded, but you can try to find times and destinations (within Italy) on one of the multilingual computer screens in the lobby. Watch out for thieves. There is a taxi stand in front, car hire booths, buses to most points in Rome from Piazza dei Cinquecento, and two underground stations. The left luggage (L5,000 per item for 12 hours) is along the first track, on the far left of the station. There are two international telephone offices, one in the lobby and one downstairs, a post office, several bars (the food is terrible; the bar downstairs is less nerve-racking), pharmacy, currency exchange, etc. Rome's other stations are **Tiburtina** on the eastern edge of town, ✆ 06 4424 5104; **Ostiense**, ✆ 06 575 0732; and **Trastevere**. Some north-south trains only stop at Tiburtina (and occasionally Trastevere) so check the timetables carefully. There is also a private railway, **Roma Nord**, with trains to Viterbo from Piazza Flaminia.

Naples, the main rail hub for southern Italy, is served by a full range of trains. From the centre (the main station is **Stazione Centrale**), funiculars, national and local lines straggle down the coast to Sorrento and beyond via Pompeii and Herculaneum. The state-run (FS) line offers a fast service between Naples and Salerno; for other coastal destinations, you will probably rely on local rail systems. For coastal journeys, the **Circumvesuviana** trundles round the Bay of Naples every half-hour or so from dawn till quite late, stopping just about everywhere. The Neapolitan terminus is on Corso Garibaldi; trains also stop at Stazione Centrale (on underground platforms). Main lines run east via Ercolano, then diverge, passing Pompeii on opposite sides. One line takes you to Sorrento (about an hour), the other to Sarno, east of Vesuvius. To get to Positano, Amalfi, Ravello, etc. it's best to take a bus.

If you're heading westwards from Naples, the Naples underground or **Metropolitana** crosses the city centre and ends up at Pozzuoli-Solfatara (30mins). The **Ferrovia Cumana** (along the coast) and the **Circumflegrea** (via Cumae) take you as far as Torregaveta.

The Italian bus system is not easy. Indications of destination and departure point are often mystifying; ask before you get on. Buy tickets in advance from tobacconists, news-stands or ticket booths at the bus stations, and validate them on the bus by punching them in the machine (you can be heavily fined for travelling without one, or with an unvalidated ticket).

Rome's orange ATAC buses and trams are the best way to get around, though the complex route system is intimidating, and until you're reasonably familiar with the city, the destinations listed on the signs can seem meaningless. If you're staying for any time it's well worth spending L8,000 on the *Roma Metro-Bus* route map, which has a comprehensive list of all routes, as well as a directory of streets listing the buses that run along them. All the news-stands at Termini sell it. Most routes run quite frequently, and most are crowded. Tickets are L1,500 and are valid for 75 minutes (during which time you can hop on and off as many buses as you want). If you reckon you'll use more than two buses or metros a day, it's worth investing in a 7-day tourist ticket valid for all the lines (L24,000), available from the **ATAC information booths** in front of Termini Station or on Piazza Risorgimento. The 'Big' is a one-day pass for L6,000, available from information kiosks and tobacconists; a monthly pass, valid from the first of each month, is L50,000 for all lines. For information, ✆ 06 4695 4444.

The main bus station in **Naples** is just in front of the central railway station. Many buses are run by the **Naples Public Transport Board**, ✆ 081 700 1111, which has information offices in Piazza Garibaldi. There are regular services to Salerno (**SITA**, ✆ 081 552 2176). **Curreri**, ✆ 081 801 5420, runs a useful service from Capodichino airport to Sorrento. Buses are the best way to get around the islands in the bay. The Circumvesuviana railway is generally more obvious for east bay destinations like Pompeii, but you can take buses too. In Naples you might want to invest in the travel pass called 'Giranapoli' (*see* p.113).

Buses come into their own on the **Amalfi coast**, which is not served by rail. SITA services run every 50mins between Sorrento and Salerno . Buy tickets in advance in bars or shops bearing the SITA sign, or from the terminus depots.

By Car

If you're planning a tour of the cities, you'll be better off not driving at all: parking is impossible, traffic impossible, deciphering one-way streets, signals and signs impossible. Much of Rome is closed to unauthorized traffic. A car is sheer hell in Naples, whether moving or stationary (*see* p.114); if you must bring one in, leave it in a guarded parking lot, with no valuables inside. On the streets, if the thieves don't get it a tow-truck may—don't leave it in a *Zona Rimozione*. Driving isn't much fun in any place of more than 10,000 people, expect solid traffic jams from about 11am to 2pm, and in the evening from about 5 until 10 or 11. If you must drive in or out of a town, try to do it at night, or when the Italians are eating.

However, if you're touring the surrounding countryside a car undoubtedly gives immeasurable freedom and is certainly the most convenient way to get to the more remote parts.

Third-party insurance is a minimum requirement in Italy (and you should be a lot more than minimally insured, as many of the locals have none whatsoever). Obtain a Green Card from your insurer, which gives automatic proof that you are fully covered. Also get hold of a

European Accident Statement form, which may simplify things if you are unlucky enough to have an accident. Always insist on a full translation of any statement you are asked to sign. Breakdown assistance insurance is obviously a sensible investment (e.g. AA's Five Star or RAC's Eurocover Motoring Assistance). *See* p.5 for more information on driving in Italy.

Italians are famously anarchic behind a wheel, especially within the big cities, where all warnings, signals and rules of the road are ignored. The only way to beat the locals is to join them by adopting an assertive and constantly alert driving style. All drivers from boy racers to elderly nuns overtake at the most dangerous bend. Speed limits (generally ignored) are 130kph on motorways (110kph for cars under 1100cc or motorcycles), 110kph on main highways, 90kph on secondary roads, and 50kph in built-up areas. Fines for speeding are up to L500,000, or L100,000 for jumping a red light (a popular Italian sport).

If you are undeterred by these caveats, you may enjoy driving in Italy, at least away from the congested tourist centres. Signposting is generally good, and roads are usually excellently maintained. Some of the roads (e.g. the Amalfi corniche) are feats of engineering that the Romans would have admired. Buy a good road map, such as the Italian Touring Club series.

The **Automobile Club of Italy** (**ACI**) has bushels of useful information on road conditions, routes, petrol stations, and addresses of garages that repair foreign cars; they offer a free breakdown service, and can be reached from anywhere by dialling ✆ 116—also use this number if you have to find the nearest service station. If you need major repairs, the ACI can make sure the prices charged are according to their guidelines. You will find them at Viale C. Colombo 261, Rome, ✆ 06 514 971; Via Marsala 8, Rome, ✆ 06 495 9352; Piazzale Tecchio 49/d, Naples, ✆ 081 239 4511; Via G. Vicinanza 11, Salerno, ✆ 089 226 677.

Also try the Automobile Club di Roma, ✆ 44 77, an extremely useful 24-hour helpline that also monitors road conditions across Italy as well as in Rome (they speak English too).

Hiring a Car

Hiring a car or camper van (*autonoleggio*) is simple but not cheap. You can reserve a car in advance through large international firms; local agencies often have lower prices. Air or train travellers should ask about discount packages. Most companies require a deposit amounting to the estimated cost of the hire and have a minimum age limit of 21 (sometimes 23). A credit card makes life easier. You will need to produce your licence and a passport when you hire.

All the major car hire firms in **Rome** have booths in Termini Station and at Fiumicino and Ciampino airports. **Avis**, Via Sardegna 38/a, ✆ 06 4282 4728; **Criss**, Via dei Prati Fiscali 273, ✆ 06 886 1920; **Europcar**, Via Lombardia 7, ✆ 06 481 9103, Via del Fiume Giallo 196, ✆ 06 520 2140; **Hertz**, Via Veneto 156, ✆ 06 321 6831; **Maggiore-Budget**, Via Tor Cervara, ✆ 06 22 9351, **Tropeo**, Via S. Basilio 60 (Piazza Barberini), ✆ 06 488 1189, 🖷 06 482 8336.

Several major companies have offices in **Naples**; mainly on Via Partenope (near the port), and at the airport or main station. A hefty surcharge is levied in Naples because of the local theft problem, and if you hire elsewhere, check you are allowed to drive within Naples without penalty. You can take a car to Capri, but rental facilities are not available.

From the UK or USA: **Avis**, (UK) ✆ (0990) 900 500, (USA) ✆ (800) 331 1084; **Hertz**, (UK) ✆ (0990) 996 699, (USA) ✆ (800) 654 3001, (Canada) ✆ (800) 263 0600, (Ireland) ✆ (01) 660 2255; **Eurodollar**, ✆ (01895) 233 300.

It is illegal to hitch on the *autostrade*, though you can get a lift near a toll booth. Don't hitch from city centres, head for suburban exit routes. For the best chances of getting a lift, travel light, look respectable and take your shades off. Hold a sign indicating your destination if you can. Risks for women are lower in northern Italy than in the south, but it is not advisable to hitch alone. Two or more men may encounter reluctance. On major roads, heading out of town, you may see scantily clad women standing or sitting on the edges of corn fields trying to attract your attention. These are not hitch-hikers, although you may still pick them up.

By Taxi

Try not to take taxis if you're on a budget. They are invariably expensive, and foreign tourists are sitting ducks for overcharging.

Rome's yellow and white taxis cruise the main roads and have stands in the major piazzas; radio taxis are on ✆ 06 3570, or ✆ 06 6645, or ✆ 06 4994, or ✆ 06 4157 or ✆ 06 88177. The meter starts at L6,400. There are supplementary charges: L3,000 between 10pm and 7am; Sunday and holidays L1,500; L1,000 per piece of baggage. Taxis to and from the airports cost around L70,000. Drivers tend to be honest and helpful—the circuitous routes they take are usually the result of the one-way system—but don't get in a taxi if it doesn't have a meter.

In **Naples** corruption is rife, and the traffic jams mean even a short trip may clock up an alarming bill. Try to negotiate the fare in advance. Don't try to flag them down on the street; head for a taxi rank on a main square, or call the **Radiotaxi Napoli**, ✆ 081 556 4444. In other resorts taxis aren't such bad news, but they are still expensive, especially on **Capri**.

By Motorcycle, Moped or Bicycle

Mopeds, vespas and scooters are the vehicles of choice for many Italians. In traffic-congested towns this is a ubiquity born of necessity; when driving space is limited, two wheels are always better than four. Despite the obvious dangers, there are benefits to moped-riding. It is cheaper than car hire and can be an excellent way to cover a town in a limited space of time. Also, Italian car drivers are conditioned to their presence and so are less likely to hurtle into them when taking corners. Nonetheless, you should only hire a moped if you have ridden one before (Italy's alarming traffic is no place to learn) and, despite local examples, you should always wear a helmet. Some travel insurance policies exclude claims resulting from scooter or motorbike accidents. You may have trouble hiring a *motorino* (moped) or scooter in **Naples** because of theft, but they are available in all the major resorts such as Sorrento, and on the islands.

You must be at least 14 for a *motorino* and 16 for anything more powerful. Helmets are compulsory. Costs for a *motorino* range from about L30,000 per day, scooters somewhat more (up to L50,000).

You can hire a **bike** in most towns. Prices start at about L20,000 per day, which may make buying one interesting if you plan to spend much time in the saddle (L190,000– L300,000). You can usually take your bike quite cheaply on slower trains. To rent a bike, you must bring your passport; to rent a scooter you must be over 21 and have a driver's licence.

Climate and When to Go

Summer comes on dry and hot in the south, with daytime temperatures soaring to an enervating 35°C, relieved by occasional bouts of torrential rain. On the coast, temperatures are more moderate, refreshed by breezes, while annual rainfall is considerably higher in Amalfi than Rome or London. It's humid and hot in much of the northern lowlands and inland hills. Take a light jacket for cool evenings. August is probably the worst month to stump through Italy. Transport facilities are jammed to capacity, prices are at their highest, and the large cities are abandoned to hordes of tourists while the locals take to the beach.

Spring and **autumn** are perhaps the loveliest times to go; the weather is mild, places aren't crowded, and you won't need your umbrella too much, at least until October. **Winter** is the best time to go if you want the museums to yourself; from December to March you can enjoy blissful solitude at reasonable temperatures anywhere close to the coasts. But beware, it can rain and rain.

Average Temperatures in °C

	January	April	July	October
Rome	7	14	25	18
Naples	9	14	25	18
Capri	11	13	24	17

Consulates

UK: Via XX Settembre 80/A, Rome, ℰ 06 482 5441.

Via Francesco Crispi 122, Naples, ℰ 081 663 511.

USA: Via Veneto 121/a, Rome, ℰ 06 487 0235 or ℰ 06 4788 8629/30.

Piazza della Repubblica 2, Naples, ℰ 081 583 8181.

Australia: Via Alessandria 215, Rome, ℰ 06 85 2721.

Canada: Via Zara 30, ℰ 06 440 3028.

Ireland: Largo del Nazareno 3, ℰ 06440 2928.

Crime and the Police

There is a fair amount of petty crime in Italy—purse-snatchings, pickpocketing, minor thievery of the white-collar kind (always check your change) and car break-ins and theft—but violent crime is rare. Nearly all mishaps can be avoided with adequate precautions. Scooter-borne purse-snatchers can be foiled if you stay on the inside of the pavement and keep a firm hold on your property (sling your bag-strap across your body, don't dangle it from one shoulder); pickpockets strike in crowded buses or trams and gatherings; don't carry too much cash, and split it so you won't lose the lot at once. In cities and popular tourist sites, beware groups of scruffy-looking women or children with placards, apparently begging for money. They use distraction techniques to perfection. The smallest and most innocent-looking child is generally the most skilful pickpocket. If you are targeted, the best technique is to grab sharply hold of any vulnerable possessions or pockets and shout furiously. (Italian passers-by or plain-clothes police will often come to your assistance if they realize what is happening.) Be extra careful in train stations, don't leave valuables in hotel rooms, and always park your car in garages, guarded lots or on well-lit streets, with portable temptations well out of sight. Purchasing small quantities of soft drugs for personal consumption is technically legal in Italy, though what constitutes a small quantity is unspecified, and if the police don't like you to begin with, it will probably be enough to get you into big trouble.

Southern Italy has more than its fair share of opportunist criminals. Naples in particular is notorious for street crime; here kindly waiters will tuck your necklace out of sight, and remind you as regularly as bus conductors to hang on tight to your camera. The local brand of *mafiosi* are known as *Camorra* in Naples (crime syndicates who keep a toehold on most walks of life, largely financed by protection rackets, drug-dealing and the proceeds of the *toto nero*, or illegal football pools). If at all possible, avoid taking a car anywhere near Naples. Theft is so tediously common that some car hire firms refuse to rent certain models for use in the city. If your car is stolen, ring the police, ☎ 081 794 1435, but don't expect much sympathy.

Political terrorism, once the scourge of Italy, has declined greatly in recent years, mainly thanks to special quasi-military squads of black-uniformed national police, the *Carabinieri*. Local matters are usually in the hands of the *Polizia Urbana*; the nattily dressed *Vigili Urbani* concern themselves with directing traffic and handing out parking fines. If you need to summon any of them, dial ☎ **113**.

Disabled Travellers

Italy has been relatively slow off the mark in its provision for disabled visitors. Uneven or non-existent pavements, the appalling traffic conditions, crowded public transport, and endless flights of steps in many public places are all disincentives. Progress is gradually being made, however. A national support organization in your own country may well have specific information on facilities in Italy, or will at least be able to provide general advice. The Italian tourist office, or CIT (travel agency) can also advise on hotels, museums with ramps, etc. If you book rail travel through CIT, you can request assistance if you use a wheelchair.

Royal Association for Disability & Rehabilitation (RADAR), 12 City Forum, 250 City Road, London EC1B 8AF ☎ (020) 7250 2222; sell a guide, *European Holidays and Travel* (£5).

Society for the Advancement of Travel for the Handicapped (SATH), 347 Fifth Avenue, Suite 610, New York 10016, ☎ (212) 725 8253.

Mobility International, PO Box 3551, Eugene, Oregon 97403, ☎ (541) 343 1284.

Australian Council for the Rehabilitation of the Disabled (ACROD), PO Box 60, Curtin, ACT 2605 ☎ (06) 282 4333.

If you need help while you are in Naples or the resorts of Campania, contact the local tourist office. Provincial tourist boards provide lists of hotels with specialized facilities, museums with wheelchair access, etc.

There are literally thousands of festivals answering to every description in Italy. Every *comune* has at least one or two honouring patron saints, at which the presiding Madonna is paraded through the streets decked in fairy lights and gaudy flowers. Shrovetide and Holy Week are great focuses of activity, but many of the celebrations also have a strong pagan flavour, especially those linked to the land and the harvest, and some of the feast-day paraphernalia is unmistakably phallic (towers and obelisks are an obvious give-away).

Some festivals are secular affairs sponsored by political parties (especially the Communists and Socialists), where everyone goes to meet friends. There are great costume pageants dating back to the Middle Ages or Renaissance, an endless round of carnivals, music festivals, opera seasons and antique fairs. Whatever the occasion, eating is a primary pastime at all Italian jamborees, and all kinds of regional specialities are prepared. Check at the local tourist office and notices in the piazzas of towns and villages for precise dates, which alter from year to year, and often slide into the nearest weekend.

17 January	Festa d'o' Cippo di Sant'Antonio, **Naples**
Jan–April	Chamber music at the Teatro delle Palme, **Naples**
Jan–mid-July	Opera at the San Carlo, **Naples**
March/April	Holy Week and Easter: Good Friday Procession led by the Pope, **Rome**. In **Campania**, celebrations have a definite Spanish flavour, many featuring processions of floats carried by robed and hooded members of confraternities
May weekends	Cultural and gastronomic events in **Naples**
May (3rd week)	Comic strip and illustration show, **Naples**
May (3rd–4th week)	International music festival in **Naples**
July and August	Outdoor opera, Terme di Caracalla, **Rome**
21 June	Infiorata, **Genzano**, Rome
27 June	Sant'Andrea, with fireworks, costumes and processions in **Amalfi**
	Festa dei Gigli, in **Nola**, near Naples—procession of enormous 'lilies' (wooden-tower floats), recalling the homecoming of Bishop Paolino after his imprisonment in Africa in 394. Challenge of the Trombonieri, arquebus shooting contest in period costume, recalling a defeat over the Angevins, at **Cava de'Tirreni** (Salerno)
15 August	Feast of the Assumption, **Positano**, ancient celebration in honour of the Virgin
1–10 September	Neapolitan song contest, fireworks, etc. at **Piedigrotta**, Naples
19 September	Feast of San Gennaro, **Naples**, where the faithful gather to watch the liquefaction of the saint's blood
December	Advent and Christmas celebrations. Christmas Fair, selling figures and decorations for the *presepi*, **Naples** and other cities

Food and Drink

There are those who eat to live and those who live to eat, and then there are the Italians, for whom food has an almost religious significance, unfathomably linked with love, La Mamma, and tradition. Few Italians are gluttons, but all are experts on what is what in the kitchen; to serve a meal that is not properly prepared and more than a little complex is tantamount to an insult. For the visitor this culinary obsession comes as an extra bonus to the senses—along with remarkable sights, music, and the warm sun, you can enjoy some of the best tastes and smells in the world, prepared in Italy's kitchens and fermented in its countless wine cellars.

Breakfast (*colazione*) is no lingering affair, but an early morning wake-up shot to the brain: a *cappuccino* (*espresso* with hot foamy milk—first thing in the morning is the only time of day at which any self-respecting Italian will touch the stuff), a *caffè latte* (white coffee) or a *caffè lungo* (a generous portion of *espresso*), accompanied by a croissant-type roll, called a *cornetto* or *briosce*, or one of the fancy pastries that are a special talent of Naples. This can be consumed in any bar and repeated during the morning as often as necessary. Breakfast in most Italian hotels seldom represents great value.

Lunch (*pranzo*), generally served around 1pm, is the most important meal of the day, traditionally with a minimum of a first course (*primo piatto*—any kind of pasta dish, broth or soup, rice dish or pizza), a second course (*secondo piatto*—a meat dish, accompanied by a *contorno*, or side dish—a vegetable, salad or potatoes usually), followed by fruit or dessert and coffee. Nowadays few restaurants blink if you only order a bowl of pasta. You can, however, begin with a platter of *antipasti*—the appetizers Italians do so brilliantly, ranging from warm seafood delicacies to raw ham (*prosciutto crudo*), salami in a hundred varieties, lovely vegetables, savoury toasts, olives, pâté and many many more. There are restaurants that specialize in *antipasti*, and they usually don't take it amiss if you decide to forget the pasta and meat and just nibble on these scrumptious *hors d'œuvres* (though in the end it will probably cost more than a full meal). Most Italians accompany their meal with wine and mineral water—*acqua minerale*, with or without bubbles (*con* or *senza gas*), which supposedly aids digestion—concluding their meals with a *digestivo* liqueur.

Cena, the **evening meal**, is usually eaten around 8pm. This is much the same as *pranzo* although lighter, without the pasta; a pizza and beer, eggs or a fish dish. In restaurants, however, they offer all the courses so, if you like, you can have a full meal in the evening.

In Italy the various terms for **restaurants**—*ristorante*, *trattoria* or *osteria*—have been confused. A *trattoria* or *osteria* can be as elaborate as a restaurant, though a *ristorante* is rarely as informal as a traditional *trattoria*. Unfortunately the old habit of posting menus and prices in the windows has fallen from fashion, so it's often difficult to judge variety or prices. Invariably the least expensive type of restaurant is the *vino e cucina*, simple places serving simple cuisine for everyday prices. Remember, the fancier the fittings, the fancier the bill, though neither of these has anything to do with the quality of the food. If you're unsure, do as you would at home—look for lots of locals. When you eat out, mentally add to the bill (*conto*) the bread and cover charge (*pane e coperto*, between L2,000 and L4,000), and a 15 per cent service charge. This is often included in the bill (*servizio compreso*); if not, it will say *servizio non compreso*, and you'll have to do your own arithmetic. Additional tipping is at your own discretion, but never do it in family-owned and -run places.

Restaurant price categories

very expensive	over L80,000
expensive	L50–L80,000
moderate	L30–L50,000
cheap	under L30,000

People who haven't visited Italy for years and have fond memories of eating full meals for under a pound will be amazed at how much prices have risen, though in some respects eating out in Italy is still a bargain, especially when you figure out how much all that wine would have cost you at home. In many places you'll often find restaurants offering a **menu turistico**—full, set meals of usually meagre inspiration for L20,000–30,000. More imaginative chefs often offer a **menu degustazione**—a set-price gourmet meal that allows you to taste their daily specialities and seasonal dishes. Both of these are cheaper than ordering the same food *à la carte*. When you leave a restaurant you will be given a receipt (*scontrino* or *ricevuto fiscale*) which according to Italian law you must take with you out of the door and carry for at least 60m. If you aren't given one, it means the restaurant is probably fudging on its taxes and thus offering you lower prices. There is a slim chance the tax police (*guardia di finanza*) may have their eye on you and the restaurant, and if you don't have a receipt they could slap you with a heavy fine.

There are several alternatives to sit-down meals. The 'hot table' (*tavola calda*) is a stand-up buffet, where you can choose a simple prepared dish or a whole meal, depending on your appetite. The food in these can be truly impressive (especially in the centre of Naples, where the sign out front may read *Degustazione*; some of these offer the best gourmet delights to be had in the south, and are always crowded). Many offer only a few hot dishes, pizza and sandwiches, though in every fair-sized town there will be at least one *tavola calda* with seats where you can contrive a complete dinner outside the usual hours. Little shops that sell pizza by the slice are common in city centres.

At any grocer's (*alimentari*) or market (*mercato*) you can buy the materials for a picnic; some places in the smaller towns will make the sandwiches for you. For really elegant picnics, have a *tavola calda* pack up something nice. And if everywhere else is closed, there's always the railway station—bars will at least have sandwiches and drinks, and perhaps (usually in the unlikeliest of locations) some surprisingly good snacks you've never heard of before. Some of the station bars also prepare *cestini di viaggio*, full-course meals in a basket for long train trips. Common snacks you'll encounter include *panini* of prosciutto, cheese and tomatoes, or other meats; *tramezzini*, little sandwiches on plain, square white bread that are always much better than they look; and pizza, of course.

Rome

Traditional Roman specialities tend to be simple, almost rustic, making use of inexpensive ingredients that are produced locally; pickled swan hearts and imported fish gut sauce went out with the Caesars. Now the most famous Roman first course, or *primo*, is *spaghetti* or *bucatini* (thin tubes) *all'amatriciana*, with a sauce of salt pork, tomatoes and chilli peppers, topped with grated *pecorino* (sharp sheep cheese). *Spaghetti alla carbonara*, another popular dish, features bacon, eggs, garlic, cheese and pepper (tradition says it was invented by

American GIs, who topped spaghetti with their breakfast rations). Other local specialities include *fettuccine al burro* (cholesterol heaven: ribbon egg noodles, with a double dose of butter, cream, and Parmesan cheese); *penne all'arrabiata* ('angry quills', with tomato sauce and lots of chilli pepper); *gnocchi di patate* (potato dumplings with butter or meat sauce, a favourite on Thursdays), or the much harder to find *gnocchi alla romana*, made of semolina and baked in the oven; *stracciatella* (broth with eggs, semolina and Parmesan cheese); and *spaghetti ad aglio e olio* (with garlic, olive oil, chilli pepper and parsley).

Typical Roman meat courses (*secondo*) are headed by the famous 'jump-in-the-mouth' *saltimbocca alla romana* (veal scallops with ham and sage, cooked in butter and white wine). For heartier fare, try *trippa alla romana* (tripe stewed with onions, carrots, mint, meat sauce and Parmesan), or *coda alla vaccinara* (stewed ox tail), or *involtini al sugo* (rolled veal cutlets filled with ham, celery and cheese, cooked in tomato sauce). *Pajata*, for intrepid diners only, is veal intestine with its mother's milk clotted inside, dressed up with garlic, chilli peppers, tomatoes and white wine. Popular, but often expensive, is *abbacchio alla scottadito*, lamb chops 'burn the finger', grilled over a flame. *Tordi matti* are a kind of grilled *involtini*. Seafood is expensive; traditional dishes are *anguillette in umido* (stewed baby eels from Lake Bracciano), *filetti di baccalà* (dried cod fried in batter), and *seppiette con i carciofi* (cuttlefish with artichokes).

The Roman *campagna* produces tender, purple 'Roman' artichokes, used in *carciofi alla giudea* (artichokes fried in oil), the famous side dish or *contorno*, one of many adopted from the Jews. A *misticanza* is a green salad composed of wild and domestic greens. In the winter try Roman cauliflower, which grows in beautiful pale green spirals (but tastes pretty much like regular cauliflower). A typical dessert (also Jewish in origin) is *crostata di ricotta*, a tart filled with cream, ricotta, cinnamon and bits of chocolate; or *zuppa inglese alla romana*, the local version of trifle. The classic Roman cheese is *pecorino*, made from sheep's milk; *caciotta romana* comes from a mixture of cow's and sheep's milk.

Modern Romans are as adventurous at the table as their classical ancestors, and include some stomach-churning offal in their diets. But the capital is an excellent place to delve into any style of regional cooking, with dozens of restaurants from all over Italy. If you are bored poring over a menu in Rome, you've been nipped in the tastebuds.

Naples and the South

Naples, of course, invented both pizza and spaghetti, the staples of Italian cuisine. A genuine Neapolitan pizza cooked in a wood-fired brick oven is the archetypal local eating experience, and watching it being made, whirled and slapped high in the air with lightning speed, is as much of an entertainment as eating it. The popular *marinara* is anointed with tomato, garlic and basil. *Calzoni* are half-moon envelopes of pizza dough, often filled with ham and cheese and sold as street snacks. Pasta often appears with engaging simplicity, smothered in oil and garlic, or tomato and basil. In the south, factory spaghetti gives way to the real monarch of pasta—nothing more than thick home-made spaghetti, but unmistakably different from the mass-produced commodity. Mozzarella, rather than parmesan, appears most often in pasta sauces. *Mozzarella in carrozza* is a fried sandwich of cheese, often sold as a street snack.

Campania tends to be overly modest about its cuisine. Its biggest favourites are simple enough: *pasta e fagioli* (pasta and beans), *spaghetti alle vongole* (with baby clams); the seafood, as everywhere else along the southern coasts, is exceptional. Besides the ubiquitous clams, squid, octopus and mussels (*zuppe di cozze*, mussels in a hot pepper sauce) appear frequently, along with oily fish like mackerel and sardines. Vegetables (often served as *contorni*, an appetising assortment) are excellent too. Aubergines and courgettes make their way into many local dishes, especially *melanzane parmigiana* (aubergine/eggplant baked with tomato and mozzarella), *misto di frittura* (deep-fried potato, aubergine and courgette flowers), or *zucchini a scapace* (courgettes in tomato sauce). In Campania, specialities tend to be hotter and spicier than in the north, and are often seasoned with condiments like capers, garlic, anchovies, lemon juice, oregano, olives and fennel. Dishes described as *alla napoletana* usually contain tomato, capers, black olives and garlic.

The local olive oil is dark and strong, closer to that of Greece than the lighter oils of Tuscany and Umbria; the olives too are smaller and fuller flavoured, coming from trees whose roots have to dig deep into the soil to reach water. As in most of southern Italy, sheep make up a great part of the livestock, and the region's sheep's cheeses include the local styles of *pecorino* and *ricotta*—look out for the unusually strongly flavoured *ricotta forte*.

Puddings and cakes are rich and sweet all over the south. *Pasteria* is one of the most celebrated local sweets: a ricotta pie full of wheat berries, candied fruit and spices, traditionally eaten at Easter. Another irresistible speciality of Naples is *sfogliatella* (flaky pastry, sometimes stuffed with ricotta and candied peel), sometimes eaten for breakfast. If this sounds too much of a good thing, the best of all (in season) is a fresh peach, naked and unadorned.

Wine and Spirits

Italy is a country where everyday wine is cheaper than Coca-Cola or milk, and where nearly every rural family owns some vineyards or has some relatives who supply most of their daily needs—which are not great. Even though they live in one of the world's largest wine-growing countries, Italians imbibe relatively little, and only at meals.

If Italy has an infinite variety of regional dishes, there is an equally bewildering array of regional wines, many of which are rarely exported because they are best drunk young. Unless you're dining at a restaurant with an exceptional cellar, do as the Italians do and order a carafe of the local wine (*vino locale* or *vino della casa*). Most Italian wines are named after the grape and district they come from. If the label says DOC (*Denominazione di Origine Controllata*) it means that the wine comes from a specially defined area and was produced according to a certain traditional method. DOCG (*Denominazione di Origine Controllata e Garantia*) is allegedly a more rigorous classification, indicating that the wines not only conform to DOC standards, but are tested by government-appointed inspectors. At present few wines have been granted this status, but the number should increase steadily.

Wine in Rome usually means a white Castelli Romani, most famously *Frascati*, which inspired the Trastevere's dialect poet Trilussa to rhapsodize: *'Dentro 'sta boccia trovi er bonumore/che canta l'inni e t'imbandiera er còre'* (something like: 'in a mouthful there's such good humour/that sings hymns and decks your heart with banners'). Straw-coloured, dry, and clear, Frascati, like all the Castelli wines, is the perfect accompaniment to Roman cooking. Other white wines worth trying from the region are *Marino*, like Frascati a DOC wine; also *Colli Albani*, from near Castel Gandolfo, a pale gold in colour, soft and fruity; *Colli*

Lanuvini, from south of Lake Nemi, good for fish and *antipasti*; and *Velletri*, both a white and a dry tannic ruby red, a friend to pasta, and roast and grilled meats. If none of these wines please, Rome is a great place to find thousands of wines from all other corners of Italy, some as inexpensive. On the whole, the *vino della casa* is usually cheap and drinkable, though it's advisable, if you're quaffing cheap wine, to do as the Romans do and dilute it with water to avoid a morning-after headache.

Campania was known for wine in Roman times. The legendary full-bodied Falerno was highly regarded by the ancients, and praised by Horace and Pliny. Today the region produces surprisingly little, and not much of any note. The most famous is Lacrima Christi, grown on the slopes of Vesuvius and only recently granted DOC status. Others to look out for include the white Greco di Tufo or Fiano di Avellino, or the deep, heavy red Taurasi.

Italians are fond of postprandial **brandies** (to aid digestion)—the famous Stock or Vecchia Romagna labels are always good. Grappa (acquavitae) is tougher, and often drunk in black coffee after a meal (a *caffè corretto*). Other favourites include Campari, a red bitter drunk on its own or in cocktails; Vermouth, Fernet Branca, Cynar and Averno, popular aperitifs/digestives; and liqueurs like Strega from Benevento, apricot-flavoured Amaretto, aniseed Sambuca, cherry Maraschino, and any number of locally brewed elixirs, often made by monks.

Health and Emergencies

Ambulance, ✆ 118. Red Cross ambulance, ✆ 5510

Citizens of EU countries are entitled to reciprocal health care in Italy's National Health Service and a 90 per cent discount on prescriptions (bring Form E111 with you). The E111 does not cover all medical expenses (no repatriation costs, for example, and no private treatment), and it is advisable to take out separate travel insurance for full cover. Citizens of non-EU countries should check carefully that they have adequate insurance for any medical expenses, and the cost of returning home. Australia has a reciprocal health care scheme with Italy, but New Zealand, Canada and the USA do not. If you already have health insurance, a student card, or a credit card, you may be entitled to some medical cover abroad.

In an **emergency**, dial ✆ 113, for an ambulance (*ambulanza*); in Naples, ✆ 081 752 0696 (24 hours), daytime only ✆ 081 752 0850. Less serious problems can be treated at a *pronto soccorso* (casualty/first aid department) at any hospital (*ospedale*), or at a local health unit (*unità sanitariale locale*—USL). Airports and main railway stations also have first-aid posts. If you have to pay for any health treatment, make sure you get a receipt.

Public hospitals in Rome with 24-hour first aid and medical services are:

Fatebenefratelli: Isola Tiberina (Tiber Island), ✆ 06 68 371
Policlinico: Viale Policlinico, ✆ 06 49971
Rome American Hospital: Via Longoni 69, ✆ 06 228 5062/64
San Camillo: Circ. Gianicolense 87, ✆ 06 58 701
Sant'Eugenio: Piazzale dell'Umanesimo (EUR), ✆ 06 591 9795
San Filippo: Via Martinotti 20, ✆ 06 33 061
San Giacomo: Via Canova 29, ✆ 06 67 261
Santo Spirito: Lungotevere in Sassia 1 (near the Vatican), ✆ 06 650 901

For a list of English-speaking doctors in Rome, call the American Embassy, © 06 487 0235.

The hospital in Naples is **Policlinico**, Via Sergio Pansini, © 081 746 1111—though this is a regular subject of horror stories in the local newspapers.

Pharmacies are generally open 8.30–1 and 4–8. Pharmacists are trained to give advice for minor ills and administer simple first aid. Any large town has a pharmacy that stays open 24 hours; others take turns to stay open. The address rota is posted in the windows of pharmacies and in the newspapers La Repubblica and Il Messagero in Rome, or by ringing © 1921 for a recorded listing; or in Il Mattino in Naples. The following are 24-hour pharmacies:

Rome: **Internazionale:** Piazza Barberini 49, © 482 5456
Piram: Via Nazionale 228, © 488 0754
Cola di Rienzo: Via Cola di Rienzo 213, © 324 3130/324 476
Brienza: Piazza Risorgimento 44, © 372 2157
Spinedi: Via Arenula 73, © 6880 3278

Naples: **Carducci**, Via Carducci 21–23, © 081 417 283.

No specific vaccinations are required or advised for citizens of most countries before visiting Italy; the main **health risks** are the usual travellers' woes of upset stomachs or the effects of too much sun. Occasional, much-publicized outbreaks of more serious disease have occurred in Naples in recent years (cholera, for example), but these are rarely likely to affect travellers. Take a supply of useful medicaments with you (e.g. insect repellent, anti-diarrhoeal medicine, sun lotion and antiseptic cream), and any drugs you need regularly. Stick to bottled water (dehydration is a serious risk in those southern climes) and avoid uncooked shellfish around the polluted Bay of Naples.

Maps and Publications

The maps in this guide are for orientation only and to explore in any detail invest in a good, up-to-date regional map before you arrive. Try the following bookshops: **Stanford's**, 12–14 Long Acre, London WC2 9LP, © (020) 7836 1321; **The Travel Bookshop**, 13 Blenheim Crescent, London W11 2EE, © (020) 7229 5260; **The Complete Traveller**, 199 Madison Ave (at W. 35th Street intersection), New York, NY 10016, © (212) 685 9007.

Touring Club Italiano, **Michelin** and **Istituto Geografico de Agostini** produce excellent maps, available at all major bookshops in Italy (e.g. Feltrinelli) or sometimes on news stands. Italian tourist offices are helpful and can often supply good area maps and town plans.

Books are more expensive in Italy than in the UK. Some English language bookshops:

Anglo-American Book Co., Via della Vite 57, Rome.
Lion Bookshop, Via del Babuino 181, Rome.
Economy Book Center, Via Torino 136, Rome.
Universal, Rione Sirignano 1, Naples.

Money and Banks

It's a good idea to order a wad of *lire* from your home bank to have on hand when you arrive in Italy, the land of strikes, unforeseen delays and quirky banking hours. Take great care how you carry it, however (don't keep it all in one place). **Banking hours** vary, but core times are usually Monday to Friday, 8.30–1.20 and 3–4, closed weekends and on local and national holidays (*see* below). Obtaining money is often frustrating, involving much queueing and form-filling. The major banks and exchange bureaux licensed by the Bank of Italy give the best exchange rates. Hotels, private exchanges in resorts and FS-run exchanges at railway stations usually have less advantageous rates, but are open outside normal banking hours. In cities, you can change money outside normal banking hours at the **post office**, in most good hotels, and at travel agents. In Rome try **Banco Nazionale delle Comunicazione**, Stazione Termini; **Thomas Cook**, Piazza Barberini 21D. In Naples: **Thomas Cook**, Piazza Municipio 70, © 081 551 8399; **CIT**, Piazza Municipio 72, © 081 552 5426; and **Partenotour**, Piazza dei Martiri 23, © 081 764 3415. Remember that Italians indicate decimals with commas and thousands with full points.

Besides traveller's cheques, most banks will give you cash on a **credit card** or **Eurocheque** with a Eurocheque card (taking little or no commission), and in big cities you can find cash-points (ATMs) to spout money on a Visa, American Express or Eurocheque card. You need a PIN number to use these. Read the instructions carefully, or your card may be retained by the machine. MasterCard (Access) is much less widely acceptable. Large hotels, resort area restaurants, shops and car hire firms will accept plastic; many smaller places will not. From sad experience, Italians are wary of plastic—you can't even use it at motorway petrol stops.

You can have money transferred to you through an Italian bank but this process may take over a week, even if it's sent urgent *espressissimo*. You will need your passport as identification when you collect it. Sending cheques by post is inadvisable.

National Holidays

Most museums, as well as banks and shops, are closed on the following national holidays:

1 January (New Year's Day)
6 January (Epiphany)
Easter Monday
25 April (Liberation Day)
1 May (Labour Day)
15 August (Assumption, or *Ferragosto*, official start of the Italian holiday season)
1 November (All Saints' Day)
8 December (Immaculate Conception)
25 December (Christmas Day)
26 December (*Santo Stefano*, St Stephen's Day)

In Naples, the feast of San Gennaro (19 September) is also a holiday.

Opening Hours, Museums and Churches

Most of Italy closes down at 1pm until 3 or 4pm to let everyone eat and digest. Afternoon hours are 4–7, sometimes 5–8 in the hot summer months. Bars are often the only places open in the early afternoon. Shops are usually closed on Saturday afternoons, Sundays and Monday mornings—although grocery stores and supermarkets open on Monday mornings.

Italy's **churches** have always been a target for art thieves, and are usually locked when there isn't a caretaker. All churches except the really important cathedrals and basilicas close in the afternoon, and the little ones often stay closed. Bring coins for the light machines in churches, or the work of art you came to inspect will remain shrouded in ecclesiastical gloom. Don't do your visiting during services, and don't come to see paintings and statues in churches the week preceding Easter—you will probably find them covered with mourning shrouds. Many churches are becoming less strict about dress, but you should cover up for cathedrals. In the frenzy of preparations for the **Giubileo** (the Holy Year in 2000), many churches are or will be undergoing various degrees of restoration. Check locally for up-to-date information.

Many of Italy's **museums** are magnificent, many are run with shameful neglect, and many have been closed for years for 'restoration' with slim prospects of reopening in the foreseeable future. With two works of art per inhabitant, Italy has a hard time financing the preservation of its national heritage; it's as well to inquire at the tourist office to find out what is open and what is 'temporarily' closed before setting off on a wild goose chase.

In general, Sunday afternoons and Mondays are dead periods for the sightseer—you may want to make them your travelling days. Places without specified opening hours can usually be visited on request—but it is best to go before 1pm. We have listed the hours of important sights and museums, and specified which ones charge admission. Expect to pay between L4,000 and L8,000 to get in. The more important sites such as Pompeii may cost up to L12,000. EU citizens under 18 and over 65 get free admission to state museums on presentation of their passports, at least in theory.

Packing

You can't overdress in Italy; whatever strides Italian designers have made on the international fashion merry-go-round, most of their clothes are purchased domestically. Whether or not you want to try to keep up with the natives is your own affair. The few places with dress codes are the major churches and basilicas (no shorts, sleeveless shirts or strappy sundresses; women should carry a scarf to throw over the shoulders), casinos and a few posh restaurants.

Your electric appliances will work if you adapt them to run on 220 AC with two round prongs on the plug.

Post Offices

Dealing with *la posta italiana* has always been a risky, frustrating, time-consuming affair. One of the scandals that has mesmerized Italy in the past few years involved the minister of the post office, who disposed of literally tons of backlog mail by tossing it in the Tiber. When the news broke, he was replaced—the new minister, having learned his lesson, burned all the mail the post office was incapable of delivering. Not surprisingly, fed-up Italians view the invention of the fax machine as a gift from the Madonna. From these harsh judgements, however, we exempt the Vatican City, whose special postal service (on angelic wings?) knocks spots off the rest of the country for speed and efficiency. In Rome, be sure to post your mail in the Holy See. You need to buy special Vatican stamps.

Post offices are usually open Mon–Sat, 9–1, or until 6 or 7pm in cities. To have mail sent *poste restante*, have it addressed to the central post office (*Fermo Posta*) and allow three to four weeks for it to arrive. Make sure your surname is very clearly written in block capitals. To pick up your mail you must present your passport and pay a nominal charge. Stamps (*francobolli*) are sold in post offices or at tobacconists (*tabacchi*, identified by their black or blue signs with a white T). Prices fluctuate. The rates for letters and postcards (depending how many words you write!) vary according to the whim of the tobacconist or postal clerk.

Rome: Posta Centrale in Piazza San Silvestro, 00186, Mon–Fri 8am–9pm, Sat 8–12, © 06 679 5530 or © 06 678 1172. **Naples**: Piazza Matteotti, © 081 551 1456, near Via Toledo, (Mon–Fri 8am–8pm, Saturday 8–12). You can also send faxes and telegrams from here.

You can also have money telegraphed to you through the post office; if all goes well, this can happen in a mere three days, but expect a fair proportion of it to go into commission.

Shopping

If you are looking for antiques, be sure to demand a certificate of authenticity—reproductions can be very, very good. To get your antique or modern art purchases home, you will have to apply to the Export Department of the Italian Ministry of Education and pay an export tax as well; your seller should know the details. Be sure to save receipts for Customs on the way home. Italians don't much like department stores, but there are a few chains— the classiest is Rinascente, while COIN stores often have good buys in almost the latest fashions. Standa and UPIM are more like Woolworth's; they have good clothes selections, housewares, etc., and often contain basement supermarkets. The main attraction of Italian shopping, however, is to buy classy luxury items; for less expensive clothes and household items you can nearly always do better at home. Prices for clothes are generally very high.

Sports and Activities

football

Soccer (*il calcio*) is a national obsession. For many Italians its importance far outweighs tedious issues like the state of the nation, the government of the day, or any international event—not least because of the weekly chance (slim but real) of becoming an instant lira billionaire in the Lotteria Sportiva. The sport was actually introduced by the English, but a Renaissance game, a cross between football and rugby, has existed in Italy for centuries. Modern Italian teams are known for their grace, precision, and teamwork; rivalries are intense, scandals, especially bribery and cheating, are rife. The tempting rewards offered by such big-time entertainment attract all manner of corrupt practices, yet crowd violence is minimal compared with the havoc wreaked by other countries' lamentable fans.

Rome has two football teams, Lazio and Roma. Both play at the Stadio Olimpico, Via dei Gladiatori 2. Matches happen twice a week (Wednesdays at 8pm and Sundays at 3pm) from September to May during the Italian league competition, the Campionato Italiano. Ticket prices range from L15,000 to L150,000.

Around Naples matches are generally played on Sunday afternoons. Tickets aren't cheap for the top matches (L25,000–100,000). In Naples, the main ground is the **Stadio di San Paolo** in Fuorigrotta (a western suburb—take Ferrovia Cumana as far as Mostra and the stadium is directly outside), © 081 239 5623.

The International Tennis Championships are held at Rome's Foro Italico in May. Those who prefer to serve themselves can get a list of tennis clubs from the Federazione Italiana Tennis, Viale dei Gladiatori 31, ✆ 06 321 9041. Reservations are essential to get a court.

S.S. Aristos, Via Aristofane 101, ✆ 06 5235 2881. Squash, tennis, football and pool. L25,000 per 45 minutes.

Forum Sport Center, Via Cornelia 495, ✆ 06 611 101. For tennis, squash or any of the other numerous activities this place offers. L10,000.

A.S. Squash Roma, Via di Pietralata 135, ✆ 06 418 2142. Closed in the summer and Sun. One of the more expensive places to play squash, tennis or pool, with a restaurant.

A.S. Squash Tevere, Via Quarantotti 50 (Isola Sacra), ✆ 06 652 2632. Only squash here, but worth visiting for the Turkish bath.

Around the Bay of Naples many of the more expensive hotels have courts, and non-residents may be able to use them by arrangement with the hotel or local tourist office. There are public courts in **Naples**, Via Giochi del Mediterraneo, ✆ 081 570 3912.

watersports and beaches

The best chance for a swim around **Rome** is to go to the coast—the further away from the mouth of the Tiber the better—or head up to Lake Bracciano. Rome's so-called public pools are actually open to members only. In summer, however, a couple of hotels with pools open them up to the public on a daily rate, and there's a pleasant outdoor pool up at EUR.

A.S. Villa Flaminia, Via Donatello 20, ✆ 322 2019. Check ahead of time to know what hours are free.

Piscina delle Rose, Viale America 20, ✆ 592 6717. Open 9am–9.30pm (closes at 7pm at weekends) from June to September. L15,000.

Hilton, Via Alberto Cadlolo 101. L45,000.

YMCA, Via Libano 68, ✆ 592 3595. Free membership, but a monthly fee: L175,000. Closed in the summer.

S.S. Lazio Nuoto, Via di Villa in Lucina 82, ✆ 541 5522. Open from September to July, free swim from 9.30am to 2pm.

At most **Bay of Naples** resorts it is possible to hire boats and equipment, and go wind-surfing, waterskiing or diving; in Naples contact the **Subacquei Napoletani**, Via Caracciolo 2, ✆ 081 764 1985. Capri is one of the best choices for such activities, with some of the cleanest waters in the bay. You can also take submarine trips around the island. For scuba diving, waterskiing, canoeing and boat hire, contact the **Sea Service Centre**, Marina Piccola, Via Mulo 63, ✆ 081 837 0221. Sorrento, Positano, Amalfi and Salerno also offer a range of watersports.

Many southern Italian beaches are disappointingly flat, and scarcely improved by regimented lines of parasols and sunbeds. Those around the Bay of Naples tend to be of grey volcanic sand and the free public ones are small, crowded and neglected with few facilities. Accept the fact, then, that to enjoy Italian beaches you will have to pay: most of the best stretches of sand (some of them artificial) are operated by private concessions. For the most attractive resort beaches, head for Positano, Minori or Maiori. Despite the appalling pollution immediately around Naples, the water off Capri is generally clean and inviting.

sailing

Almost all the islands have some facilities for **yachts**, though they may not be equipped for a long stay. You can bring your own boat to Italy for six months without any paperwork if you bring it by car; if you arrive by sea you must report to the port authority. The harbour-master (*capitaneria di porto*) at your first Italian port of call will give you a document called a *costituto*, which you will have to produce for subsequent harbour-masters; this permits the purchase of tax-free fuel. For further information, contact the Italian State Tourist Office or write to:

Mare Club d'Italia (MA.C.I.), Via A. Bargoni 8, 00135 Rome, ✆ 06 589 4046/✉ 06 589 7084.

Other useful addresses are:

Federazione Italiana Vela (Italian Sailing Federation), Via Brigata Bisagno 2/17, Genoa.

Federazione Italiana Motonautica (Italian Motorboat Federation), Via Piranesi 44/b, Milan.

The main Bay of Naples yacht harbours are Posillipo in Naples; Capri; Procida; and Porto, Casamicciola, Lacco Ameno and Forio d'Ischia on Ischia.

Telephones

In Rome telephone numbers can be anywhere between 4 and 9 digits long, so if it looks strange it probably isn't a misprint. To make things even more confusing, telephone numbers in the city are in the process of changing. Some new numbers are listed in the telephone directory, others are not. For around two months after a number has changed there will be a message, in Italian and then English, telling you what the new number is. After two months, there will be a message in Italian which simply states that the number is unobtainable, and that you should check the directory or phone directory enquiries (✆ 12, known as SIP Dodici). If you're lucky there may be an English-speaking operator at SIP.

For information (in English) on international calls, on calling with your credit card or to get an on-line translation into Italian and vice versa (L3,000 a minute) dial ✆ 170.

Public telephones for **international calls** may be found in the offices of Telecom Italia (Italy's telephone company). They are the only places where you can make reverse-charge calls (*erre*, collect calls) but be prepared for a wait. Rates for long-distance calls are among the highest in Europe. To make direct calls dial the international prefix (UK ✆ 0044, Ireland ✆ 00353, USA and Canada ✆ 001, Australia ✆ 0061, New Zealand ✆ 0064).

Calls within Italy are cheapest after 10pm; international calls after 11pm. Most phone booths now take either coins or phone cards (*schede telefoniche*)—L5,000, L10,000 or L15,000—on sale from tobacconists and news-stands. In smaller villages and islands you can usually find *telefoni a scatti*, with a meter on them, in at least one bar (a small commission is generally charged). Try to avoid telephoning from hotels, which often add 25 per cent to the bill.

Note that you now have to dial the whole of the area prefix when making a call. In other words, if you are calling a Naples number from within Naples you have to dial '℡ 081' followed by the number, and if calling from abroad you have to dial '℡ 00 39 081' followed by the number.

Rome is well supplied with phones: try Termini station and post offices. The code is ℡ 06. **Phone centres in Naples** are at the Stazione Centrale, at Via Depretis 40, and in the Galleria Umberto I. The code for Naples is ℡ 081.

Time

Italy is one hour ahead of Greenwich Mean Time and six hours ahead of Eastern Standard Time. From the last weekend of March to the end of September, Italian Summer Time (daylight saving time) is in effect.

Toilets

You will find public conveniences in places like train and bus stations and bars: ask for the *bagno, toilette* or *gabinetto*. In stations and the smarter cafés there are washroom attendants who expect a few hundred lire for keeping the place clean. You'll probably have to ask them for paper (*carta*). Don't confuse the Italian plurals: *signori* (gents), *signore* (ladies).

Tourist Offices Abroad

Tourist information offices: *open 8–12.30 or 1 and 3–7, possibly longer in summer. Few open on Saturday afternoons or Sundays.*

Known as EPT, APT or AAST, information booths provide hotel lists, town plans and terse information on local sights and transport. Queues can be maddeningly long. English is spoken in the main centres. If you're stuck, you may get more sense out of a friendly travel agency than an official tourist office.

Australia   c/o Italian Embassy,1 Macquarie Street, Sydney 2000, NSW, ℡ (02) 9392 7900.

Canada   1 Place Ville Marie, Suite 1914, Montréal, Quebec H3B 3M9, ℡ (418) 529 9801.

UK   **Italian State Tourist Board**, 1 Princes Street, London W1R 8AY, ℡ (020) 7408 1254; **Italian Travel Centre**, 30 St James' Street, London SW1A 1HB, ℡ (020) 7853 6464.

USA   **Italian Government Travel Office**, 630 Fifth Ave, Suite 1565, New York NY 10111, ℡ (212) 245 4822;

Italian Government Travel Office, 12400 Wilshire Blvd, Suite 550, LA, CA 90025, ℡ (310) 820 1959;

Italian Government Travel Office, 500 N. Michigan Ave, Suite 2240, Chicago IL 60611, ℡ (312) 644 0996.

All accommodation in Italy is classified by the provincial tourist boards. Price control, however, has been deregulated since 1992. After a period of rapid and erratic price fluctuation, tariffs are at last settling down again to more predictable levels. The quality of furnishings and facilities has generally improved in all categories in recent years. But you can still find plenty of older style hotels and *pensioni* whose eccentricities of character and architecture (in some cases undeniably charming) may frequently be at odds with modern standards of comfort or even safety. In Naples, particularly, good accommodation is scarce and should be booked ahead. Campania's tariffs are generally lower than further north, but Capri's ritziest establishments vie with any in Italy on price.

Accommodation price ranges

Category	Double with bath
luxury (*****)	L450,000 and over
very expensive (****)	L300–450,000
expensive (***)	L200–300,000
moderate (**)	L120–200,000
cheap (*)	up to L120,000

Hotels and Guesthouses

Italian **alberghi** come in all shapes and sizes. They are rated from one to five stars, depending on their facilities (not character, style or charm). The star ratings are some indication of price levels, but for tax reasons not all hotels choose to advertise themselves at the rating to which they are entitled, so you may find a modestly rated hotel just as comfortable (or more so) than a higher rated one. Conversely, you may find that a hotel offers few stars in order to attract budget-conscious travellers, but charges just as much as a higher-rated neighbour. **Pensioni** are generally more modest establishments, though nowadays the distinction between these and ordinary hotels is becoming blurred. **Locande** are traditionally an even more basic form of hostelry, but these days the term may denote somewhere fairly chic.

Other cheap accommodation is sometimes known as *alloggi* or *affittacamere*. There are usually plenty of cheap dives around railway stations; for somewhere more salubrious, head for the historic quarters. Whatever the shortcomings of the décor, furnishings and fittings, you can usually rely at least on having clean sheets.

Price lists, by law, must be posted on the door of every room, along with meal prices and any extra charges (such as air conditioning, or even a shower in cheap places). Many hotels display two or three different rates, depending on the season. Low-season rates may be about a third lower than peak-season tariffs. Some resort hotels close down altogether for several months a year. During high season you should always book ahead to be sure of a room (a fax reservation may be less frustrating to organize than one by post). If you have paid a deposit, your booking is valid under Italian law, but don't expect it to be refunded if you have to cancel. Tourist offices publish annual regional lists of hotels and pensions with current rates, but do not make reservations for visitors. Major railway stations generally have accommodation booking desks; inevitably, a fee is charged. Chain hotels or motels are generally the easiest hotels to book, but are often less interesting to stay in.

If you arrive without a reservation, begin looking or phoning round for accommodation early in the day. If possible, inspect the room (and bathroom facilities) before you book, and check the tariff carefully. Italian hoteliers may legally alter their rates twice during the year, so printed tariffs or tourist board lists (and prices quoted in this book) may be out of date. Hoteliers who wilfully overcharge should be reported to the local tourist office. You will be asked for your passport for registration purposes.

You can expect to pay about two-thirds the rate for single occupancy, though in high season you may be charged the full double rate in a popular resort. Extra beds are usually charged at about a third of the room rate. Rooms without private bathrooms are generally 20–30 per cent less, and most establishments offer discounts for children sharing parents' rooms, or children's meals. A *camera singola* (single room) may cost anything from L30,000 upwards. Double rooms are normally twin-bedded (*camera doppia*). If you want a double bed, specify a *camera matrimoniale*. Breakfast is usually optional in hotels and *pensioni*. You can usually get better value in a bar or café if you have any choice. In high season you may be expected to take half-board in resorts if the hotel has a restaurant, and one-night stays may be refused.

Youth Hostels

There aren't many of these in Italy (where they are known as *alberghi* or *ostelli per la gioventù*), but they are generally pleasant and sometimes located in historic buildings. The **Associazione Italiana Alberghi per la Gioventù** (Italian Youth Hostel Association, or AIG) is affiliated to the International Youth Hostel Federation. For a full list of hostels, contact **AIG**, Via Cavour 44, 00184 Roma, ✆ 06 487 1152, ✉ 06 488 0492. An international membership card will enable you to stay in any of them (cards can be purchased on the spot in many hostels if you don't already have one). You can obtain these in advance from the following organizations.

UK, Youth Hostels Association of England and Wales, 14 Southampton Street, London WC2, ✆ (01629) 581 418.

USA, American Youth Hostels, Box 37613, Washington DC 20013-7613, ✆ (202) 783 6161.

Australia, Australian Youth Hostel Association, 60 Mary Street, Surry Hills, Sydney, NSW 2010, ✆ (02) 9565 1699.

Canada, Canadian Hostelling Association, 205 Catherine Street, Ottawa, Ontario K2P 1C3, ✆ (613) 237 7884.

Rome's youth hostel is out of the city and hard to reach. Hostels around Naples include Agerola-S. Lazzaro or Mergellina (Naples) and Irno (Salerno). Rates are usually between L12,000 and L18,000 (L23,000 in Rome) for a place in a dormitory and breakfast. Discounts are available for senior citizens, and some family rooms are available. You generally have to check in after 5pm, and pay for your room before 9am. Hostels usually close for most of the daytime, and many operate a curfew. During the spring, noisy school parties cram hostels for field trips. In the summer, it's advisable to book ahead. Contact the hostels directly.

History and Art

The First Italians

Some 50,000 years ago, Neanderthal man graced the Ligurian Riviera with his low-browed presence. Neither he nor any of his successors left much in terms of art or culture, and the peninsula remained a backwater until about the 8th century BC. At that time, most of the population were lumped together as 'Italics', powerful tribes with related languages. Among them were the **Samnites**, who dominated much of Campania and the south and a boiling kettle of contentious peoples in the centre: **Sabines**, **Aequi**, **Volscii** and **Latins**. The mighty walls of their cities, called *cyclopean walls*, can still be seen today around southern Lazio.

750–509 BC: Greeks and Etruscans

Two relative newcomers contributed much towards bringing Italy out of its primitive state: the **Etruscans** and **Greeks**. The Etruscans are one of the puzzles of ancient history. They came from somewhere in western Anatolia about 900 BC, probably as a warrior aristocracy that imposed itself on Tuscany and north Lazio. By the 8th century BC they were the strongest people in Italy, grouped in a loose confederation of 12 city-states called the *Dodecapolis*. At the same time, the Greeks, whose trading routes had long covered Italy's southern coasts, began to look upon that country as a New World, ripe for exploration and colonization. Cumae, on the Campanian coast, became the first Greek foundation in 750 BC, a convenient base for trading with the Etruscans, who had recently discovered iron mines. A score of others soon followed in Sicily and along the Ionian Sea and soon they were rivalling the cities of Greece itself in wealth and culture.

Conflict between the Greeks and the Etruscans was inevitable and serious. Warfare began in 524 BC with an unsuccessful Etruscan siege of Cumae. The Greeks got the better of it from then on, and finally defeated the Etruscans at sea in the decisive Battle of Cumae (474 BC). Their southern colonies straggled on for a while, but the taking of Capua by the Samnites in 432 BC put an end to Etruscan hopes in the south forever.

Greek Campania by this time was the northernmost province of *Magna Graecia*, a land of rich culture and wealthy cities that included Sicily and all of southern Italy's coasts save the Adriatic. Greek Italy's painters and sculptors were among the greatest of Greece's golden age, but its most memorable contributions were in philosophy. The famous Elean School (from Elea in the Cilento) included some of the most important pre-Socratics: Parmenides, who invented the concept of atoms, and Zeno, with his pesky paradoxes.

Italy was ripe for civilization. The Etruscans spread their rule and culture over the north while the Italic tribes learned from Etruscans and Greeks alike. Some of them, especially the Latins and the Samnites, developed into urbanized, cultured nations in their own right. For the Greek cities it was a golden age for trade, but they dissipated their energies in constant wars between cities and civil wars within them, with the losers usually massacred or sold as slaves. Parthenope, which once stood on the hill that now divides the old and new quarters of Naples, and on the nearby island where the Castel dell'Ovo is now, slugged it out with Cumae until the latter triumphed. The Cumaeans may have destroyed their rival; in any case they founded a new city—*Neapolis*—right next to it. Some Greek cities were completely destroyed, and by *c.* 400 BC the failure of the rest to work together sent them into a slow but irreversible economic decline.

The Etruscan story is much the same. By about 600 BC the 12 cities and their allies ruled almost all northern Italy, and wealth from their Tuscan mines made them a political force on a Mediterranean scale. Their decline was as rapid as Magna Graecia's. Repeated defeats by the Gauls weakened them, but the economic decline that led to Etruria's evaporation in the 4th century BC is harder to account for. **Rome**, a border city between the Etruscans and Latins, threw out its Etruscan king and established a Republic in 509 BC (*see* **Rome**, 'History', p.55). Somehow, probably by absorbing conquered populations, this relatively new city managed to grow to perhaps 100,000 people, ranking it as one of the largest on the peninsula. With an economy insufficient to support so many Romans, the city could only live by a career of permanent conquest.

509–91 BC: The Roman Rollercoaster

In the 6th century BC Rome began terrorizing the towns and tribes of central Italy. By the 4th century BC, she had gobbled up the lot, and the borders of the Roman state extended into Campania. About 358 BC the senators turned their attention to the only power in Italy capable of competing with Rome: the Samnites. These rugged highlanders of the southern Apennines had seized parts of coastal Campania from the Greeks. The Romans drove them out in 341 BC, but lost to them in the Second Samnite War (Battle of the Caudine Forks, in 321 BC). In the third war, surrounded by Roman allies,

the Samnites formed an alliance with the northern Etruscans and Celts, leading to a general Italian commotion in which the Romans beat everybody, annexing almost all of Italy by 283 BC.

After the Samnites, it was the turn of the Greeks. The frightened cities of Magna Graecia sent for Pyrrhus of Epirus, a brilliant adventurer with a big army, to keep the barbarians out. Pyrrhus won a string of inconclusive 'Pyrrhic' victories, but after finally losing a battle in 275 BC he quit and returned home, letting the Romans snatch up the deserted Greek cities. Now the conquest was complete. All along the Romans had been diabolically clever in managing their new demesne, maintaining most of the tribes and cities as nominally independent states, while planting Latin colonies in or near the ruins of cities they had destroyed, such as Paestum, Puteoli (Pozzuoli) and Benevento.

After this, Rome deserved a shot at the Mediterranean heavyweight title. The current champ, the powerful merchant thalassocracy of Carthage, was alarmed at the successes of its precocious neighbour, and proved happy to oblige. Rome won the first bout, beating Carthage and her ally Syracuse in the **First Punic War** (264–41 BC), and gained Sicily, Sardinia, and Corsica. For the rematch, the **Second Punic War** (219–202 BC), Carthage sent **Hannibal** and his elephants from Spain into Italy over the Alps to bring the war into the Romans' backyard. Undeterred by the brilliant African general's victory at Cannae in 216 BC, where four legions were destroyed, the Romans hung on tenaciously even when Hannibal appeared at the gates of Rome. In Hannibal's absence, they took Spain and much of Africa, and after Scipio Africanus' victory at Zama in 202 BC, Carthage surrendered. The **Third Punic War** was a sorry affair. Rome only waited for Carthage to miss a step in its treaty obligations before razing her to the ground. The west conquered, Rome looked east. Already by 200 BC she had been interfering in Greek affairs. The disunited Greeks and successor states of Alexander's empire proved easy targets, and by 64 BC the legions were camped on the Cataracts of the Nile, in Jerusalem, and half across Asia Minor.

Nothing corrupts a state like easy conquests, and all this time things in Italy were going very wrong. Taxation ceased for Roman citizens as booty provided the state with all the revenues it needed, and tens of thousands of slaves were imported. Italy became a parasite nation. Vast amounts of cheap grain from Africa and Egypt ruined the Italian farmer, who had the choice of selling his freehold and becoming a sharecropper, joining the army, or moving to Rome as part of the burgeoning lumpenproletariat. The men who profited the most from the wars bought tremendous amounts of land, turning Italy into a country of huge estates (*latifundia*), and becoming a new aristocracy powerful enough to stifle attempts at reform. Only Rome and a few other cities prospered. The 1st century BC witnessed a continuous political and social crisis, breaking out into a series of civil wars and rebellions that did not end until the accession of Augustus and the end of the Roman Republic.

91–31 BC: Sixty Years of Civil War

91 BC saw a coordinated revolt among the southern peoples called the **Social War**, which was defeated by the campaigns of Marius and **Sulla**, and by an offer to extend Roman citizenship to all Italians. A military coup by Sulla followed, with the backing of the Senate. An effective dictatorship was created, and all opponents murdered or exiled. Italy careered into anarchy, with many rural districts reverting to bandit-ridden wastelands, a setting for the remarkable revolt in 73 BC of **Spartacus**, an escaped gladiator who led a motley army of dispossessed farmers and runaway slaves— some 70,000 of them— back and forth across the south until the legions finally defeated him in 71 BC.

All this exhausted both sides and discredited senatorial rule. After Sulla's death, no one minded when the consulship and real power passed to **Pompey**, a successful general who cared little for politics. Pompey set out for the east, where the most glory and booty were to be gained, and left the stage in Rome to **Julius Caesar**, a clever soldier-politician, but a good man anyhow. With his surpassing talents for rhetoric and attracting money, he took up the popular cause in better style than anyone before him. After Pompey's return, he, Caesar, and a wealthy building contractor named Licinius Crassus sliced up the republic between them, forming the **First Triumvirate** (59 BC).

What Caesar really wanted was a military command. He bought one in the north, and undertook the conquest of most of Gaul, with well-known results. In his four years as ruler of Rome, Caesar surprised everyone; everything received a good dose of reform, even the calendar, and a beginning was made towards sorting out the economic mess and getting Italy back on its feet. His assassination by a clique of Republican bitter-enders in 44 BC plunged Italy into civil war again. A **Second Triumvirate** was formed, of Caesar's adopted son Octavian, a senatorial figurehead named Lepidus,

and Caesar's old friend, the talented, dissipated Marcus Antonius (Mark Antony), who according to one historian spent the equivalent of $3 billion (of other people's money) in his brief lifetime. While he dallied in the east with Cleopatra, Octavian was consolidating his power in Italy. The inevitable battle came in 31 BC, at Actium in Greece, and it was a complete victory for Octavian.

31 BC–AD 251: The Empire

With unchallenged authority through all the Roman lands, Octavian (soon to rename himself **Augustus**) was free to complete Caesar's reforms. For his career, and those of his successors, read the gossipy, shocking and wonderfully unreliable *Lives of the Caesars* by Suetonius. All Rome tittered at the scandals of the later Julian Emperors, but reality was usually more prosaic. **Tiberius** (AD 14–37) may have been a monster to his partners, but he was an intelligent and just ruler otherwise; his criminally insane successor **Caligula** lasted only four years (37–41) while the bureaucracy kept things going. **Claudius** (41–54) governed well and conquered southern Britain, while **Nero** (54–68) made a nuisance of himself in Rome but did little to disturb the system. Nevertheless, **Galba**, a commander in Spain, declared him unfit to rule and marched on Rome to take his place; Nero just managed to commit suicide before they caught him. Now the genie was out of the bottle again, as the soldiers realized that they had the real power. **Otho**, commander of the Praetorian Guard, beat Galba, then lost to **Vitellius**, commander on the Rhine. The fourth emperor of AD 68–69 was **Vespasian**, leader of the eastern armies. He had the strongest legions and so kept the job; his reign (69–79) and those of his sons **Titus** (79–81) and **Domitian** (81–96), the three Flavian Emperors, were a period of prosperity. Vespasian began the Colosseum, an incomparable charnel house that made a perfect symbol for the renewed decadence and militarization of the state.

For the moment, however, things looked rosy. After the assassination of Domitian, Rome was ruled by a series of high-minded and intelligent military men, who chose their successors in advance to avoid civil war. The **Antonine Emperors** presided over the greatest age of prosperity the Mediterranean ever knew; in Italy they ran a surprisingly modern state (albeit based on slave labour) with public libraries, water boards to maintain aqueducts, rent control, agricultural price supports, low-cost loans to start new businesses and many other innovations. The first Antonine was **Nerva** (96–98), then **Trajan** (98–117) and **Hadrian** (117–138), both great soldiers and builders on a monumental scale, especially in Rome; after them came **Antoninus Pius** (138–61), little known only because his reign was so peaceful, and **Marcus Aurelius** (161–80), soldier, statesman and Stoic philosopher. His choice for successor was his useless son **Commodus** (180–93), and the string of good emperors was broken.

The 2nd-century prosperity had a darker side. The arts were in serious decline, as if the imagination of the Graeco-Roman Mediterranean was failing. Education was in poor shape, and fatuous mysticism permeated thought. The rural south sank deeper into decline, while Magna Graecia's commerce began to fail, ruined by competition, high taxes and bureaucracy. The eruption of Vesuvius in AD 79 must have increased the economic disarray; three sizeable towns—Pompeii, Herculaneum and Stabiae—completely disappeared, and vast tracts of fertile land withered under volcanic ash. In northern Italy, meanwhile, a sounder, more stable economy was leading to the growth of new centres—Milan, Padua, Verona, Florence and others. The economic north-south divide, a problem for which no solution is in sight even today, was already beginning.

251–475: Decline and Fall

For all it cost to maintain them, the legions were no longer Augustus' formidable military machine. They were bureaucratic and tired, and their tactics and equipment were no longer the best. The Goths showed this in 251 when they overran the Balkans, Greece and Asia Minor. Five years later Franks and Alemanni invaded Gaul, and in 268 Odenathus of Palmyra detached much of the east from the empire. Somehow the empire recovered under dour soldier-emperors like **Aurelian** (270–5), who built Rome's walls, and **Diocletian** (284–305), who completely revamped the structure of the state and economy. His fiscal reforms, such as the fixing of prices and a decree that every son had to follow the trade of his father, ossified the economy and made the creeping decline of Italy and all western Europe harder to arrest.

More than ever, the Empire was a military dictatorship, whose waning energies were devoted to supporting an all-devouring army and bureaucracy. The confused politics of the 4th century are dominated by **Constantine** (306–37), who ruled both halves of the Empire, defeated other contenders and founded the new eastern capital of Constantinople. He adroitly moved to increase his and the Empire's political support by favouring Christianity. Though still a minority in most of the Empire, the Christians' strong organization and determination made them a good bet for the future.

The military disasters began in 406, with Visigoths, Franks, Vandals, Alans and Suevi overrunning Gaul and Spain. Visigoths invaded Italy in 408; Alaric sacked Rome in 410. St Augustine, probably echoing the thoughts of most Romans, wrote that it seemed the end of the world must be near. Judgement was postponed long enough for **Attila the Hun** to pass through Italy in 451. Then Gaiseric the Vandal, who had set up a pirate kingdom in Africa, raided Italy and sacked Rome in 455. By now it was scarcely possible to tell the Romans from the barbarians. By the 470s, the real ruler was a Gothic general, **Odoacer**, who led a half-Romanized Germanic army and probably thought he was the heir of the Caesars. In 476, he dispensed with the lingering charade of the Western Empire. The last emperor, silly Romulus Augustulus, was packed off to premature retirement in Naples, and Odoacer was crowned King of Italy at Pavia.

475–1000: The Dark Ages

At first the new Gothic-Latin state showed some promise. The average man was no worse off than he had been under the last emperors; trade and cities even revived a bit. In 493, Odoacer was replaced (and murdered) by a rival Ostrogoth, **Theodoric**, nominally working on behalf of the Eastern Emperor at Byzantium.

A disaster as serious as those of the 5th century began in 536, with the invasion of Italy by the Eastern Empire, part of the relentlessly expansionist policy of the great **Justinian**. In the ancient homeland of the Roman Empire, Roman troops now came as foreign, Greek-speaking conquerors. The south, still largely Greek by race and sentiment, welcomed the Greek army, but much of the worst fighting took place in the region; Naples, the largest city in the south, was sacked by both sides. Justinian's brilliant generals, Belisarius and Narses, prevailed over the Goths in a series of terrible wars that lasted until 563, but the damage to an already stricken society and economy was incalculable. Italy's exhaustion was exposed just five years later, when the **Lombards**, a Germanic tribe who worked hard to earn the title of barbarian, overran northern Italy and parts of the south, establishing a kingdom at Pavia and duchies in Benevento and Spoleto. A new pattern of power appeared, with semi-independent Byzantine dukes defending coastal areas and Lombard chiefs ruling most of the interior. Byzantine control was always tenuous, and cities like Naples and Salerno achieved a *de facto* independence. The popes in Rome, occasionally allied with the Lombards against Byzantium, became a force during this period, especially after the papacy of the clever, determined **Gregory the Great** (590–604). Scion of the richest family in Italy, Gregory took political control in Rome during desperate times, and laid the foundations for the papacy's claims to temporal power.

With trade and culture at their lowest ebb, the 7th century marks the rock bottom of Italian history. The 8th showed some improvement; **Venice** was beginning its remarkable career as a trading city, and independent Amalfi and Naples emulated its success on the Tyrrhenian coast. The popes intrigued to increase their influence; they finally cashed in with a Frankish alliance in the 750s. At the time the Lombard kings were doing well, finally conquering Ravenna (751) and considerable territories formerly under the dominion of the popes, who invited in **Charlemagne** to protect them.

When Charlemagne's empire disintegrated following his death in 814, Italy reverted to a finely balanced anarchy. In the 9th century Italy was caught between Arab raiders and the endless wars of petty nobles in the north. The 10th century proved better—perhaps much better than the scanty chronicles of the time attest. A big break came in 961 with the invasion of the German **Otto the Great**, heir to the imperial pretensions of the Carolingians. He deposed the last King of Italy, Berengar II of Ivrea, and was crowned Holy Roman Emperor the following year. The Italians weren't happy to see him, but the strong government of Otto and his successors beat down the nobles and allowed the growing cities to expand their power and influence. A new pattern was established; Germanic emperors would be meddling in Italian affairs for centuries, not powerful enough to establish total control, but at least usually able to keep out important rivals.

1000–1154: The Rise of the *Comuni*

On the eve of the new millennium, most Christians were convinced that the turn of the calendar would bring the end of the world. If there had been economists and social scientists around, though, they would have had ample evidence that things were looking up. Especially in the towns, business was very good, and political prospects even better. The first mention of a truly independent *comune* (plural: *comuni*; meaning a free city state; the best translation might be 'commonwealth') was in Milan, where in 1024 a popular assembly is recorded, deciding which side the city would take in the Imperial Wars.

Throughout this period the papacy had declined greatly, becoming a political football kicked by the emperors and the piratical Roman nobles. Beginning in the 1050s, a remarkable monk named Hildebrand controlled papal policy, working behind the scenes to reassert the influence of the Church. When he became Pope himself, in 1073, **Gregory VII** immediately set himself in conflict with the emperors over investiture—whether the Church or secular powers could name Church officials. The various Italian (and European) powers took sides on the issue, and 50 years of intermittent war followed.

Southern Italy knew a different fate. The first **Normans** arrived about 1020, and soon younger sons of feudal families were moving into the south, first as mercenaries but gradually gaining large tracts of land in exchange for their services. One of their greatest chiefs, Robert Guiscard, came to control much of the south as Duke of Puglia. In 1084 he descended on Rome for a grisly sack that put the best efforts of the Goths and Vandals to shame. His less destructive brother, Roger de Hauteville, began the conquest of Sicily in 1060. Naples fell to the Norman armies in 1139.

Roger de Hauteville eventually united all of the south into the 'Kingdom of Sicily', and by the 1140s, under Roger II, this strange Norman-Arab-Jewish-Italian-Greek state, with its glittering, half-oriental capital of Palermo, had become the cultural centre of the Mediterranean, a refuge of religious tolerance and serious scholarship. Under Roger and his successors it remained one of the strongest and best-organized states in Europe.

1154–1300: Guelphs and Ghibellines

Meanwhile, the First Crusade (1097–1130) occupied the headlines. It was in part a result of the new militancy of the papacy; for Italy it meant pure profit. Trade was booming everywhere, and the accumulation of money helped the Italians to create modern Europe's first banking system. It also financed the continued independence of the *comuni*, which flourished everywhere, with a big enough surplus for building projects like Pisa's cathedral complex. Culture and science were flourishing, too, with a big boost from contact with the Byzantines and the Muslims of Spain and Africa. By the 12th century, far in advance of most of Europe, Italy had attained a prosperity unknown since Roman times.

Emperors and popes were still embroiled in the north. **Frederick I Barbarossa** made it the cornerstone of his policy to reassert imperial power in Italy. Beginning in 1154, he crossed the Alps five times, molesting free cities that asked nothing more than to fight one another. He spread terror, utterly destroying Milan in 1161, but a united front of cities (the 'Lombard League') defeated him in 1176. His greatest triumph in Italy came by arranging the marriage with the Normans that left his grandson **Frederick II** not only Emperor but King of Sicily, giving him a strong power base in Italy itself.

The second Frederick's career dominated Italian politics from 1220 to 1250. With his brilliant court, in which Italian was used for the first time (alongside Arabic and Latin), his half-Muslim army, his processions of dancing girls, eunuchs, and elephants, he provided Europe with a spectacle the like of which it had never seen. He founded universities (as at Naples), gave Sicily a written constitution (perhaps the world's first), and built geometrically arcane castles and towers all over the south. The popes excommunicated him at least twice.

The battle of pope and emperor was now serious. Italy divided into factions: the **Guelphs**, led by the popes, supported religious orthodoxy, the liberty of the *comuni*, and the interests of the emerging merchant class. The **Ghibellines** stood for the Emperor, statist economic control, the interests of the rural nobles, and religious and intellectual tolerance. Frederick's campaigns and diplomacy in the north met with very limited success, and his death in 1250 left the outcome much in doubt.

His son **Manfred**, not Emperor but merely King of Sicily, took up the battle with better luck; Siena beat Florence in 1260, gaining that city and most of Tuscany for the Ghibellines. The next year, however, Pope Urban IV set a disastrous precedent by inviting in **Charles of Anjou**, a powerful, ambitious leader, brother of the King of France and protector of the Guelphs. Charles defeated Manfred (1266) and murdered the last of the Hohenstaufens, Conradin (1268). He held unchallenged sway over Italy until 1282, when the famous revolt of the Sicilian Vespers started the party wars up again. By now, however, the terms *Guelph* and *Ghibelline* had ceased to have much meaning; men and cities changed sides as they found expedient.

Cities were falling under the rule of military *signori* whose descendants would style themselves counts and dukes—the Visconti of Milan, the della Scala of Verona. Everywhere the freedom of the *comuni* was in jeopardy; after so much strife the temptation to submit to a strong leader often proved overwhelming. During Charles of Anjou's reign the popes extracted the price for their invitation: the Papal State, including much of central Italy, was established in 1278. But the Italian economy never seemed to mind the trouble. Trade and money flowed as never before; cities built new cathedrals and created incredible skyscraper skylines, with the tall tower-fortresses of the now urbanized nobles. And it was, in spite of everything, a great age for culture—the era of Guelphs and Ghibellines was also the time of Dante (b. 1265) and Giotto (b. 1266).

1300–1494: Renaissance Italy

This paradoxical Italy continued into the 14th century, with a golden age of culture and an opulent economy side by side with almost continuous war and turmoil. With no serious threats from foreign powers, the Italian states menaced each other joyfully without outside interference. War became a sort of game, conducted on behalf of cities by paid mercenaries led by *condottieri*, who were never allowed to enter the cities themselves.

By far the biggest event of the 14th century was the **Black Death** of 1347–8, in which it is estimated Italy lost one-third of its population. The shock brought a rude halt to 400 years of almost continuous growth and prosperity, though its effects did not prove a permanent setback for the economy. In fact, the plague's grim joke was that it actually made life better for most of the Italians who survived; working people in the cities, no longer overcrowded, found their rents lower and their labour worth more, while in the country farmers were able to increase their profits by tilling only the best land.

Despite its unity under Normans and Hohenstaufens, the south was falling behind politically and economically. The Normans ruled their domains fairly and intelligently, but they also introduced feudalism into a country that had never known it, just as the mercantile states of the north were breaking loose from the feudal arrangements brought in by the Goths and Lombards. Now the 'Kingdom of Naples', as the southern state had become known, was a tapestry of battling barons, each busily building or improving his castle and increasingly less inclined to listen to kings or popes or anyone. The trading cities, especially Naples, Amalfi and Bari, saw increasingly strong competition from the Venetians and Genoese. With little encouragement from king or barons, they could only continue to decline.

Robert the Wise (1309–43) was a good king, patron of Giotto, Petrarch and Boccaccio. He left a granddaughter, Giovanna I, under whose unsteady hand the barons increased their power and contentiousness. Her reign witnessed the beginnings of civil war between Angevin factions, something that would continue fitfully through a century of intrigue and insurrections. It ended in the hands of another foreigner, Alfonso the Magnanimous, King of Aragon, who conquered Naples and tossed out the last Angevins in 1442. Once more the Kingdom was reunited with Sicily, part of the Aragonese crown since the Sicilian Vespers. Alfonso and his successor, the cruel King Ferrante, ruled Naples with harshness and skill; both were typical Renaissance princes who, as leaders of the only kingdom in Italy, played major roles in the eternal petty wars and intrigues of the age.

And what of the Renaissance? No word has ever caused more mischief for the understanding of history and culture—as if Italy had been Sleeping Beauty, waiting for some Prince Charming of classical culture to come and awaken it from a thousand-year nap. On the contrary, Italy even in the 1200s was richer, more technologically advanced, and far more artistically creative than it had ever been in the days of the Caesars. The new art and scholarship that spread across the nation in the 1400s grew from a solid foundation of medieval accomplishment. The opulent Italy of the 15th century felt complacently secure in its cultural and economic pre-eminence. A long spell of freedom from outside interference lulled the nation into believing that its political disunity could continue forever; except perhaps for the clear-eyed realistic Niccolò Machiavelli, no one realized that Italy was a plum waiting to be picked.

1494–1529: The Wars of Italy

The terrible series of conflicts that eventually rang down the curtain on the Renaissance and on Italian liberty began in 1494 with a quarrel over Naples. Charles VIII, King of France, took advantage of Italian disunity when Duke Ludovico of Milan invited him to cross the Alps and assert his claim through the Angevins to the throne of Milan's enemy, Naples. Charles did just that, and the failure of the combined Italian states to stop him (at the inconclusive Battle of Fornovo, 1494) showed just how helpless Italy was at the hands of emerging monarchies like France or Spain. The last Aragonese king of Naples, the ineffectual Alfonso II, fled the city rather than face him. Spain sent Gonsalvo di Córdoba, with a strong army, who restored Naples to its Spanish king the following year. More fighting between Aragonese factions followed, and when the dust settled, in 1502, Naples and its kingdom were directly under the Spanish crown, and ruled by a viceroy.

Before long the German Emperor and even the Swiss entered this new market for Italian real estate. The popes did as much as anyone to keep the pot boiling. Alexander VI and his son Cesare Borgia carried the war across central Italy in an attempt to found a new state for the Borgia family, and Julius II egged on the Swiss, French and Spaniards in turn, before finally crying, 'Out with the barbarians!' when it was already too late.

By 1516, with the French ruling Milan and the Spanish in control of the south, it seemed as if a settlement would be possible. The worst possible luck for Italy, however, came with the accession of the insatiable megalomaniac **Charles V** to the throne of Spain in that year; in 1519 he bought himself the crown of the Holy Roman Empire, making him the most powerful ruler in Europe since Charlemagne. Charles felt he needed Milan as a base for communications between his Spanish, German and Flemish possessions, and as soon as he had emptied Spain's treasury, driven her to revolt, and plunged Germany into civil war, he turned his attentions to Italy. The wars began anew, bloodier than anything Italy had seen for centuries, climaxing with the sack of Rome by an out-of-control Imperial army in 1527. The French invaded once more, in 1529, and were defeated this time at Naples by the treachery of their Genoese allies. All Italy, save only Venice, was now at the mercy of Charles and the Spaniards.

1529–1600: Italy in Chains

The broader context of these events was the bitter struggles of the Reformation and Counter-Reformation. In Italy, this new religious angle made the Spaniards and the popes natural allies. With most of the peninsula still nominally controlled by local rulers, and an economy that remained sound, both the Spaniards and the popes realized that the only real threat was from ideas. Under the banner of combating Protestantism, they began a reign of terror across Italy. In the 1550s, the revived Inquisition began its manhunt for free-thinkers of every variety. A long line of Italian intellectuals trudged to the stake, while many more buried their convictions or left for exile in Germany or England.

Despite the oppression, the average Italian at first had little to complain about. Spanish domination brought peace and order to a country that had long been a madhouse of conflicting ambitions. Renaissance artists attained a new virtuosity, just in time to embellish the scores of churches, palaces, and villas of the mid 16th-century building boom. The combined Christian forces had turned back the Turkish threat at Malta (1566) and Lepanto (1571), and some Italians were benefiting greatly from Spanish imperialism in the New World—especially the Genoese, who rented ships, floated loans, and snatched up a surprising amount of the gold and silver arriving from America.

Nevertheless, the first signs of decay were already apparent. Palladio's villas for Venetian magnates, and Michelozzo's outside Florence, are landmarks in architecture but also one of the earliest symptoms. In both cities, the old mercantile economies were failing, and the wealthy began to invest their money unproductively in land instead of risking it in business or finance.

1600–1796: The Age of Baroque

After 1600 nearly everything started to go wrong for the Italians. The textiles and banking of the north, long the engines of the economy, withered in the face of foreign competition, and the old port towns (with the exceptions of Genoa and Livorno) began to look half empty as the English and Dutch muscled them out of the declining Mediterranean trade. Worst off of all was the south, under direct Spanish or papal rule. Combining incompetence and brutality with outrageously high taxes (the Spaniards' to finance foreign wars, the popes' to build up Rome), they rapidly turned the already poor south into a nightmare of anarchic depravity, haunted by legions of bandits and beggars, and controlled more tightly than ever by its violent feudal barons. To everyone's surprise, the south rose up and staged an epic rebellion. Beginning in Naples (Masaniello's Revolt, 1647), the disturbances soon spread all over the south and Sicily. For over a year peasant militias ruled some areas, and makeshift revolutionary councils defended the cities. When the Spanish finally defeated them, however, they massacred some 18,000, and tightened the screws more than ever.

Bullied, humiliated and increasingly impoverished, 17th-century Italy tried hard to keep up its prominence in the arts and sciences. Galileo looked through telescopes, Monteverdi wrote the first operas, and hundreds of talented if uninspired artists cranked out pretty pictures to meet the continuing high demand. Bernini and Borromini turned Rome into the capital of baroque—the florid, expensive coloratura style that serves as a perfect symbol for its age of political repression and thought control where art became a political tool. Baroque's grandeur and symmetry helped to impress everyone with the majesty of Church and state. At the same time, baroque scholars wrote books that went on for hundreds of pages without saying anything, but avoided offending the government or Inquisition.

By the 18th century, there were very few painters, or scholars or scientists. There were no more heroic revolts either. Italy in this period hardly has any history: with Spain's increasing decadence, the great powers decided the future of Italy's major states, and used the minor ones to hold surplus princes and those dispossessed by wars elsewhere (the most famous being Napoleon on Elba). In 1713, after the War of the Spanish Succession, the Habsburgs of **Austria** came into control of Milan and Lombardy, Mantua and the Kingdom of Naples. The House of Lorraine, related to the Austrians, won Tuscany upon the extinction of the Medici in 1737. These new rulers improved conditions somewhat.

1796–1830: Napoleon, Restoration, and Reaction

Napoleon, that greatest of Italian generals, arrived in the country in 1796 on behalf of the French revolutionary Directorate, sweeping away the Piedmontese and Austrians and setting up republics in Lombardy (the 'Cisalpine Republic'), Liguria, and Naples (the 'Parthenopean Republic'). Italy woke with a start from its baroque slumbers, and local patriots gaily joined the French cause. In 1799, however, while Napoleon was off in Egypt, the advance through Italy by an Austro-Russian army, aided by Nelson's fleet, restored the status quo. This was often accompanied by bloody reprisals, as peasant mobs led by clerics like the 'Army of the Holy Faith' marched across the south massacring liberals and French sympathizers.

In 1800 Napoleon returned in a campaign that saw the great victory at Marengo, giving him the opportunity once more to reorganize Italian affairs. Napoleon crowned himself King of Italy; Joseph Bonaparte and later Joachim Murat ruled at Naples. Rome was annexed to France, and the Pope was carted off to Fontainebleau. Napoleonic rule lasted only until 1814, but in that time important public works were begun and laws and education reformed after the French model; Church properties were expropriated, and medieval relics everywhere put to rest. The French, however, soon wore out their welcome. Besides hauling much of Italy's artistic heritage off to the Louvre, implementing high war taxes and conscription (some 25,000 Italians died in the invasion of Russia), and brutally repressing a number of local revolts, they systematically exploited Italy for the benefit of the Napoleonic élite and the crowds of speculators who came flocking over the Alps. When the Austrians and English came to chase all the little Napoleons out, no one was sad to see them go.

The 1815 Congress of Vienna put the clock back to 1798: the Bourbons pretended the Napoleonic upheavals had never happened, and the political reaction in their territories was fierce (from this time on, incidentally, the *Regno* of Naples and Sicily was officially and confusingly called the 'Kingdom of the Two Sicilies'). But the experience had given Italians a taste of the opportunities offered by the modern world, as well as a sense of national feeling that had been suppressed for centuries. Almost immediately, revolutionary agitators and secret societies like the famous *Carbonari* kept Italy convulsed in plots and intrigues. A big revolt in Naples forced King Ferdinand, now a bitter old reactionary after his experiences with the French, to grant a constitution (1821), but when Austrian troops came down to crush the rebels he took it back.

1848–1915: The Risorgimento and United Italy

Conspirators of every kind, including the legendary **Giuseppe Mazzini**, had to wait 18 years for their next chance. Mazzini, a patriot and democrat, agitated all through the years 1830–70, beginning by founding the *Young Italy* movement, all with little practical effect.

The big change came in the revolutionary year of 1848, when risings in Palermo and Naples anticipated those in Paris itself. Soon all Italy was in the streets. Piedmont and Tuscany won constitutions; the people of Milan chased out the Austrians; the Venetian Republic was restored. Carlo Alberto marched against the Austrians, but his bungled campaigns let the enemy re-establish control over the peninsula. By June 1849, only Venice, under Austrian blockade, and the recently declared Roman Republic were left. Rome, led by Mazzini, and with a small army under **Giuseppe Garibaldi**, beat off several attacks from foreign troops invited in by the Pope. The republic finally succumbed to a force sent by, of all people, the republic of President Louis Napoleon (soon to declare himself Napoleon III) in France.

At least the Italians knew they would get another chance. Unification was inevitable, but there were two irreconcilable contenders for the honour of accomplishing it. On one side, the democrats and radicals dreamed of a truly reborn, revolutionary Italy, and looked to the popular hero Garibaldi to deliver it; on the other, moderates wanted the Piedmontese to do the job, ensuring a stable future by making **Vittorio Emanuele II** King of Italy. Vittorio Emanuele's Minister, the polished, clever **Count Camillo Cavour**, spent the

1850s getting Piedmont in shape for the struggle, building its economy and army, participating in the Crimean War to earn diplomatic support, and plotting with the French for an alliance against Austria.

War came in 1859, and French armies did most of the work in conquering Lombardy. Tuscany and Emilia revolted, and Piedmont was able to annex all three. In May 1860, Garibaldi and his red-shirted 'Thousand' sailed from Genoa—Cavour almost stopped them at the last minute—and landed in Sicily, electrifying Europe by repeatedly beating the Bourbon forces in a quick march across the island as the Thousand became 20,000. On 7 September, Garibaldi entered Naples; he proclaimed himself temporary dictator on Vittorio Emanuele's behalf, but the Piedmontese were alarmed enough to occupy Umbria and the Marches. The King met Garibaldi in October, and after finding out what little regard the Piedmontese had for him, the greatest and least self-interested leader modern Italy has known went off to retirement on the island of Caprara.

Just as the French made all this possible, some more unexpected help from outside allowed the new Italy to add two missing pieces and complete its unification. When the Prussians defeated Austria in the war of 1866, Italy was able to seize the Veneto. Only Rome was left, defended by a French garrison, and when the Prussians beat France at Sedan in 1870, the Italian army marched into Rome almost without opposition.

The first decades of the Italian Kingdom were just as unimpressive as its wars of independence. A liberal constitutional monarchy was established, but the parliament almost immediately split into cliques and cartels. Finances started in disorder and stayed that way, and corruption was widespread. Peasant revolts occurred in the south, as people felt cheated after the promises of the Risorgimento, and organized brigandage became a problem, partially instigated by the Vatican as part of an attempt to discredit the new regime. The outlines of foreign policy often seemed to change monthly, though like the other European powers Italy felt it necessary to snatch up some colonies. The attempt revealed the new state's limited capabilities, with embarrassing military disasters at the hands of the Ethiopians at Dogali in 1887, and again at Adowa in 1896.

After 1900, with the rise of a strong socialist movement, strikes, riots and police repression often occupied centre stage in Italian politics. Even so, important signs of progress, such as the big new industries in Turin and Milan, showed that at least the northern half of Italy was becoming part of the European economy. The 15 years before the war, prosperous and contented ones for many, came to be known by the slightly derogatory term *Italietta*, the 'little Italy' of modest bourgeois happiness, sweet Puccini operas, motorcars, 'Liberty'-style architecture, and Sunday afternoons at the beach.

1915–1945: War, Fascism, and War

Italy could have stayed out of the First World War, but missed the chance in the hope of gaining some new territory, especially Trieste. Also, part of the intelligentsia found the *Italietta* boring and disgraceful: irredentists of all stripes, some of the futurists, and the perverse, idolized poet **Gabriele D'Annunzio**. They helped Italy leap blindly into the conflict in 1915, with a big promise of boundary adjustments dangled by the beleaguered Allies. Italian armies fought with their accustomed flair, masterminding a catastrophe at Caporetto (1917) that any other nation but Austria would have parleyed into a total victory. No thanks to their incompetent generals, the poorly armed and equipped Italians somehow held firm for another year, until Austria's total exhaustion allowed them to prevail at the Battle of Vittorio Veneto, capturing some 600,000 prisoners in November 1918.

In return for 650,000 dead, a million casualties, severe privation on the home front, and a huge war debt, Italy received Trieste, Gorizia, the South Tyrol and a few other scraps. Italians felt they had been cheated, and nationalist sentiment increased, especially when D'Annunzio led a band of freebooters to seize the half-Italian city of Fiume in September 1919, after the peace conferences promised it to Yugoslavia. The Italian economy was in a shambles, and in the north revolution was in the air; workers in Turin raised the Red Flag and organized themselves into soviets. The troubles encouraged extremists of both sides, and many Italians became convinced that the liberal state was finished.

Enter **Benito Mussolini**, a professional intriguer of no fixed principles. In the post-War confusion, he found his opportunity. A bit at a time, he developed the idea of **Fascism**, at first less a philosophy than an astute use of mass propaganda and a sense for design. With a little discreet money supplied by frightened industrialists, Mussolini had no trouble in finding recruits for his black-shirted gangs, who found their first success beating up Slavs in Trieste and working as a sort of private police for landowners in stoutly socialist Emilia-Romagna.

Mussolini's accession to power came on an improbable gamble. In the particularly anarchic month of October 1922, he announced that his followers would march on Rome. Vittorio Emanuele III refused to sign a decree of martial law to disperse them, and there was nothing to do but offer Mussolini the post of prime minister. At first he governed Italy with competence. Industry advanced, great public works were undertaken, with special care for the backward south, and the Mafia and Camorra (*see* pp.51–2) took some heavy blows. Order was restored, and the economy and foreign policy handled intelligently by non-Fascist professionals. In the 1924 elections, despite the flagrant rigging and intimidation, the Fascists only won a slight majority. During 1925 and 1926 the Fascists used parliamentary methods to convert Italy into a permanent Fascist dictatorship.

In the words of one of Mussolini's favourite slogans, painted on walls all over Italy, 'Whoever stops is lost'. Mussolini couldn't stop, and the only possibility for new diversions lay with the chance of conquest and empire. His invasion of Ethiopia and meddling in the Spanish Civil War, both in 1936, compromised Italy into a close alliance with Nazi Germany. Mussolini's confidence and rhetoric never faltered as he led an entirely unprepared nation into the biggest war ever. Once more, Italian ineptitude at warfare produced embarrassing defeats on all fronts, and only German intervention in Greece and North Africa saved Italy from being knocked out of the war as early as 1941. The Allies invaded Sicily in July 1943, and the Italians began to look for a way out. They seized Mussolini during a meeting of the Grand Council and sent him off first to Ponza, then to a little ski hotel up in the Apennines. The new government under Marshal Badoglio didn't know what to do, and confusion reigned supreme.

As British and American forces slogged northwards, the Germans poured in divisions to defend the peninsula. They rescued Mussolini, and set him up in a puppet state called the Italian Social Republic in the north. In September 1943, the Badoglio government signed an armistice with the Allies, too late to keep the war from dragging on another year and a half, as the Germans used Italy's difficult terrain to slow the Allied advance. Meanwhile Italy finally gave itself something to be proud of: a determined, resourceful Resistance that established free zones and harassed the Germans with sabotage and strikes. After the Salerno landings, the successful short cut that put the Allies on Naples' doorstep, the city surprised everyone, perhaps even itself, by staging an entirely spontaneous popular revolt, the 'Four Days in Naples', that drove the Germans from the city. The *partigiani* caught Mussolini in April 1945, while he was trying to escape to Switzerland; after shooting him and his mistress, they hung him by his feet from the roof of a petrol station in Milan.

1945–the Present

Post-war Italian *cinema verità*—Rossellini's *Rome, Open City*, or de Sica's *Bicycle Thieves*—captures the atmosphere better than words ever could. In a period of serious hardships, the nation slowly picked itself up and returned things to normal. A referendum in June 1946 made Italy a republic by a narrow margin. The first governments fell to the new Christian Democrat Party, which has run the show ever since in coalitions with a preposterous band of smaller parties.

The fifties was Rome's decade, when Italian style and Italian cinema caught the imagination of the world. A little economic miracle was happening; *Signor Rossi*, the average Italian, started buzzing around in his first classic Fiat *cinquecento*, northern industries boomed, and life cruised slowly back to normal. The south continued to lag behind, despite the sincere efforts of the government and its special planning fund, the *Cassa per il Mezzogiorno*. Though the extreme poverty and despair of the post-War years gradually disappeared, even today there is little evidence that the region is catching up with the rest of the country. The *Democristiani*-controlled government soon evolved a Byzantine style of politics. Through the constant parade of collapsing and reforming cabinets, nothing changed; all deals were made in the back rooms and everyone, from the Pope to the Communists, had a share in the decision-making. One wouldn't call it democracy with a straight face, but for four decades it worked well enough to keep Italy on its wheels. The dark side of the arrangement was the all-pervasive corruption that the system fostered. Italy was run by an unprincipled political machine, whose members were raking in as much for themselves as they could grab, and everyone knew it, only it couldn't be said openly, for lack of proof. Even more sinister was the extent to which the machine would go to keep on top.

The seventies—Italy's 'years of lead'—witnessed the worst of the political sleaze, along with a grim reign of terrorism, culminating in the kidnapping and murder in 1978 of an honourable Christian Democrat prime minister, Aldo Moro. All along, the attacks were attributed to 'leftist groups', though even at the time many suspected that some of the highest circles in the government and army were controlling or manipulating them, with the possible collusion of the CIA. They were indeed, and only recently has some of the truth begun

to seep out. On another front, Italians woke up one morning in 1992 to find that the government had magically vacuumed 7 per cent of the money out of all their savings accounts, an 'emergency measure' to meet the nation's colossal budget deficit—a deficit caused largely by the thievery of the political class and its allies in organized crime.

The lid has now blown off, and at the time of writing Italy is well into a very Italian revolution. In the early nineties, heroic prosecutors Giovanni Falcone and Paolo Borsellino went after the Sicilian Mafia with some success, and were assassinated for it, causing national outrage. Meanwhile, in Milan, a small group of prosecutors and judges found a minor political kickback scandal that led them, through years of quiet and painstaking work, to the golden string that is currently unravelling the whole rotten tangle of Italian political depravity—what Italians call the *tangentopoli*, or 'bribe city'. For over a year, the televised hearings of Judge Antonio di Pietro and his Operation *Mani Pulite* ('clean hands') team from Milan were the nation's favourite and most fascinating serial. The future of the Italian 'revolution' looks more uncertain than ever. Expect bigger and stranger surprises in the years to come.

Art and Architecture

You'd have to spend your holiday in a baggage compartment to miss Italy's vast piles of architecture and art. The Italians estimate there is one work of art per capita in their country, which is more than anyone could see in a lifetime—especially since so much of it is locked away in museums that are in semi-permanent 'restoration'. Although you may occasionally chafe at not being able to see certain frescoes, or at finding a famous palace completely wrapped up in the ubiquitous green netting of the restorers, the Italians on the whole bear the burden of keeping their awesome patrimony dusted off and open for visitors very well. Some Italians find it insupportable living with the stuff all around them; the futurists, for instance, were worried that St Mark's might be blown up by foreign enemies in the First World War—but only because they wanted to do it themselves, as was their right as Italian citizens.

Pre-Etruscan Art

To give a chronological account of the first Italian artists is an uncomfortable task. The peninsula's mountainous terrain saw many isolated developments and many survivals of ancient cultures even during the days of the sophisticated Etruscans and Romans. Most ancient of all is the palaeolithic troglodyte culture on the Riviera, credited with creating some of the first artworks in Europe—chubby images of fertility goddesses. The most remarkable works from the Neolithic period up until the Iron Age are the thousands of graffiti rock incisions in several isolated Alpine valleys north of Lake Iseo.

After 1000 BC Italic peoples all over the peninsula were making geometrically painted pots, weapons, tools and bronze statuettes. The most impressive culture was the tower-building, bronze-working Nuraghe civilization on **Sardinia**, of which echoes are seen in many cultures on the mainland. Among the most intriguing and beautiful artefacts to have survived are those of the Villanova culture; the statues and inscriptions of the little-known Middle Adriatic culture, and the statue-steles of an unknown people north of Viareggio.

Etruscans and Greeks (8th–2nd centuries BC)

With the refined, art-loving Etruscans we begin to have architecture as well as art. Not much has survived, thanks to the Etruscans' habit of building in wood and decorating with terracotta, but we do have plenty of distinctive rock-cut tombs, many of which contain exceptional frescoes that reflect Aegean Greek styles. The best of their lovely sculptures, jewellery, vases and much more are in the Villa Giulia in Rome, where you can also see a reconstructed temple façade.

The Etruscans imported and copied many of their vases from their ancient Greek contemporaries, from Greece proper and the colonies of Magna Graecia in southern Italy; there are many other excavated Greek cities, but usually only foundations remain. The Archaeological Museum in the Vatican has an impressive collection of ancient Greek vases, statues and other types of art.

Roman (3rd century BC–5th century AD)

Italian art during the Roman hegemony is mostly derivative of the Etruscan and Greek, with a special talent for mosaics, wall paintings, glasswork and portraiture; architecturally, the Romans were brilliant engineers, the inventors of concrete and grand exponents of the arch. Even today their constructions, such as aqueducts, amphitheatres, bridges, baths, and of course the Pantheon, are most impressive.

Of course Rome itself has no end of ancient monuments; also in the vicinity are Ostia Antica, Rome's ancient port, and Tivoli, site of Hadrian's great villa.

Rome has a stellar set of museums filled with Roman antiquities—the National Museum in Diocletian's Baths, the Vatican Museum, the Capitoline Museums, and the Museum of Roman Civilization at EUR.

Early Middle Ages (5th–10th century)

After the fall of the Roman Empire, civilization's lamp flickered most brightly in Ravenna, where Byzantine mosaicists adorned the glittering churches of the Eastern Exarchate. Theirs was to be the prominent style in pictorial art and architecture until the 13th century. There are fine mosaics and paintings of the period in Rome, in a score of churches such as Sant'Agnese, San Clemente and Santa Prassede; in Rome the Italian preference for basilican churches and octagonal baptistries began in Constantine's day, and the development of Christian art and architecture through the Dark Ages can be traced there better than anywhere else. There are also many paintings in the catacombs.

'Lombard' art (by the native population under Lombard rule) revealed original talent in the 7th–9th centuries, as well as a new style presaging the Romanesque.

Romanesque (11th–12th centuries)

At this point, when an expansive society made new advances in art possible, north and south Italy went their separate ways, each contributing distinctive styles in sculpture and architecture. We also begin to learn the identities of some of their makers. The great Lombard cathedrals are masterworks of brick art and adorned with blind arcading, bas-reliefs and lofty campaniles. Florence developed its own particularist black and white style, exemplified in truly amazing buildings like the Baptistry and San Miniato.

The outstanding architectural advance of this period is the Puglian Romanesque, a style closely related to contemporary Norman and Pisan work—it is impossible to say which came first. This period also saw the erection of urban skyscrapers by the nobility: family fortress-towers built when the *comuni* forced local barons to move into the towns. Larger cities once had literally hundreds of them, before the townspeople succeeded in getting them demolished.

Late Medieval–Early Renaissance (13th–14th centuries)

In many ways this was the most exciting and vigorous phase in Italian art history, an age of discovery when the power of the artist was almost like that of a magician.

Great imaginative leaps occurred in architecture, painting, and sculpture. From Milan to Assisi, a group of masons and sculptors known as the *Campionese Masters* built magnificent brick cathedrals and basilicas. Some of their buildings reflect the Gothic style of the north while in others you can see the transition from that same Gothic to Renaissance. This was also an era of transition in sculpture, from stiff Romanesque stylization to the more realistic, classically inspired works of the great Nicola Pisano, his son Giovanni, and his pupil Arnolfo di Cambio.

Painters, especially in Rome and Siena, learned from the new spatial and expressive sculpture. Most celebrated of the masters in the dawn of the Italian Renaissance is, of course, the solemn Giotto. Sienese artists Duccio di Buoninsegna, Simone Martini and Pietro and Ambrogio Lorenzetti gave Italy its most brilliant exponents of the International Gothic style—though they were also important precursors of the Renaissance. The works of Orcagna, Gentile da Fabriano and Lorenzo Monaco laid a foundation for Florence's launching of the Renaissance.

Rome, for one of the few times in its history, achieved artistic prominence with home-grown talent. The city's architecture from this period (as seen in the campaniles of Santa Maria in Cosmedin and Santa Maria Maggiore) has largely been lost under baroque remodellings, but the paintings and mosaics of Pietro Cavallini and his school, and the intricate, inlaid stone pavements and architectural trim of the Cosmati family and their followers (derived from the Amalfi coast style) can be seen all over the city; both had an influence that extended far beyond Rome itself.

The Renaissance (15th–16th centuries)

The origins of this high noon of art are very much the accomplishment of quattrocento Florence, where sculpture and painting embarked on a totally new way of educating the eye. The idea of a supposed 'rediscovery of antiquity' has confused the understanding of the time. In general, artists broke new ground when they expanded from the traditions of medieval art; when they sought merely to copy the forms of ancient Greece and Rome the imagination often faltered.

Florentine art soon became recognized as the standard of the age. By 1450 artists were spreading the new style to the north, where Leonardo da Vinci and Bramante spent several years. Michelangelo and Bramante, among other noted artists, carried the Renaissance to Rome, where it thrived under the

patronage of enlightened popes. The most significant art in the north came out of Venice, which had its own distinct school led by Mantegna and Giovanni Bellini.

Despite the brilliant triumphs in painting and sculpture, the story of Renaissance architecture is partially one of confusion and retreat. Florence's dignified austerity proved difficult to transplant elsewhere. In most of Italy the rediscovery of the works of Vitruvius, representing the authority of antiquity, helped to kill off Italians' appreciation of their own architectural heritage; with surprising speed the dazzling imaginative freedom of medieval architecture was lost forever.

High Renaissance and Mannerism (16th century)

At the beginning of the cinquecento an Olympian triumvirate of Michelangelo, Raphael and Leonardo da Vinci held court at the summit of European art. But in this time when Italy was losing her self-confidence, and was soon to lose her essential liberty, artistic currents tended towards the dark and subversive. More than anyone, it was Michelangelo who tipped the balance from the cool, classical Renaissance into the turgid, stormy, emotionally fraught movement the critics have labelled Mannerism. Among the few painters left in exhausted Florence, he had the brilliant, deranged Jacopo Pontormo and Rosso Fiorentino to help. Other painters lumped in with the Mannerists, such as Giuliano Romano in Mantua and Il Sodoma around Siena, broke new ground while maintaining the discipline and intellectual rigour of the early Renaissance. Elsewhere, and especially among the fashionable Florentine painters and sculptors, art was decaying into mere interior decoration. For Venice, however, it was a golden age, with the careers of Titian, Veronese, Tintoretto, Sansovino and Palladio.

In architecture, attempts to recreate ancient styles and the classical orders won the day. In Milan, and later in Rome, Bramante was one of the few architects able to do anything interesting with it, while Michelangelo's great dome of St Peter's put a cap on the accomplishments of the Renaissance. Other talented architects found most of their patronage in Rome, which after the 1520s became Italy's centre of artistic activity: Ligorio, Peruzzi, Vignola and the Sangallo family among them.

Baroque (17th–18th centuries)

Rome continued its artistic dominance to become the capital of baroque, where the socially irresponsible genius of artists like Bernini and Borromini was approved by the Jesuits and indulged by the tainted ducats of the popes. As an art designed to induce temporal obedience and psychical oblivion, its effects are difficult to describe, but you can see for yourself in the three great churches along Corso Vittorio Emanuele in Rome and a host of other works (Bernini's Piazza Navona fountains and St Peter's colonnades).

More honest cities chose to sit out the baroque era. Not all artists fitted the baroque mould; genius could survive in a dangerous, picaresque age, most notably in the person of Caravaggio.

Neoclassicism and Romanticism (late 18th–19th centuries)

Baroque proved to be a hard act to follow, and in these centuries Italian art and architecture almost ceased to exist. Two centuries of stifling oppression had taken their toll on the national imagination, and for the first time Italy not only ceased to be a leader in art, but failed even to make significant contributions.

The one bright spot in 18th-century Italian painting was Venice, with Giambattista Tiepolo and son, Antonio Canaletto and Francesco Guardi. In the 19th century, the Italian Impressionist movement, the *Macchiaioli*, was led by Giovanni Fattori. In sculpture, the neoclassical master Antonio Canova, a favourite in the days of Napoleon, stands almost alone. Some of his best works may be seen in Rome's Villa Borghese. In architecture, it was the age of grand opera houses and the late 19th-century Gallerias in Milan and Naples.

20th Century

The turn-of-the-century Liberty Style (Italian Art Nouveau) failed to spread as widely as its counterparts in France and central Europe. The age did, however, see the construction of new Grand Hotels, casinos and villas in nearly every resort.

In the 20th century two Italian art movements have attracted international attention. Futurism, a response to Cubism, is concerned with the relevancy to the present ('the art that achieves speed, achieves success'). The movement is led by Boccioni, Gino Severini and Giacomo Balla (well-represented in the National Gallery of Modern Art, Rome). There is also the mysterious, introspective metaphysical world of Giorgio De Chirico, whose brethren—Modigliani, Giorgio Morandi and Carlo Carrà—were masters of silences. Their works, and others by modern Italian and foreign artists, are in the museums of Rome.

Architecture in this century reached its (admittedly low) summit in the Fascist period (the EUR suburb in Rome, and public buildings everywhere in the south). Mussolinian architecture often makes us smile but, as the only Italian school in the last 200 years to have achieved a consistent sense of design, it presents a challenge to all modern Italian architects—one they have so far been unable to meet. In Rome you can see the works of the most acclaimed Italian architect of this century, Pier Luigi Nervi; good post-war buildings are very difficult to find, and the other arts have never yet risen above the level of dreary, saleable postmodernism. Much of the Italians' artistic urge has been sublimated into the shibboleth of Italian design—clothes, sports cars, suitcases, kitchen utensils, etc. At present, though business is good, Italy is generating little excitement in these fields. Europe expects more from its most artistically talented nation; after the bad centuries of shame and slumber a free and prosperous Italy may well find its own voice and its own style to help interpret the events of the day. If Italy ever does begin to speak with a single voice, whatever it has to say will be worth hearing.

Snapshots

If they had had postcards back in the Roman Empire, your Aunt Vulpecula would certainly have sent you one from Campania—*Having a Wonderful Time in Baiae on the Sinus Puteolanus.* The photo on the front would show gaily painted pleasure-boats in the bay, with silken canopies and slaves waving golden fans over the languorous occupants; in the background would be a row of delicious villas, each with two or three levels of gleaming marble porticoes perched on the cliffs over the blue Tyrrhenian. This playground of the Roman world is the place where holidays as we know them were invented. The young world had never seen anything like it. Everyone in the Empire, from Londinium to Baalbek, had heard of the bay and its prodigies of beauty and luxury; no doubt everyone dreamed of actually going there.

The first mention of a villa on the bay comes from the early 2nd century BC. The Roman state, which had seized all the land in the area after conquering it, was now selling it off to help finance the Second Punic War, the bloody and expensive struggle against Hannibal and the Carthaginians. One of the first buyers was Scipio Africanus, the general who brought that war to a successful conclusion, and who became the richest man in Rome in the process. He built himself a villa near Liternum, overlooking the sea, and other members of the Roman elite soon followed. Over the next two centuries, as Rome spread its rule over the Mediterranean world and the booty rolled in, the dour senators and knights found something they had never had before—*otium*, or leisure. Thanks to contact with the cultured Greek world, in Campania and in Greece itself, Rome was growing up, even becoming a tiny bit civilized in its awkward and bumptious way.

If they hadn't yet acquired many of the accomplishments of culture, at least the Romans knew how to tack up a good façade: the villas housed copies of Greek statues, frescoes, Greek cooks, poets and musicians. The nabobs affected Greek dress, the elegant *chlamys* worn by the locals, instead of their impractical togas. Some of them even learned the language, and impressed their friends at dinner parties by extemporizing a few lines of verse. In the 1st century BC everyone who was anyone in Rome had a villa, and the Campanian coast entered its golden age of opulence. The populist dictator Marius had one, and the reactionary dictator Sulla who followed him built an even bigger model, which he shared with his family, a few hundred of his picked slaves, kept ladies, whichever of his clients and hangers-on were lucky enough to be invited, and plenty of entertainment—among others, 'Roscius the comedian, Sorex the mime, and Metrobius the female impersonator', as a historian of the time solemnly recorded. Julius Caesar owned a few villas, and his murderers plotted the deed at Cinna's place just up the coast.

These famous names of history, and the clique of politicians and speculators that went with them, had serious money; when Rome conquered the world a select few raked in the lion's share of the loot, amassing fortunes that make the greatest private hoards of our day seem pocket change in comparison. The honest Cicero often wrote disapprovingly of his fellow Romans' ostentatious displays of wealth—but he had three villas on the bay himself, and a string of lodges all the way to Rome so he would always have somewhere cosy to sleep as he travelled back and forth; we can imagine how the folks in the fast lane must have been carrying on.

The holiday trip was called the *peregrinatio*, and everyone would come down in mid-April. In the heat of summer they would go back to Rome if there was money to be made or intrigues to be hatched, or else retire to a cooler villa up in the mountains. Most would be back on the bay in autumn, and stay as long as there was blessed *otium* left to enjoy. In whatever season, amusements were never lacking. There were the famous baths of Baiae, the most sumptuous such establishment in the ancient world, and above all the dinner parties, which would fill up nearly every evening.

For the afternoon, lazy cruises on the bay were in favour, or rides in slave-born litters to Puteoli or Neapolis or the countryside. In Caesar's time pet fish were a craze among the bay set—bearded mullets decorated with jewels, trained to leap up and eat out of their masters' hands. Humbler citizens must have been as fascinated with the doings of the rich as they are today, and even if they had no patron to invite them to stay, they must have come in great numbers to gawk and dream.

The bay, having invented holidays, can also probably take credit for the first secular souvenirs. Archaeologists have dug up plenty of examples: small items of Puteoli's famous glassware decorated with hand-painted scenes of the coastline and its villas. Almost incredibly, contemporaries describe the entire bay, from Misenum to Sorrentum, as being solidly lined with these palaces, giving the impression of a single, tremendous marble city. It must have been the grandest sight of the classical world, and it isn't certain that our own time has anything to match it.

The bay remained in fashion well into the imperial age. Augustus bought Capri from the city of Neapolis, and covered it with pavilions and terraced gardens; his house was decorated with whale bones and other marvels of the sea, and with relics of classical heroes. All the other early emperors spent much of their time there, notably Tiberius (*see* pp.135–6). Some of the glamour wore off in greyer times, under Vespasian and after, when the wealth and glory of the emperors shamed everyone else's into the shade; later emperors would build their own pleasure palaces in places closer to the necessities of power or military leadership; some of these were huge cities in themselves, such as Trajan's, near Tivoli, or Diocletian's, which survives today as the city of Split, Croatia.

By the late 5th century there were no more pleasure boats in the bay—only prowling Vandal pirate craft from Africa. The last mention of any of the villas in antiquity was when Romulus Augustulus, the last pathetic emperor of the west, was sent off to live under close guard in the Villa of Lucullus (now Naples' Castel dell'Ovo) by his Gothic conqueror, Odoacer. Many of the villas must have been destroyed in this era; earthquakes, Vesuvius, time and stone quarriers have done for the rest.

So often, in and around Naples, the most affecting and unforgettable sights are the ones no longer present. Constant reminders of the impermanence of all our glories may be a major contributor to the melancholy many visitors to Naples have always felt. But there's no need to be melancholy; the Neapolitans, true heirs of antiquity, hardly ever are. Or as Martial put it, gazing at Caesar's tomb through the window of his Roman flat:

> *The great dead themselves, with jovial breath,*
> *Bid us be merry, and remember death.*

'Italy', begins the 1948 Constitution, 'is a republic based on labour'—an unusual turn of phrase, perhaps, but one entirely in keeping with a time when a thoroughly humbled Italy was beginning to get back on its feet after the War. The sorrows of the common man occupied the plots of post-War *cinema verità*, and artists and writers began to celebrate themes of Faith, Bread and Work as if they were in the employ of the Church's *Famiglia Cristiana* magazine. To outsiders it must have seemed that Italy was undergoing a serious change, but careful observers would have noted only another oscillation in the grandest, oldest dichotomy in Italian history. Brick Italy was once more in the driver's seat.

Brick Italy is a nation of hard work, humility and piety that knows it must be diligent and clever to wrest a comfortable living from the thin soil of this rocky, resource-poor peninsula. Marble Italy knows its citizens are perfectly capable of doing just that, just as they always have, and seeks to celebrate that diligence and cleverness by turning it into opulence, excess and foreign conquest. The two have been contending for Italy's soul ever since Roman quarrymen discovered the great veins of Carrara marble during the Republican era. Brick Italy's capital in former times was brilliant, republican Siena; right now it is virtuous, hard-working socialist Bologna, a city with more bricks that Woolworth's has nickels. Its triumphs came with the Age of the Comunes, with the modest genius of the Early Renaissance, and with the hard-won successes of the last 40 years. Marble Italy reached its height in the days of Imperial Rome; its capital is Rome, always and forever. After the medieval interlude, marble made its great comeback with the High Renaissance, Spaniardism and Michelangelo, the high priest of marble. The Age of Baroque belonged to it completely, as did the brief era of Mussolini.

Some confirmed Marble cities are Naples, Genoa, Turin, Pisa, Parma, Trieste, Perugia and Verona. Brick partisans include Pavia, Livorno, Lucca, Arezzo, Cremona and Mantua. Florence and Venice, the two medieval city-republics that eventually became important states on their own, are the two cities that most successfully straddle the fence. Look carefully at their old churches and palaces: you will often find marble veneer outside and solid brick underneath.

Keep all this in mind when you ponder the infinite subtleties of Italian history. It isn't always a perfect fit; medieval Guelphs and Ghibellines each had a little brick and a little marble in them, and the contemporary papacy changes from one to the other with every shift of the wind. Mussolini would have paved Italy over in marble if he had been able—but look at the monuments he could afford, and you'll see more inexpensive travertine and brick than anything else. For a while in the eighties, with Italy's economic successes and the glitz of Milanese fashion and design, it looked as if Marble Italy was about to make another comeback. But today, with Italy in the midst of its long and torturous revolution, the situation is unclear. If and when a new regime emerges, will its monument to itself be a beautiful symbol of republican aspirations, like Siena's brick Palazzo del Pubblico, or a florid marble pile like Rome's Altar of the Nation, the monument to Italian unification (and one of the biggest hunks of kitsch on this planet)?

Sub-Roma

Compared to the transit systems of other European capitals, Rome's Metropolitana seems a paltry affair: only two lines, both of which studiously avoid going near any place you want to visit. But consider the problems of building an underground in Rome, where some buildings rest on four levels of earlier foundations, with all the world's archaeologists looking over your shoulder waiting for something interesting to turn up, something that can stop the work for years (in one scene in Fellini's *Roma*, beautiful frescoes are discovered in one such underground foray, though on contact with the air they crumble away before your eyes).

Underground Rome, in fact, may be as interesting as what lies on the surface. Some of it can be visited: the street of ancient pagan tombs under, of all places, the crypt of St Peter's, or the sanctuary of Mithras below San Clemente. Beyond these, no one has ever attempted to catalogue the hundreds of chambers, cellars, monuments, and tombs the Romans have under their houses. Below these run underground streams, like the one under the Quirinale that once flowed through Catullus' famous gardens, or the lake beneath Palazzo Colonna. Julius Caesar built a network of tunnels under the Forum, linked to the Cloaca Maxima, surely the world's most famous sewer, built by the Tarquins and still in use today. This was overshadowed by a later tunnel, built for horse-drawn wagons to transport firewood from the Campus Martius docks all the way to the Baths of Caracalla. The strangest part of this sub-Roma may be the Capitoline itself, a veritable Great Pyramid of ancient chambers and tunnels and half-excavated, half-forgotten temples.

Not surprisingly, this secret city below has evolved some new life forms fitted to its peculiar environment. We hear of a poor soul trying to excavate a basement for a new pizzeria in Trastevere, and unearthing battalions of monster flatworms, giant albino water scorpions (supposedly harmless, however disgusting) and plenty of specimens of Rome's true totem animal, the mighty, cat-eating Royal Pantagana rat. The authorities aren't sure whether Rome has ten rats per person, like any normal city, or thirty, like Naples.

Pasquinade

As you cross over the Ponte Garibaldi, have a look at the monument to Gioacchino Belli, the top-hatted Roman dialect poet who stands in his piazza welcoming you to Trastevere. On the back of the pedestal you'll see a relief with a group of old-time Romans, gathered excitedly around a queer broken statue. What makes this shapeless marble lump different from the other ten thousand in Rome is that it is a talking statue. His name is Pasquino, and you can see him today behind Palazzo Braschi, just a block west of Piazza Navona.

Political graffiti, and particularly the habit of making statues talk by hanging placards on them, has been a Roman speciality since ancient times. During the siege of AD 545, friends of King Totila set up such placards by night to chastise the Romans for their treachery towards the Goths. In the Renaissance it was big business; Pasquino could hold running dialogues with Rome's other 'talking' statues—'Marforio', an old marble river god who now resides in the courtyard of the Capitoline Museum, and 'Madama Lucrezia', a cult figure of Isis moved in front of San Marco. One of their favourite subjects, understandably, was the insane acquisitiveness of the popes and cardinals—Pasquino once appeared with a tin cup, begging 'alms for the completion of the Palazzo Farnese,' and when the Barberini pope, Urban VIII, robbed the Pantheon of its bronze ceilings, Pasquino remarked 'What the Barbarians didn't do, the Barberini did.' One irritated pope was ready to toss the statue in the Tiber, but thoughtfully refrained when a subtle counsellor warned him that it would 'infect the very frogs, who would croak pasquinades day and night'.

Coffee Culture

Some people like it straight, a short sharp shot of rich dark liquid, usually downed in one gulp while standing at the bar. Others temper their favourite brew with a dash of hot milk—a *caffè macchiato*, literally, a stained coffee. In Italy, there are almost as many ways of taking a *caffè* as there are of eating pasta, and Naples is generally regarded as the capital of the country's coffee culture.

There is also the *latte macchiato*—a long glass of hot milk with a dash of coffee to give it colour and flavour, a wimp's drink by macho Neapolitan standards. The cappuccino, an espresso coffee topped with steam-whipped milk, is known to all, but it can be ordered in a myriad number of ways, *con schiuma* (with froth), *senza schiuma* (without froth), *freddo*, *tepido* or *bollente* (cold, warm or piping hot). It may be *scuro* or *chiaro*, depending on the amount of milk desired. And it will always be restricted to the first coffee of the day. The foreign tourists' habit of ordering a milky cappuccino after lunch or dinner is enough to make any Neapolitan stomach heave.

In Naples, more than anywhere else, the all-important act of going out to the bar for a fix of caffeine is a ritual that is repeated every few hours. For Neapolitans, coffee is a sacred thing, its preparation an art form. At the best bars in town, barmen in starched white jackets with gleaming brass buttons serve the dark syrupy brew with a glass of water, to prepare the palate for the treat in store. In Naples your coffee will usually be served already sugared. If you want it without, you must ask the barman for a *caffè amaro*.

Every Neapolitan has his favourite bar—and his favourite barman—but the 150-year-old Caffè Gambrinus on Piazza Trieste e Trento is widely recognised as the most venerable temple of them all. Also favoured are the Verdi in Via Verdi, the Caflish, in Via Toledo, and La Caffettiera in Piazza dei Martiri, a popular spot with well-dressed Neapolitan ladies after a busy morning's shopping.

On summer evenings, outside the bars along the seafront at Mergellina, you'll see Neapolitans indulging in the ultimate bliss, a cup of coffee served to them in the comfort of their own car, on trays which slot conveniently over the window of the driver's seat.

As any Neapolitan barman worth his salt will tell you, the perfect espresso is made with a blend of arabica coffees, with water passed through at a temperature of 90°C, for precisely 30 seconds. Connoisseurs can tell whether the coffee will be good or not before they even taste it. The foam is the give-away. It should be a uniform light brown colour, dappled with darker brown. Very dark brown or greyish foam is a clear warning sign that the barman is an amateur, or the coffee second rate. Most self-respecting Neapolitans would rather leave such a brew untouched on the counter and head for another bar. A bad cup of coffee can cast a blight over the entire day.

Sotto questo cielo non nascono sciocchi
(Under these skies no fools are born)

Neapolitan proverb

Camorra means a short jacket, of the kind the street toughs of Naples used to wear in the days of the Bourbon kings. But, as with Sicily's Mafia, the origin of the Neapolitan Camorra is lost in legend. Some accounts put it in the slums of the *Quartiere Spagnuole*, under the rule of the Spanish viceroys of the 16th century. Spanish soldiers of that time lived the life of picaresque novels—or at least tried to—and the fathers and brothers of the district did their best to defend their girls from such picaresqueness, which usually meant a knife in the back in some dark alley. There may be some truth to that, or it could all be romantic bosh. Criminals in southern Italy seem always to have been well organized, with a hierarchy, initiations, a set of rules, and a code of *omertà*. Foreign visitors to the city in the 1700s wrote that, when something was stolen, they were able to get in touch with the 'King of Thieves' who would magically get it restored—stealing from guests, after all, was a discourtesy.

It's doubtful they were ever so polite to their fellow citizens, for as long as there has been a Camorra it has lived mainly by extortion, with a fat finger in whatever rackets of the age looked most profitable. For a long time the gang's biggest takings came from the prisons, which they controlled. In the old days prisoners in Naples, as anywhere else, had to pay for their upkeep, and each new arrival would be met by the Camorristi with a subtle request for 'money for oil for the Madonna': that is, to keep the light burning at the shrine in the Camorra's favoured church, the Madonna del Carmine in the Piazza del Mercato; you can imagine that the Madonna required a lot of fuel.

Relations between the Camorra and the authorities have always been rather complex. In the last days of the *Regno*, Ferdinand II made use of them as a kind of anti-liberal secret police. In 1860 it was claimed that Garibaldi was forced to make a deal with them, handing over control of the city government in return for nobody shooting at him and his army when they entered the city. The new Italian state, run by northerners, could not see the logic in this, and tried to wipe out the Camorra by vigorous police action. The mob trumped that ploy easily by going into politics, setting the pattern of close alliance between organized crime and centre-rightist parties that continues in Italy to this day. In a typical irony of parliamentary democracy, the titled gentry of the ruling class and the thugs found that their interests coincided perfectly, and by 1900 the theory and practice of southern machine politics had been refined to an art. As people used to say: 'the government candidate always wins'. In another place that might seem a cliché; in Naples it was a piece of the deepest folk wisdom.

Like the Mafia in Sicily, the Camorra took some hard knocks under Mussolini. If there was any cream to be skimmed, the Fascists wanted it all for themselves, and the ambience of the dictatorship proved wonderfully convenient for getting around the legal niceties of arrest and conviction. And, like the Mafia, the Camorra was able to manipulate easily the Allied Military Government after 1944 to get back on its feet. Perhaps the Americans were sincerely convinced that the mobsters would be a useful ally in an impossible situation, or maybe they had got a message that a little cooperation would save their army a lot of trouble (accidents can happen...). In any case it seems always to have been Allied policy on the Italian front to throw open the prisons in every town they captured.

In 1944 top American mobster Lucky Luciano went to Sicily to arrange things. He was swindled royally by his supposed brothers; there has always been less of a connection between the native and foreign Mafias than one might suppose. One of his New York lieutenants, Vito Genovese, was from around Naples; he went back there, and had better luck than Lucky, insinuating his way into the confidences of the Allied High Command. From the old Camorra stronghold of the 'Triangle of Death', in the villages north of the city, and from the *bancarelle* of the Forcella market, Genovese oversaw an incredible orgy of black-market wheeling and dealing, largely over stolen army supplies, while the old Camorra hands revived the hallowed traditions of extortion.

Today it is estimated that 60 per cent of all businesses in the Naples area pay protection money to the Camorra. The gang takes its cut from most sorts of common crime and, like the Mafia, has become heavily involved in drugs—not so much exporting them as pushing them on their neighbours. If the old Camorra ever knew any bounds or limits, or had any sense of decency, the current model has forgotten it; even the youngest children are tricked into crime. Unlike the Mafia, the Camorra has no recognized central authority; factions settle their differences with reciprocal assassinations—spectacles conducted out in the streets of the old quarters where all may enjoy them. The politicians in league with the Camorra have cheated Naples of fantastic amounts, enough to make the difference between the modern European metropolis it could be and the decomposing live body it is.

As late as 1992, newspapers managed to cover events in the south without ever daring to mention the obvious fact that government and organized crime were one and the same; it wasn't 'proved', and so even the most discreet insinuation might have been risky. Today, when Italy is in the midst of a revolution, things aren't so clear. The Camorra and the Mafia are undergoing a possibly serious crisis, thanks to the disgust of the electorate and the determined efforts of a few incorruptible policemen, prosecutors and judges. They are trying to make their arrangements with the new powers that be, wherever they can; meanwhile we all may wonder, as the Italians do, just what our newspapers aren't telling us now.

Rome

To know what Rome is, you might pay a visit to the little church of San Clemente, unobtrusively hidden away on the back streets behind the Colosseum. The baroque façade conceals a 12th-century basilica with a beautiful marble choir screen 600 years older. In 1857 a cardinal from Boston discovered the original church of 313 underneath the church, one of the first great Christian basilicas. And beneath that have been discovered the remains of two ancient buildings and a Temple of Mithras from the time of Augustus; from it you can walk out into a Roman alley that looks exactly as it did 2,000 years ago, now some 30ft below ground level. There are commemorative plaques in San Clemente, placed there by a Medici duke, a bishop of New York, and the last chairman of the Bulgarian Communist Party.

You are not going to get to the bottom of this city, or even begin to understand it, whether your stay is for three days or a month. With its legions of headless statues, acres of paintings, 913 churches and megatons of artistic sediment, this metropolis of aching feet will wear down even the most resolute of travellers (and travel writers). The name Rome passed out of the plane of reality into legend some 2,200 years ago, when princes as far away as China first began to hear of the faraway city and its invincible armies building an empire in the West. At the same time the Romans were cooking up a personified goddess, the Divine Rome, and beginning the strange myth of their city's destiny to conquer and pacify the world, a myth that would still haunt Europe a thousand years later.

You may find it requires a considerable effort of the imagination to break through to the past Romes of the Caesars and popes. You will need to peel away the increasingly thick veneer of the 'Third Rome', the thoroughly up-to-date creation of post-Reunification Italy. Ancient Rome at the height of its glory had perhaps a million and a half people; today there are four million, and at any given time at least half of them will be pushing their way into the Metro train while you are trying to get off. The popes, for all their experience in spectacle and ceremony, rarely steal the show, sharing the stage with an overabundance of preposterous politicians, with Cinecittà and the rest of Italy's cultural apparatus, and of course with the tourists, who sometimes put on the best show in town. The old-guard Romani, now a minority, often bewail the loss of old Rome's slow and easy pace, its vintage brand of *dolce vita* that once impressed other Italians, let alone foreigners. Lots of money, lots of traffic and an endless caravan of tour buses have a way of compromising even the most beautiful cities. Don't worry; the present is only one snapshot from a 2,600-year history, and no one has ever left Rome disappointed.

History

Historians believe the settlement of the Tiber Valley began in about 1000 BC, when volcanic eruptions in the Alban Hills forced the Latin tribes down to the lowlands. But, remembering that every ancient legend conceals a kernel of truth, it would be best to follow the accounts of Virgil, the poet of the empire, and Livy, the great 1st-century Roman chronicler. When Virgil wrote, in the reign of Augustus, Greek culture was an irresistible force in all the recently civilized lands of the Mediterranean. For Rome, Virgil concocted the story of Aeneas, fleeing from Troy after the Homeric sack and finding his way over the sea to Latium. Descent from the Trojans, however specious, connected Rome to the Greek world and made it seem less of an upstart in its Imperial age. As Virgil tells it, Aeneas' son Ascanius founded Alba Longa, a city that by the 800s was leader of the Latin Confederation. Livy takes up the tale with Numitor, a descendant of Ascanius and rightful King of Alba Longa, tossed off the throne by his usurping brother Amulius. In order that Numitor should have no heirs, Amulius forced Numitor's daughter Rhea Silvia into service as a Vestal Virgin. Here Rome's destiny begins, with an appearance in the Vestals' chambers of the god Mars, staying just long enough to leave Rhea Silvia pregnant with the precocious twins Romulus and Remus.

When Amulius found out he of course packed them away in a little boat, which the gods directed up the Tiber to a spot somewhere near today's Piazza Bocca della Verità. The famous she-wolf then looked after the babies, until they were found by a shepherd, who brought them up. When Mars revealed to the grown twins their origin, they returned to Alba Longa to sort out Amulius, and then returned home (in 753 BC, traditionally) to found the city the gods had ordained. Romulus soon found himself constrained to kill Remus, who would not believe the auguries that declared his brother should be king, and this sets the pattern for the bloody millennium of Rome's history to come. The legends portray early Rome as a glorified pirates' camp, and the historians are only too glad to agree. Finding themselves short of women, the Romans stole some from the Sabines. Not especially interested in farming or learning a trade, they adopted the hobby of subjugating their neighbours and soon polished it to an art.

Seven Kings of Rome

Romulus was the first, followed by Numa Pompilius, who by divine inspiration laid down the forms for Rome's cults and priesthoods, its auguries and its College of Vestals. Tullius Hostilius made Rome ruler of all Latium, and Ancus Martius founded the port of Ostia. Tarquinius Priscus was an Etruscan, and probably gained his throne thanks to a conquest by one of the great Etruscan city-states. Tarquin made a city of Rome, building the first real temples, the Cloaca Maxima and the first Circus Maximus. Servius Tullius restored Latin rule, inaugurated the division of the citizens between patricians and plebeians, and built a great wall to keep the Etruscans out. It apparently did not work, for as next king we find the Etruscan Tarquinius Superbus (about 534 BC), another great builder. His misfortune was to have a hot-headed son like Tarquinius Sextus, who imposed himself on a noble and virtuous Roman matron named Lucretia (cf. Shakespeare's *Rape of Lucrece*). She committed public suicide in the morning; the enraged Roman patricians, under the leadership of Lucius Junius Brutus, then chased out proud Tarquin and the Etruscan dynasty forever. The Republic was established before the day was out, with Brutus as First Consul, or Chief Magistrate.

The Invincible Republic

Taking an oath never to allow another king in Rome, the patricians designed a novel form of government, a republic (*res publica*—public thing) governed by the two consuls elected by the Senate (the patricians' assembly); later innovations in the constitution included a tribune, an official with inviolable powers elected by the plebeians to protect their interests. The two classes fought like cat and dog at home but combined with impressive resolve in their foreign wars. Etruscans, Aequi, Hernici, Volscii, Samnites and Sabines were all defeated by Rome's citizen armies. By 270 BC Rome had eliminated all its rivals to become master of Italy. It took about 200 years, and in the next 200 Roman rule would be established from Spain to Egypt. In the three Punic Wars against Carthage (264–146 BC) Rome gained most of the western Mediterranean; Greece, North Africa and Asia Minor were absorbed in small bites over the next 100 years. Rome's history was now the history of the western world.

Imperial Rome

When the Romans took Greece they first met Culture, and it had the effect on them that puberty has on little boys. After some bizarre behaviour, evidenced in the continuous civil wars, the Romans began tarting up their city in the worst way, vacuuming all the gold, paintings, statues, cooks, poets and architects out of the civilized East. Beginning perhaps with Pompey, every contender for control of the now constitutionally deranged Republic added some great work to the city centre: Pompey's theatre, the Julian Basilica, and something from almost every emperor up to Constantine. Julius Caesar and Augustus were perhaps Rome's greatest benefactors, initiating every sort of progressive legislation, turning dirt lanes into paved streets and erecting new forums, temples and the vast network of aqueducts. In their time Rome's population probably reached the million mark, surpassing Antioch and Alexandria as the largest city in the western world.

It was Augustus who effectively ended the Republic in 27 BC by establishing his personal rule and reducing the old constitution to a series of formalities. During the Imperial era that followed, Rome's position as administrative and judicial centre of the Empire created a new cosmopolitan population as people from every province, from Britain to Mesopotamia, crowded in. The city became the capital of banking and the financial markets, and of religion; Rome's policy was to induct everyone's local god as an honorary Roman, and every important cult image and relic was abducted to the Capitoline Temple. The Emperor himself was *Pontifex Maximus*, head priest of Rome, whose title derives from the early Roman veneration of bridges (*pontifex* means 'keeper of bridges'). St Peter, of course, arrived, and was duly martyred in AD 67. His successor, Linus, became the first pope—or *pontiff*.

For all its glitter, Rome was still the complete economic predator, producing nothing and consuming everything. At some points in this period, almost half the population of Roman citizens (as opposed to slaves) was on the public dole. Uncertain times made Aurelian give Rome a real defensive wall in 275. By 330 the necessity of staying near the armies at the front led the Western Emperors to spend most of their time at army headquarters in Milan. Rome became a bloated backwater and, after three sacks of the city, there was no reason to stay. The sources disagree: perhaps 100,000 inhabitants were left by the year 500, perhaps as few as 10,000.

Rome in the Shadows

Rome never quite went down the drain in the Dark Ages. Its lowest point in prestige undoubtedly came in the 14th century, when the popes were at Avignon, but the number of important churches built and mosaics created (equal in number if not quality to those of Ravenna) testify to the city's continuing importance. There was certainly enough to attract a few more sacks. Rome at this time must have been a fascinating place, much too big for its population though still thinking of itself as the centre of the western world. The Forum was mostly abandoned, as were the gigantic baths, rendered useless as the aqueducts decayed and no one had the means to repair them. Almost all of the temples and basilicas survived, converted to Christian churches. Hadrian's massive tomb on the banks of the Tiber was converted into a fortress, the Castel Sant'Angelo, an impregnable haven of safety for the popes in times of trouble.The popes deserve credit for keeping Rome alive, but the tithe money trickling in from across Europe confirmed the city in its parasitical behaviour. Charlemagne visited the city in 800; during a prayer vigil in St Peter's on Christmas Eve, Pope Leo III sneaked up behind him and set an imperial crown on his head. The surprise coronation established the precedent of Holy Roman Emperors having to cross over the Alps to receive their crown from the pope; for centuries to come Rome was able to keep its hand in the political struggles of all Europe.

Arnold of Brescia and Rienzo

Not that Rome ever spoke with one voice; over the next 500 years it was only the idea of Rome, as the spiritual centre of the universal Christian community, that kept the actual city of Rome from disappearing altogether. Down to some 20–30,000 people, Rome evolved a sort of stable anarchy, in which the major contenders for power were the popes and various noble families. Very often outsiders would get into the game. A remarkable woman named Theodora seized the Castel Sant'Angelo in the 880s; with the title of Senatrix she and her daughter Marozia ruled Rome for decades. Various German emperors seized the city, but could never hold it. In the 10th century, things got even more complicated as the Roman people began to assert themselves, and nine of the 24 popes managed to get murdered. In the 1140s a Jewish family, the Pierleoni, held power, and a Jewish antipope sat enthroned in St Peter's. Mighty Rome occupied itself with a series of wars against its neighbouring village of Tivoli, and usually lost. A sincere monkish reformer appeared, the Christian and democrat Arnold of Brescia; he recreated the Senate and almost succeeded in establishing Rome as a free *comune*, but somehow in 1155 he fell into the hands of the German Emperor Frederick Barbarossa, who sold him to the English pope (Adrian IV) for hanging.

Too much of this made Rome uncomfortable for the popes, who frequently removed themselves to Viterbo during the 13th century. The final indignity came when, under French pressure, the papacy decamped entirely to Avignon in 1309. Pulling strings from a distance, the papacy only made life more complicated for the Romans left behind. Cola di Rienzo stepped into the vacuum they created. An innkeeper's son, he had a good enough education to read Latin inscriptions and the works of Livy, Cicero and Tacitus. Obsessed by the idea of re-establishing Roman glory, he talked at the bewildered inhabitants until they caught the fever too. With Rienzo as Tribune of the People, the Republic was reborn in May 1347. Corrupted by power, however, an increasingly fat and ridiculous Rienzo was hustled out of

Rome by the united nobles before the year was out. His return to power in 1354 ended with his murder by a mob after only two months. Rome was now at its lowest ebb, with only some 15,000 people, and prosperity and influence were not restored until after 1447.

The New Rome

In the more settled conditions of the 15th century, a new papacy emerged, richer and more sophisticated. Political power was always its goal, and a series of talented Renaissance popes saw their best hopes for achieving this by rebuilding Rome. Under Julius II (1503–13) the papal domains for the first time were run like a modern state; Julius also laid plans for the rebuilding of St Peter's, beginning, with his architect, Bramante, the great building programme that was to transform the city. New streets were laid out, especially the Via Giulia and the grand avenues radiating from the Piazza del Popolo.

Over the next two centuries hundreds of churches were either built or rebuilt, and cardinals and nobles lined the streets with imposing new palaces. A new departure in urban design was developed in the 1580s, under Sixtus V, and piazzas were cleared in front of the major religious sites, each with its Egyptian obelisk, linked by a network of straight boulevards. The New Rome, symbol of the Counter-Reformation and the majesty of the popes, was, however, bought at a terrible price. Besides Bramante's destruction of medieval Rome, buildings that had survived substantially intact for 1,500 years were cannibalized for their marble and, to pay for their programme, the popes taxed the economy of the Papal States out of existence. Worst of all, the new papacy in the 16th century instituted terror as an instrument of public policy. The popes tried to extend their power by playing a game of high-stakes diplomacy between Emperor Charles V of Spain and King Francis I of France, but reaped a bitter harvest in the 1527 sack of Rome. An out-of-control, destructive Imperial army occupied the city for almost a year, while Pope Clement VII looked on helplessly from the Castel Sant'Angelo. The popes subsequently became part of the Imperial-Spanish system and political repression was fiercer than anywhere else in Italy; the Inquisition was refounded in 1542, and book-burnings, the torture of freethinkers and executions became more common than in Spain itself.

The End of Papal Rule

By about 1610 workmen were adding the last stones to the cupola of St Peter's. It was the end of an era, but the building continued. A thick accretion of baroque, like coral, collected over Rome. Bernini did his Piazza Navona fountain in 1650, and the Colonnade for St Peter's 15 years later. The political importance of the popes, however, disappeared with surprising finality as they drifted into irrelevance during the Thirty Years War and after.

Rome was left to enjoy a decadent but pleasant twilight. A brief interruption came when revolutionaries in 1798 once again proclaimed the Roman Republic, and a French army sent the pope packing. Rome later became part of Napoleon's empire, but papal rule was restored in 1815. Another republic appeared in 1848, but this time a French army besieged the city and had the Pope propped back on his throne by July 1849. For twenty years Napoleon III maintained a garrison in Rome to look after the Pope, and consequently Rome became the last part of Italy to join the new Italian kingdom. After the French defeat in the war of 1870, Italian troops blew a hole in the old Aurelian wall near the Porta Pia and marched in. Pius IX locked himself in the Vatican and pouted; the popes were to be 'prisoners' until Mussolini's

Concordat of 1929, by which they recognized the Italian state. As capital of the new state, Rome underwent another building boom; new streets made circulation a little easier; villas and gardens disappeared under endless blocks of speculative building; long-needed projects like the Tiber embankments were built; and, at the same time, the kingdom strove to impress the world with gigantic, absurd public buildings and monuments, such as the Altar of the Nation and the Finance Ministry on Via XX Settembre. Growth has been steady; from some 200,000 people in 1879, Rome has since increased twentyfold.

The Twentieth Century

1922 the city saw Mussolini's 'March on Rome', when he used his blackshirts to claim complete power in the Italian government. Mussolini wanted to revive the greatness of ancient Rome and create a 'New Roman Empire' for Italy; it was under Fascism that many of Rome's relics were first opened as public monuments to remind Italians of their heritage. His greatest legacy, however, was the EUR suburb to the south—the projected site of a world exhibition for 1942, and a huge showcase of his preferred Fascist-classical architecture. Since the War Rome has grown fat as the capital of the often ramshackle, notoriously corrupt, never-changing political system thrown up by the Italian Republic, and the headquarters of the smug *classe politica* that ran it. Nevertheless, Romans have joined in Italy's 'Moral Revolution', abusing the old-style political bosses, despite the fact that many in this city of civil servants themselves benefited from the system. The city has been led by a mayor from the Green Party since 1993, and is currently in the throes of preparation for the Holy Year 2000. Many promises are being made for what will be one of the great tourist onslaughts of the century—local officials are estimating as many as 30 million visitors to the capital over the year. Just whether the city will get its act together in time remains to be seen.

Art and Architecture

The Etruscans

Although Rome stood on the fringes of the Etruscan world, the young city could hardly help being overwhelmed by the superior culture almost on its doorstep. Along with much of its religion, customs and its engineering talent, early Rome owed its first art to the enemies from the north. Thanks to the Villa Giulia Museum, Rome can show you much of the best of Etruscan art. Enigmatic, often fantastical, and always intensely vital, Etruria's artists stole from every Greek style and technique, and turned it into something uniquely their own.

The Romans Learn Building and Just Can't Stop

The Romans learned how to build roads and bridges from the Etruscans, perfected the art, and built works never dreamed of before. Speaking strictly of design, the outstanding fact of Roman building was its conservatism. Under the Republic, Rome adopted Greek architecture, preferring the more delicate Corinthian order. When the money started rolling in, the Romans began to build in marble. But for 400 years, until the height of Empire under Trajan and Hadrian, very little changed. As Rome became the capital of the Mediterranean, its rulers introduced new building types to embellish it: the series of Imperial Fora, variations on the Greek agora, the first of which was begun by Julius Caesar; public baths, a custom imported from Campania; colonnaded streets, as in Syria and Asia Minor; and theatres.

Concrete may not seem very romantic, but in the hands of Imperial builders it changed both the theory and practice of architecture. Volcanic sand from the Bay of Naples, used with rubble as a filler, allowed the Romans to cover vast spaces cheaply. First in the palaces, and later in the Pantheon's giant concrete dome and in the huge public baths, an increasingly sophisticated use of arches and vaults was developed. Concrete seating made the Colosseum and the vast theatres possible, and allowed *insulae*—Roman apartment blocks—to climb six storeys and occasionally more. Near the Empire's end, the tendency towards gigantism becomes an enduring symptom of Roman decadence; the clumsy forms of late monsters like Diocletian's Baths and the Basilica of Maxentius show a technology far outstripping art.

Roman Sculpture, Painting and Mosaics

Even after the conquests of the 2nd century BC and the looting of the East, it was a long time before Rome produced anything of its own. As in architecture, the other arts were dependent for centuries on the Greeks. Portrait sculpture, inherited from the Etruscans, is the notable exception, with a tradition of almost photographic busts and funeral reliefs. Sculpture, most of all, provides a vivid psychological record of Rome's history. In the 3rd century, as its confidence was undergoing its first crisis at the hands of German and Persian invaders, sculpture veered slowly towards the introverted and strange. Under the late Antonines the tendency is apparent, with grim, realistic battle scenes on Marcus Aurelius' column, and troubled portraits of the Emperor himself. Later portraits are even more unsettling, with rigid features and staring eyes, concerned more with psychological depth than outward appearances.

During the 3rd and 4th centuries there was little public art. There was a brief revival under Constantine, and no work better evokes the Rome of the psychotic, totalitarian late Empire than his weird, immense head in the Capitoline Museum. Gigantism survived the final disappearance of individuality and genuinely civic art, while the Imperial portraits freeze into eerie icons. Painting and mosaics were present from at least the 1st century BC, but Romans considered them little more than decoration, rarely entrusting to them any serious subjects.

Early Christian and Medieval Art

Almost from the beginning, Rome's Christians sought to express their faith in art. On dozens of finely carved sarcophagi and statues the figure of Christ is represented as the 'Good Shepherd', a beardless youth with a lamb slung over his shoulder. Occasionally he wears a Roman toga. Familiar New Testament scenes are common, along with figures of the early martyrs. The 4th-century building programme financed by Constantine filled Rome with imposing Christian basilicas, though little remains. Through the 5th and early 6th centuries, Christian art—now the only art permitted—changed little in style but broadened its subject matter, including scenes from the Old Testament and the Passion of Christ.

An impressive revival of Roman building came in the late 8th century, with peace, relative prosperity, and enlightened popes such as Hadrian, Leo III and Paschal I. New churches went up, decorated with mosaics by Greek artists. A return of hard times after the collapse of the Carolingian Empire put an end to this little Renaissance. When Rome began building again, it was largely with native artists, and stylistically was almost a clean break with the past. The **Cosmati**, perhaps originally a single family, but eventually a name for a whole school, ground up fragments of coloured glass and precious stone and turned them into intricate pavements, altars, candlesticks and pulpits, geometrically patterned in styles derived from southern Italy, and ultimately from the Muslim world. Perhaps the greatest Roman artist of the Middle Ages was **Pietro Cavallini** (c. 1250–1330), whose freedom in composition and talent for expressive portraiture make him a genuine precursor of the Renaissance, equally at home in mosaics and fresco painting.

The Renaissance in Rome

Rome's High Renaissance begins with Julius II (1503–13). **Michelangelo Buonarroti** had already arrived, to amaze the world of art with his *Pietà* in St Peter's (1499), but the true inauguration of Rome's greatest artistic period was the arrival of **Donato Bramante**. This new marriage of the Renaissance and ancient Rome can best be seen at Bramante's *Tempietto* at S. Pietro in Montorio (1503), or at his cloister for S. Maria della Pace (1504). For painting and sculpture, the High Renaissance meant a greater emphasis on emotion, movement and virtuosity. **Raphael**, following in Bramante's footsteps, arrived from Florence in 1508 and was the most influential painter of his time, with his skill and sunny personality that patrons found irresistible. In the frescoes in the Vatican Stanze, he combined the grand manner from antique sculpture and the ancient approach to decoration from Nero's recently unearthed Golden House to create one of the definitive achievements of the age, and also excelled at portraiture, mythological frescoes, and even almost visionary religious work.

The Sack of Rome in 1527 rudely interrupted artistic endeavours, and many artists left Rome for ever. Among those who returned was, of course, Michelangelo, who in 1536 began the *Last Judgement* in the Sistine Chapel, whose sombre tones and subject matter illustrate more clearly than any other work the change in mood that had come over Roman art.

The Art of the Counter-Reformation

The Counter-Reformation and the Inquisition put a chill on the Italian imagination that would never really be dispelled. In 1563 the Council of Trent decreed the new order for art: it was to be conformist and naturalistic, propaganda entirely in the service of the totalitarian Church, with a touch of Spanish discipline and emotionalism. Rome was to become the symbol of the Church resurgent, the most modern and beautiful city in the world. Under Sixtus V, **Domenico Fontana** and other architects planned a scheme to unite the sprawling medieval city with a network of straight avenues sighted on obelisks in the major piazzas.

The Age of Baroque

During this period art was reduced to mere decoration, forbidden to entertain any thoughts that might be politically dangerous or subversive to Church dogma. But in this captive art there was still talent and will enough for new advances to be made, particularly in architecture. Plenty of churches, fountains and palaces were built, and there was every opportunity for experimentation. In sculpture it meant a new emphasis on cascading drapery and exaggerated poses, typecasting emotion, saintliness or virtue in a way the Renaissance would have found slightly trashy. Here **Bernini** led the way, with such works as his *David* in the Galleria Borghese (1623). Painting was on a definite downward spiral, though one usually had to look up to see it. Decorative ceiling frescoes, such as those of **Pietro da Cortona**, were all the rage, though few artists could bring anything like Cortona's talent to the job.

The Last of Roman Art

From Rome, the art of the high baroque reached out to all Europe—just as the last traces of inspiration were dying out in the city itself. After the death of Pope Alexander VII (1667) there was less money and less intelligent patronage, and by this time, a more introspective Rome was looking backwards. Meaningful sculpture and painting were gone for ever.

In the 19th century art in Rome continued to lose ground. After 1870 the fathers of the new Italy believed that liberation and Italian unity would unleash a wave of creativity, and spent tremendous sums to help it along. They were mistaken. The sepulchral, artless monuments they imposed on Rome helped ruin the fabric of the city and provided an enduring reminder of the sterility of the Risorgimento and the subsequent corrupt regimes. Mussolini too wanted his revolution to have its artistic expression. The sort of painting and sculpture his government preferred is best not examined too closely, but his architecture, mashing up Art Deco simplicity with historical pomposity, now and then reached beyond the level of the ridiculous. Rome today is moribund as an art centre, and even architecture has not recovered. There are no first-rate contemporary buildings. Not few—none. Efforts at planning the city's post-war growth resulted in confusion and concrete madness, and the hideous apartment and office blocks of the suburbs. Until recently it seemed impossible that Rome could ever again produce inspired architecture. However, Paolo Portoghesi's mosque, a playful postmodern extravaganza near the Villa Ada, could be a sign that the tide is about to turn.

A Little Orientation

two walls

Of Rome's earliest wall, built by King Servius Tullius before the republic was founded, little remains; one of the last surviving bits is right outside Stazione Termini. The second, built by Aurelian in AD 275, is one of the wonders of Rome. With its 19km length and 383 towers, it is one of the largest ever built in Europe—and certainly the best-preserved of antiquity. In several places you can see almost perfectly preserved bastions and monumental gates.

three Romes

Classical Rome began on the Monte Palatino, and all through its history its business and administrative centre stayed nearby, in the original Forum and the great Imperial Fora. Many of the busiest parts of the city lay to the south. After Rome's fall these areas were never really rebuilt, and even now substantial ruins like Trajan's Baths remain unexcavated. The Second Rome, that of the popes, had its centre in the Campus Martius, the plain west and north of the Monte Capitolino, later expanding to include the 'Leonine City' around St Peter's and the new baroque district around Piazza del Popolo and the Spanish Steps. The Third Rome, capital of united Italy, has expanded in all directions, its centre the Via del Corso.

seven hills

Originally they were much higher; centuries of building, rebuilding and river flooding have made the ground level in the valleys much higher, and various emperors and popes have shaved bits off the tops. The **Monte Capitolino**, smallest but most important, now has Rome's city hall, the Campidoglio, roughly on the site of ancient Rome's greatest temple, that of Jupiter Greatest and Best. The **Palatino**, originally the most fashionable district, eventually got entirely covered by the palaces of the emperors. The usually plebeian **Aventino** lies to the south, across from the Circus Maximus. Between the Colosseum and the Stazione Termini, the **Esquilino**, the **Viminale** and the **Quirinale** stand in a row. The Quirinale was the residence of the popes, and later of the Italian kings. The **Monte Celio**, south of the Colosseum, is now a charming oasis of parkland and ancient churches in the centre of Rome. Rome has other hills not included in the canonical seven: **Monte Vaticano**, from which the Vatican takes its name, **Monte Pincio**, including the Villa Borghese, Rome's biggest park, and the **Gianicolo**, the long ridge above Trastevere the ancients called the Janiculum.

Getting Around

On the map, Rome seems to be a city made for getting around on foot. This may be so in the centro storico around Piazza Navona, but elsewhere it will always take you longer than you think to walk. If you fancy more of a stroll, head for the old districts west of the Corso, around the Tiber Island, in the old parts of Trastevere and around the Monte Celio.

by metro

The two Metro lines, A and B, cross at Stazione Termini; one or the other will take you to the Colosseum, around the Monte Aventino, to Piazza di Spagna, St John Lateran, St Paul's outside the walls, Piazza del Popolo, or within eight blocks of St Peter's. Single tickets (*L1,500*), also good for city buses—within 75mins of validation—are available from Metro stations, tobacconists, bars and newspaper kiosks.

by bus and tram

Buses are by far the best way to get around. Pick up a map of the bus routes from the **ATAC** (city bus company) information booth outside Stazione Termini. Bus tickets cost L1,500, and are good for travel on any ATAC city bus or tram and one Metro ride; stamp them in the machines in the back entrance of buses or trams or in the Metro turnstiles. There are also special-price full-day, weekly and monthly passes.

Three lines are of particular interest to visitors. The **Circuito Turistico ATAC** (bus 110, special ticket L15,000) leaves from Piazza dei Cinquecento in front of the station at 3.30pm (in winter at 2.30pm, sometimes on Saturdays and Sundays only) for a three-hour tour of the principal sights of the city. Rickety little **tram 30** makes a fun ride when your feet are sore; it circles the city centre, passing many sights. Catch it in Piazza del Risorgimento, near the Vatican; by St John Lateran; the Colosseum; Porta San Paolo; Viale Trastevere; or by the zoo or Villa Giulia in the Villa Borghese. **Electric minibus 119** tours the medieval lanes between Piazza del Popolo and the Pantheon, a relaxing introduction to Rome's neighbourhoods.

by taxi

It's easiest to get official taxis (painted yellow or white) at a rank (in most of the main piazzas). To phone for a taxi, call © 06 3570, or © 06 4994; there's no specific surcharge, but expect to pay for the time it takes for it to reach you.

by car

Much of the old centre is closed to unauthorized traffic, and ought to be avoided altogether (you should be walking anyway in this compact area). This includes the

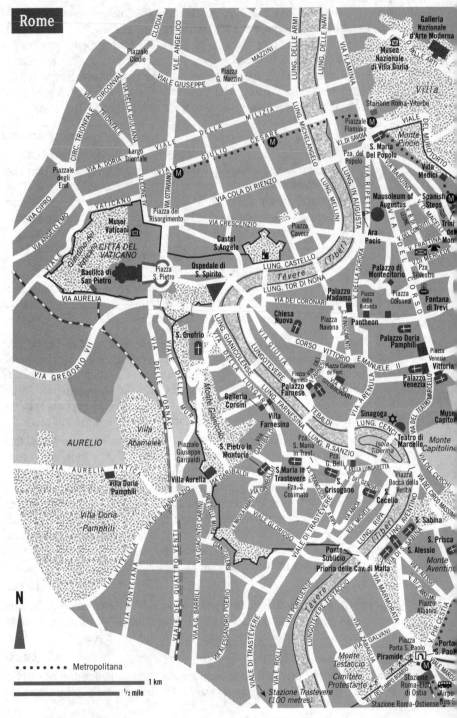

Rome

- ••••••• Metropolitana

1 km

½ mile

64

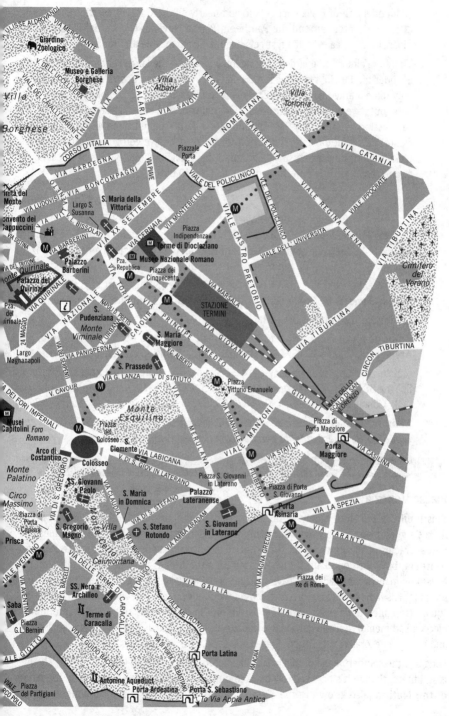

'Trident' south of Piazza del Popolo and nearly all the Campus Martius outside the main boulevards, around the Pantheon, Piazza Navona, Campo de' Fiori and the Tiber. In this area even main streets like the Corso may be arbitrarily closed.

There are almost no guarded parking lots in Rome—the largest and most convenient is under the Pincio, near Piazza del Popolo. Parking in the *centro storico* is resident-only (blue-marked zones, as in Trastevere, are designed to make non-residents pay to park, but have met massive resistance). If you park on a street and return to find your car missing, contact the Vigili Urbano at Via della Conciliazione 4, ℘ 67 691, and ask the Uffizio Rimozione if it's been towed away before you go to the police. Cars picked up in the centre usually end up in the Villagio Olimpio. If it's been clamped, phone the number left on the car; the fine is L140,000.

Tourist Information

EPT: main office: Via Parigi 5, ℘ 06 4889 9253 (*open Mon–Fri 8.15–7.15, Sat 8.15–1.30*); also Stazione Termini, Fiumicino Airport, the Colosseum, Castel Sant'Angelo and Via Nazionale next to Palazzo Esposizione (*all slightly varying hours*).

Two weeklies available from news-stands, *Romac'e'*(with a short English section at the back) and *Time Out* (in Italian), have listings for arts, culture and entertainment.

General emergencies: ℘ 113.

24-hour pharmacies: Piram, Via Nazionale 228, ℘ 06 488 0754; **Arenula**, Via Arenula 73, ℘ 06 6880 3278. Duty pharmacists are listed outside all pharmacies.

Outside banking hours money can be exchanged at **American Express**, Piazza di Spagna 38, ℘ 06 67641 (*open Mon–Fri 9–5.30, Sat 9–12.30*); **Thomas Cook**, Via della Conciliazione 23–25, ℘ 06 6830 0435 (*open Mon–Sat 8.30–6, Sun 9–1.30*).

Main post office: Piazza San Silvestro, ℘ 06 6771 (*open Mon–Fri 8.30–6, Sat and Sun 8.30–2; other branches generally open 8.30–1.30*).

Around the City

Piazza Venezia

This traffic-crazed, thoroughly awful piazza may be a poor introduction to Rome, but it makes a good place to start, with the ruins of old Rome on one side and the boutiques and bureaucracies of the new city on the other. The piazza takes its name from the **Palazzo Venezia**, built for Pope Paul II in 1455, but long the Embassy of the Venetian Republic. Mussolini made it his residence, leaving a light on all night to make the Italians think he was working. His famous balcony, from which he would declaim to the 'oceanic' crowds in the square (renamed the Forum of the Fascist Empire in those days) still holds its prominent place, a bad memory for the Italians. Nowadays the palazzo holds a **museum** of Renaissance and baroque decorative arts (*open Tues–Sat 9–1.30, Sun 9–1; adm exp*).

Long ago the southern edge of this piazza had approaches up to the Capitoline Hill. The hill is still there, though it's now entirely blocked out by the mammoth white bulk of the **Altar of the Nation** (also known as the *Vittoriano*, the Vittorio Emanuele Monument or, less respectfully, the 'Wedding Cake' or the 'Typewriter'), Risorgimento Italy's own self-inflicted satire and one of the world's apotheoses of kitsch.

The Capitoline Hill and Museums

Behind the *Vittoriano*, two stairways lead to the top of the hill. In 121 BC the great reformer Tiberius Gracchus was murdered here by a right-wing death squad. Almost a millennium and a half later Cola di Rienzo was trying to escape Rome in disguise when a mob recognized him by his rings and tore him to pieces here. Rienzo built the left-hand staircase, which leads to the church of **Santa Maria in Aracoeli**, begun in the 7th century over the temple of Juno Moneta—the ancient Roman Mint was adjacent to it. The Aracoeli, which in Rienzo's time served as a sort of council hall, is one of the most revered of Roman churches.

The second stairway takes you to the real heart of Rome, Michelangelo's **Piazza del Campidoglio**, passing on the way a rather flattering statue of Rienzo set on a bronze pedestal. At the top, bordering the piazza, a formidable cast of statues includes the Dioscuri, who come from Pompey's Theatre, and Marforio (in the Capitoline Museum courtyard), a river god once employed as one of the 'talking statues' of Rome, decorated with graffiti and placards commenting on current events. The great 2nd-century bronze equestrian statue of the philosophical emperor **Marcus Aurelius** that stood on the plinth in the middle of the piazza from the 16th century until 1981 has been fully restored and regilded and is now on show in the security of the Capitoline Museums; fortunately, since it was an old Roman saying that the world would end when all the original gold flaked off. The Christians of old only refrained from melting him down for cash because they believed he was not Marcus Aurelius, but Constantine. A copy of the original now stands at the centre of the piazza.

Michelangelo's original plans may have been adapted and tinkered with by later architects, but nevertheless his Campidoglio has come out as one of the triumphs of Renaissance design. The centrepiece, the **Palazzo Senatorio**, Rome's city hall, with its distinctive stairway and bell tower, is built over the ruins of the Roman *tabularium*, the state archive. At the base of the stair note the statue of Minerva, in her aspect as the allegorical goddess Roma. Flanking it, Michelangelo redesigned the façade of **Palazzo dei Conservatori** (on the right), and projected the matching building across the square, **Palazzo Nuovo**, built in the early 18th century. Together they make up the **Capitoline Museums**.

Founded by Pope Clement XII in 1734, and so the oldest true museum in the world, the Capitoline (*open Tues–Sun 9–7; adm*) displays both the heights and depths of ancient society and culture. For the heights, there are the reliefs from the triumphal arch of Marcus Aurelius—first-class work in scenes of the emperor's clemency and piety, and his triumphal receptions in Rome. Marcus always looks a little worried in these, perhaps considering his good-for-nothing son Commodus, and the empire he would inherit, sinking into corruption and excess. What was to come is well illustrated by the degenerate art of the 4th century, like the colossal bronze head, hand and foot of Constantine, parts of a gigantic statue in the Basilica of Maxentius (now in the courtyard).

In between these extremes come roomfuls of statuary, including the famous *Capitoline She-Wolf*, the very symbol of Rome; statues of most of the emperors, and busts of Homer, Sophocles and Pythagoras; the voluptuous *Capitoline Venus*; a big baby Hercules (who may have inspired Donatello's famous *Amor* in Florence); and the *Muse Polyhymnia*, one of the most delightful and beautiful statues of antiquity. Later works include lots of papal paraphernalia, a statue of Charles of Anjou by Florence's Arnolfo di Cambio and—in a small **Pinacoteca** in the Palazzo dei Conservatori—some dignified Velázquez gentlemen looking scornfully at the other paintings and two major works by Caravaggio, the *Fortune Teller* and *John the Baptist*. There are also some lovely, though at times silly, 18th-century porcelains— orchestras of monkeys in powdered wigs, and such.

From behind the Palazzo Senatorio a stairway leads down, offering the best overview of the Forum; the entrance is a little further down Via dei Fori Imperiali. The southern end of the Capitol, one of the quietest corners of Rome, was the site of Jupiter Optimus Maximus (Greatest and Best), a temple built originally by the Etruscan kings. At the time it was the largest in Italy, testimony to Rome's importance as far back as 450 BC. Along the southern edge of the hill, the cliffs you see are the somewhat reduced remains of the **Tarpeian Rock**, from which traitors and other malefactors were thrown in Rome's early days.

Along the Tiber

The early emperors did their best to import classical Greek drama to Rome, and for a while, with the poets of the Latin New Comedy, it seemed the Romans would carry on the tradition. Great theatres were built in Rome, like the **Theatre of Marcellus** at the foot of the Capitoline, begun by Caesar and completed by Augustus. By the 2nd century AD, however, theatre had already begun to degenerate into music-hall shows, lewd performances with naked actresses and grisly murders (condemned prisoners were sometimes butchered on stage), and shows by celebrity actors probably much like some unseemly spectacles of our own time. Marcellus' theatre (Augustus named it after his favourite nephew) survived into the Middle Ages, when the Orsini family converted it into their palace-fortress, the strongest in Rome after the Castel Sant'Angelo. Today it presents one of Rome's more curious sights, the tall arches of the circumference surmounted by the rough medieval walls of the Orsini.

The streets to the west contain a mix of some of Rome's oldest houses with new buildings; the latter have replaced the old walled **ghetto**, demolished only a century ago. There has been a sizeable Jewish community in Rome since Pompey and Titus first brought them to Rome as slaves. They helped finance the career of Julius Caesar, who would prove to be their greatest benefactor. For centuries they lived near this bend in the river and in Trastevere. Paul IV took time off from burning books and heretics to wall them into the tiny ghetto in 1555; at the same time he forced them to wear orange hats, attend Mass on Sunday, and limited them to the rag and old iron trades. Tearing down the ghetto walls was one of the first acts of the Italian kingdom after the entry into Rome in 1870. The exotic, eclectic main **synagogue** was built in 1904, after the last of the ghetto was demolished.

Opposite the synagogue, the **Tiber Island** is joined to both sides of the river by ancient bridges. In Imperial times, the island was sacred to Aesculapius, god of healing; a legend records how some serpents brought from the god's shrine in Greece escaped and swam to the spot, choosing the site by divine guidance. Now, as in ancient times, most of the lovely island is taken up by a hospital, the Ospedale Fatebenefratelli; in place of the Temple of Aesculapius, there is also the church of **San Bartolomeo**, most recently rebuilt in the 1690s.

Piazza Bocca della Verità

The two well-preserved Roman temples here, the round **Temple of Vesta**, used as an Armenian church in the Middle Ages, and the **Temple of Fortuna Virilis**, have probably been misnamed—it's almost certain that they were actually dedicated to Hercules Victor and Portunus (the god of harbours) respectively. Some bits of an exotic, ornate Roman cornice are built into the brick building opposite, part of the **House of the Crescenzi**, a powerful family in the 9th century, descended from Theodora Senatrix. Look over the side of the Tiber embankment here, and you can see the outlet of the **Cloaca Maxima**, the great ancient sewer begun by King Tarquin. Big enough to drive two carriages through, it is still in use. Just upstream, past the Palatine Bridge, a single arch decorated with dragons in the middle of the river is all that remains of the ancient *Pons Aemilius*. Originally built in the 2nd century BC, it collapsed twice and was last restored in 1575 by Gregory XIII, only to fall down again 20 years later. Now it is familiarly known as the 'broken bridge', or **Ponte Rotto**.

The handsome medieval church with the lofty campanile is **Santa Maria in Cosmedin**, built over an altar of Hercules in the 6th century and given to Byzantine Greeks escaping from the Iconoclast heretic emperors in the 8th. The name (like 'cosmetic') means 'decorated', but little of the original art has survived; most of what you see is from the 12th century, including some fine Cosmatesque work inside. In the portico, an ancient, ghostly image in stone built into the walls has come down in legend as the Bocca della Verità—the 'Mouth of Truth'. Medieval Romans would swear oaths and close business deals here; if you tell a lie with your hand in the image's mouth he will most assuredly bite your fingers off. Try it.

The Heart of Ancient Rome

In the 1930s Mussolini built the **Via dei Fori Imperiali**, a grand boulevard between the Vittoriano and the Colosseum designed to ease traffic congestion and show off the ancient sites, and named after the Imperial Fora which it partly covers. The **Imperial Fora** of Augustus, Nerva and Trajan were built to relieve congestion in the original Roman Forum. **Trajan's Forum**, built with the spoils of his conquest of Dacia (modern Romania), was perhaps the grandest architectural and planning conception ever built in Rome, a broad square surrounded by colonnades, with a huge basilica flanked by two libraries and a covered market outside. A large part of **Trajan's Market** still stands, with entrances on Via IV Novembre and down the stairs just to the side of the Trajan Column (*open Tues–Sun 9–one hour before sunset; adm*).

Behind it, you can see Rome's own leaning tower, built in the 12th century and called the **Torre delle Milizie**. All that remains of Trajan's great square is some paving and its centrepiece, the **Trajan Column**. The spiralling bands of sculptural reliefs, illustrating the Dacian Wars, reach to the top, some 100ft high. They rank with the greatest works of Roman art. Plaster casts taken during a lengthy restoration are on display at the Museum of Roman Civilization in the EUR suburb. Behind the column, the church of **Santa Maria di Loreto** is a somewhat garish High Renaissance bauble, built by Bramante and Antonio da Sangallo the Younger, starting in 1501. The Romans liked it so much they built another one just like it next door, the **Santissimo Nome di Maria**, from the 1730s. Scanty remains of the **Forum of Caesar** and the **Forum of Augustus** can be seen along the boulevard to the south.

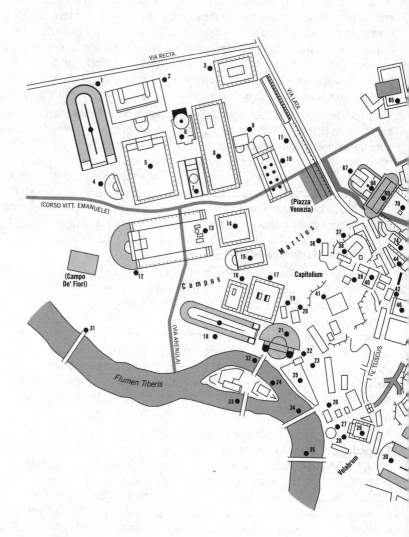

Central Rome 300 AD

VIA RECTA

VIA LATA

(CORSO VITT. EMANUELE)

(Piazza Venezia)

(Campo De' Fiori)

Martius

Capitolium

Campus

(VIA ARENULA)

Flumen Tiberis

V. TUSCUS

Velabrum

* before names of
sights indicates
significant remains.

Modern streets and
squares shaded in to
help orientation.

CAMPUS MARTIUS
1 Stadium of Domitian
2 Baths of Nero
3 *Temple of Hadrian
4 Domitian's Odeon
5 Stagnum Agrippae
6 *Pantheon
7 Baths of Agrippa
8 Saepta Julia
9 Temple of Isis
10 Porticus Divorum
11 Portico of Vipsania
12 Pompey's Theatre
13 *Republican Temples (Largo
   Argentina)
14 Portico of Minucia
15 Theatre of Balbus
16 Porticus Philippi
17 *Portico of Octavia
18 Circus Flaminius
19 *Temple of Apollo
20 Temple of Bellona
21 *Temple of Marcellus
22 *Temple of Hope
23 Forum Holitorium
24 Temple of Aesculapius
25 Warehouses

VELABRUM AND TIBER ISLAND
26 *Temple of Portumnus
27 *Temple of Hercules Victor
28 Forum Boarium
29 Statio Annonae/Altar of
   Hercules
30 Circus Maximus
31 Bridge of Valentinian

32 *Pons Cestius
33 *Pons Fabricius
34 *Pons Aemilius
35 Pons Probus

CAPITOL
36 *Insula (apartment house)
37 Arx (citadel)
38 Temple of Juno Moneta
39 Asylum—Temple of Veiovis
40 *Tabularium
41 Temple of Jupiter

FORUM
42 *Temple of Saturn
43 *Arch of Septimius Severus
44 *Curia
45 Basilica Aemilia
46 Basilica Julia
47 *Temple of the Dioscuri
48 *House of the Vestal Virgins
49 *Basilica of Maxentius
50 *Arch of Titus
51 *Temple of Venus and Rome
52 Temple of Elagabalus
53 Nero's Colossus
54 *Arch of Constantine
55 *Colosseum

PALATINE
56 *Palace of Tiberius
57 Temple of Cybele
58 *House of Augustus
59 *Stadium
60 Septizonium

CAELIAN AND QUIRINAL
61 Temple of Claudius
62 *Ludus Magnus
63 Baths of Titus
64 Baths of Trajan
65 Temple of Serapis
66 Baths of Constantine

IMPERIAL FORA
67 Temple of Trajan
68 *Trajan's Column
69 Basilica Ulpia
70 Forum of Trajan
71 *Trajan's Market
72 *Forum of Augustus
73 *Forum of Nerva—
   Temple of Minerva
74 Temple of Venus Genetrix
75 Forum of Caesar
76 Forum of Vespasian

The Roman Forum

Though this was once the centre of the Mediterranean world, there is surprisingly little to see; centuries of use as a quarry have seen to that. *'Forum'* originally meant 'outside' (like Italian *fuori*), a marketplace outside the original Rome that became the centre of both government and business as the city expanded around it. The entrances are on the Via dei Fori Imperiali at Via Cavour, and at the end of the ramp that approaches the Forum from the Colosseum side (*open April–Oct daily 9–one hour before sunset; May–Sept Mon–Sat 9–3, Sun 9–1*).

The **Via Sacra**, ancient Rome's most important street, runs the length of the Forum. At the end of it beneath the Capitol you will be facing the **Arch of Septimius Severus** (AD 203), with reliefs of some rather trivial victories over the Arabs and Parthians. The arch also commemorated Septimius' two sons, Geta and Caracalla; when the nasty Caracalla did his brother in, he had his name effaced from it. In front of it, the **Lapis Niger**, a mysterious stone with an underground chamber beneath it, is the legendary tomb of Romulus. The inscription down below—a threat against the profaning of this sacred spot—is one of the oldest ever found in the Latin language. The famous Golden Milestone also stood here, the 'umbilicus' of Rome and the point from which all distances in the Empire were measured. To the right is the **Curia** (the Senate House), heavily restored after centuries' use as a church (the good baroque church behind it is **SS. Luca e Martina**, built by Pietro di Cortona in the 1660s). To the left of the arch the remains of a raised stone area were the **Rostra**, the speakers' platform in public assemblies under the republic, decorated with ships' prows (*rostra*) taken in a sea-battle about 320 BC. Of the great temples on the Capitol slope only a few columns remain; from left to right, the **Temple of Saturn**, which served as Rome's treasury, the **Temple of Vespasian** (three columns standing) and the **Temple of Concord**, built by Tiberius to honour the peace—so to speak—that the emperors had enforced between the patricians and plebeians.

Behind the Rostra, in the open area once decorated with statues and monuments, the simple standing **column** was placed by the Romans in honour of Phocas, Byzantine Emperor in 608—the last monument ever erected in the Forum, and they had to steal the column from a ruined building. Just behind it a small pool once marked the spot of one of ancient Rome's favourite legends. In 362 BC, according to Livy, an abyss suddenly opened across the Forum, and the sibyls predicted that it would not close unless the 'things that Rome held most precious' were thrown in. A consul, Marcus Curtius, took this as meaning a Roman citizen and soldier. He leapt in fully armed, horse and all, and the crack closed over him.

This section of the Forum was bordered by two imposing buildings, the **Basilica Aemilia** to the north and the **Basilica Julia** to the south, built by Caesar with the spoils of the Gallic Wars. The **Temple of Caesar** closes the east end, built by Augustus as a visual symbol of the new Imperial mythology. The adjacent **Temple of the Dioscuri** makes a good example of how temples were used in ancient times. This one was a meeting hall for men of the equestrian class (the knights, though they were really more likely to be businessmen); they had safe-deposit boxes in the basement, where the standard weights and measures of the Empire were kept. Between them, the round pedestal was the foundation of the small **Temple of Vesta**, where the sacred hearth-fire was kept burning by the Vestal Virgins; ruins of their extensive apartments can be seen next door.

Two more Christian churches stand in this part of the Forum. **SS. Cosma e Damiano** was built on to the **Temple of Antoninus Pius and Faustina** in the 6th century; most of the columns of the temple survive, with a fine sculptural frieze of griffons on top. **Santa Francesca Romana** is built over a corner of ancient Rome's largest temple, that of **Venus and Rome**. The temple, built by Hadrian, was a curious, double-ended shrine to the state cult; one side devoted to the goddess Roma and the other to Venus—in the Imperial mythology she was the ancestress of the family of the Caesars. Between the two churches the mastodonic **Basilica of Maxentius**, finished by Constantine, remains the largest ruin of the Forum, its clumsy arches providing an illustration of the ungainly but technically sophisticated 4th century.

Near the exit, the **Arch of Titus** commemorates the victories of Titus and his father Vespasian over the rebellious Jews (AD 60–80), one of the fiercest struggles Rome ever had to fight. The reliefs on the arch show some of the booty being carted through Rome in the triumphal parade—including the famous seven-branched golden candlestick from the holy of holies in the Temple at Jerusalem. South of the arch a path leads up to the **Palatine Hill** (*open April–Oct daily 9–one hour before sunset; May–Sept Mon–Sat 9–3, Sun 9–1; adm*). Here, overlooking the little corner of the ancient world that gave our language words like *senate, committee, rostrum, republic, plebiscite* and *magistrate*, you can leave democracy behind and visit the etymological birthplace of *palace*. The ruins of the imperial *Palatium* once covered the entire hill. As with the Forum, almost all the stone has been cannibalized, and there's little to see of what was once a palace complex three-quarters of a kilometre long, to which a dozen of the emperors contributed. There are good views across the Circus Maximus from just above what was once a big portico from which the Emperor could watch the races. Don't miss the chance to stroll through the gardens planted by the Farnese family over what were the Imperial servants' quarters—one of the most peaceful spots in the city.

The Colosseum

Its real name was the Flavian Amphitheatre, after the family of emperors who built it, beginning with Vespasian in AD 72; Colosseum refers to the *Colossus*, a huge gilded statue of Nero (erected by himself) that formerly stood in the square in front. There isn't much evidence that Christians were literally thrown to lions here—there were other places for that—but what did go on was perhaps the grossest and best-organized perversity in history. Gladiatorial contests began under the Republic, designed to make Romans better soldiers by rendering them indifferent to the sight of death. Later emperors introduced new displays—men versus animals, lions versus elephants, women versus dwarfs, sea-battles (the arena could be flooded at a moment's notice), public tortures of criminals, and even genuine athletics, a Greek import the Romans never much cared for. In one memorable day of games, 5,000 animals were slaughtered, about one every 10 seconds. The native elephant and lion of North Africa and Arabia are extinct thanks to such shenanigans.

However hideous its purpose, the Colosseum ranks with the greatest works of Roman architecture and engineering; all modern stadiums have copied most of its general plan. One surprising feature was a removable awning that covered the stands. A detachment of sailors from Cape Misenum was kept to operate it; they also manned the galleys in the mock sea-battles. Originally there were statues in all of the arches and a ring of bronze shields all around the cornice. The concrete stands have eroded away, showing the brick structure underneath. Renaissance and baroque popes hauled away half the travertine exterior—enough to build the Palazzo Venezia, the Palazzo Barberini, a few other palaces and bridges and part of St Peter's. Almost all of the construction work under Vespasian and Titus was performed by Jewish slaves, brought here for the purpose after the suppression of their revolt (*open Tues–Sat 9–one hour before sunset, Sun and Mon 9–2; adm*).

Just outside the Colosseum, the **Arch of Constantine** marks the end of the ancient Triumphal Way (now Via di San Gregorio) where victorious emperors and their troops would parade their captives and booty. The arch, with a coy inscription mentioning Constantine's 'divine inspiration' (the Romans weren't sure whether it was yet respectable to mention Christianity), is covered with reliefs stolen from older arches and public buildings—a sad commentary on the state of art in Constantine's day.

The Domus Aurea

When Nero decided he needed a new palace, money was no object. Taking advantage of the great fire of AD 64 (which he apparently did *not* start), he had a huge section of Rome (temporarily renamed Neropolis) cleared to make a rural estate in the middle of town. The **Golden House** was probably the most sumptuous palace ever built in Rome, decorated in an age when Roman art was at its height, but Nero never lived to see it finished—he committed suicide during an army coup by Spanish legions. When the dust settled the new emperor Vespasian realized that this flagrant symbol of imperial decadence had to go. He demolished it, and Titus and Trajan later erected great bath complexes on its foundations; Nero's gardens and fishponds became the site of the Colosseum. In the 1500s some beautifully decorated rooms of the Domus Aurea were discovered underground on what is now the Colle Oppio; they had been saved for use as the basement of Titus' baths. Raphael and other artists studied them closely and incorporated some of the spirit of the fresco decoration into the grand manner of the High Renaissance (our word 'grotesque', originally referring to the leering faces and floral designs of this time, comes from the finds in this 'grotto').

The rooms have been restored and reopened. 32 of the 150 rooms can be visited; due to the delicate frescoes, only 25 visitors at a time are admitted. Book, on © 06 3974 9907. *Guided tours in English available. Open 9–8; adm L10,000, free for under-16s and over-60s.*

San Clemente

This church, a little way to the east of the Colosseum on Via San Giovanni in Laterano, is one of the more fascinating remnants of Rome's many-layered history. One of the first substantial building projects of the Christians in Rome, the original basilica of *c.* 375 burned along with the rest of the quarter during a sacking by the Normans in 1084. It was rebuilt soon afterwards with a new Cosmatesque pavement, and the 6th-century choir screen—a rare example of sculpture from that ungifted time—saved from the original church. The 12th-century mosaic in the apse represents the *Triumph of the Cross*, and the chapel at the entrance contains a beautiful series of quattrocento frescoes by Masolino, partly uncovered after restoration. From a vestibule, nuns sell tickets to the **Lower Church** (*open daily 9–12 and 3.30–6.30; adm*). This is the lower half of the original San Clemente, and there are remarkable, though deteriorated, frescoes from the 900s and the 12th century, some of the oldest medieval paintings to have survived anywhere in Italy. The plaque from Bulgaria, mentioned on p.54, commemorates Saints Cyril and Methodius, who went from this church to spread the Gospel among the Slavs; they translated the Bible into Old Slavonic, and invented the first Slavic alphabet (Cyrillic) to do it.

From here, steps lead down to the lowest stratum, 1st- and 2nd-century AD buildings divided by an alley; this includes the **Mithraeum**, the best-preserved temple of its kind after the one in Capua. The larger, neighbouring building was filled with rubble to serve as a foundation for the basilica, and the apse was later added over the Mithraeum. Father Mulhooly of Boston started excavating in the 1860s, and later excavations have revealed a Mithraic antechamber with a fine stuccoed ceiling, the Mithraic school with an early fresco, and the temple proper, a small cavern-like hall with benches for the initiates to share a ritual supper.

Mithraism was a mystery religion, full of secrets closely held by the initiates (all male, and largely soldiers) and it is difficult to say what else went on down here. Two altars were found, each with the usual image of the Persian-import god Mithras dispatching a white bull, including a snake, a scorpion and a crow, and astrological symbolism in the decorative scheme. Underneath all this, there is yet a fourth building level, some foundations from the Republican era. At the end of the 1st-century building you can look down into an ancient sewer or underground stream, one of a thousand entrances to the surreal sub-Roma of endless subterranean caves, buildings, rivers and lakes, mostly unexplored and unexplorable. A century ago a schoolboy fell in the water here; they found him, barely alive, in open country several kilometres from the city.

Along Corso Vittorio Emanuele

This street, chopped through the medieval centre of Rome in the 1880s, still hasn't quite been assimilated into its surroundings; nevertheless, this ragged, smoky traffic tunnel will come in handy when you find yourself lost in the tortuous, meandering streets of Rome's oldest quarter. Starting west from Piazza Venezia, the church of the **Gesù** (1568–84) was a landmark for a new era and the new aesthetic of cinquecento Rome. The transitional, pre-baroque fashion was often referred to as the 'Jesuit style', and here in the Jesuits' head church architects Vignola and della Porta first laid down baroque's cardinal principle: an intimation of Paradise for the impressionable through decorative excess. It hasn't aged well, though at the time it must have seemed to most Romans a perfect marriage of Renaissance art and a reformed, revitalized faith. St Ignatius, the Jesuits' founder, is buried in the left transept right under the altar, Spanish-style; the globe incorporated in the sculpted Trinity overhead is the biggest piece of lapis lazuli in the world. A little way further west the street opens into a ghastly square called Largo Argentina. Remains of several Republican-era temples, unearthed far below ground level, can be seen in the square's centre.

One of the earliest and best of the palaces on Corso Vittorio Emanuele, the delicate **Piccola Farnesina** by Antonio da Sangallo the Younger, houses another little museum, a collection of ancient sculpture called the **Museo Barracco** (*open Tues–Sat 9–7, Sun 9–1.30; adm*). A third museum—not a well-known one—is just around the corner from Sant'Andrea on Via Sudario. The **Burcardo Theatre Museum** (*open by appointment, call the custodian, © 06 684 0001*) is a collection of fascinating old relics from the Roman theatrical tradition.

The biggest palace on the street, attributed to Bramante, is **Palazzo della Cancelleria**, once the seat of the papal municipal government. St Philip Neri, the gifted, irascible holy man who is patron saint of Rome, built the **Chiesa Nuova** near the eastern end of the Corso (1584). Philip was quite a character, with something of the Zen Buddhist in him. He forbade his followers any sort of philosophical speculation or dialectic, but made them sing and recite poetry; two of his favourite pastimes were insulting popes and embarrassing new initiates— making them walk through Rome with a foxtail sewn to the back of their coat to learn humility. As was common in those times, sincere faith and humility were eventually translated into flagrant baroque. The Chiesa Nuova is one of the larger and fancier of the species. Its altarpiece is a *Madonna with Angels* by Rubens. Even more flagrant, outside the church you can see the curved arch-baroque façade of the **Philippine Oratory** by Borromini. The form of music called the *oratorio* takes its name from this chapel.

Campo de' Fiori

Around Campo de' Fiori, one of the spots dearest to the hearts of Romans themselves, you may think yourself in the middle of some scruffy south Italian village. Rome's market square, disorderly, cramped and chaotic, is easily the liveliest corner of the city, full of market barrows, buskers, teenage bohemians and the folkloresque types who have lived here all their lives—the least decorous and worst-dressed crowd in Rome. During papal rule the old square was also used for executions—most notoriously the burning of Giordano Bruno in 1600. This well-travelled philosopher was the first to take Copernican astronomy to its logical extremes—an infinite universe with no centre, no room for heaven, and nothing eternal but change. The Church had few enemies more dangerous. Italy never forgot him; the statue of Bruno in Campo de' Fiori went up only a few years after the end of papal rule.

Just east of the square, the heap of buildings around Piazzetta di Grottapinta is built over the cavea of **Pompey's Theatre**, ancient Rome's biggest. This complex included a *curia*, where Julius Caesar was assassinated in 44 BC. Walk south from Campo de' Fiori, and you will be thrown back from cosy medievalism into the High Renaissance with the **Palazzo Farnese**, one of the definitive works of that Olympian style. The younger Sangallo began it in 1514, and Michelangelo contributed to the façades and interiors. The building now serves as the French Embassy, and it isn't easy to get in to see it. Most of the palaces that fill up this neighbourhood have one thing in common—they were made possible by someone's accession to the papacy, the biggest jackpot available to any aspiring Italian family. Built on the pennies of the faithful, they provide the most outrageous illustration of Church corruption at the dawn of the Reformation. Alessandro Farnese, who as Paul III was a clever and effective pope— though perhaps the greatest nepotist ever to decorate St Peter's throne—managed to build this palace 20 years before his election, with the income from his 16 absentee bishoprics.

Palazzo Spada, just to the east along Via Capo di Ferro, was the home of a mere cardinal, but its florid stucco façade (1540) almost upstages the Farnese. Inside, the **Galleria Spada** (*open Tues–Sat 9–7, Sun 9–1; adm*) is one of Rome's great collections of 16th- and 17th-century painting. Guido Reni, Guercino and the other favourites of the age are well represented. To the south, close to the Tiber, **Via Giulia** was laid out by Pope Julius II: a famous and pretty thoroughfare lined with churches and palazzi from that time. Many artists (successful ones) have lived here, including Raphael.

Piazza Navona

In 1477 the area now covered by one of Rome's most beautiful piazzas was a half-forgotten field full of huts and vineyards, tucked inside the still-imposing ruins of the Stadium of Domitian. A redevelopment of the area covered the long grandstands with new houses, but the decoration had to wait for the Age of Baroque. In 1644, with the election of Innocent X, it was the Pamphili family that won the papal sweepstakes. Innocent, a great grafter and such a villainous pope that when he died no one—not even his newly wealthy relatives—would pay for a proper burial, built the ornate **Palazzo Pamphili** (now the Brazilian Embassy) and hired Borromini to complete the gaudy church of **Sant'Agnese in Agone**, begun by Carlo and Girolamo Rainaldi.

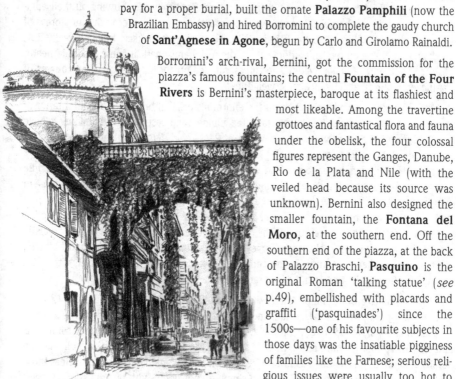

Borromini's arch-rival, Bernini, got the commission for the piazza's famous fountains; the central **Fountain of the Four Rivers** is Bernini's masterpiece, baroque at its flashiest and most likeable. Among the travertine grottoes and fantastical flora and fauna under the obelisk, the four colossal figures represent the Ganges, Danube, Rio de la Plata and Nile (with the veiled head because its source was unknown). Bernini also designed the smaller fountain, the **Fontana del Moro**, at the southern end. Off the southern end of the piazza, at the back of Palazzo Braschi, **Pasquino** is the original Roman 'talking statue' (*see* p.49), embellished with placards and graffiti ('pasquinades') since the 1500s—one of his favourite subjects in those days was the insatiable pigginess of families like the Farnese; serious religious issues were usually too hot to touch, even for a statue.

The Pantheon

When we consider the fate of so many other great buildings of ancient Rome we begin to understand what a slim chance it was that allowed this one to come down to us. The first Pantheon was built in 27 BC by Agrippa, Emperor Augustus' son-in-law and right-hand man, but was destroyed by fire and replaced by the present temple in 119–28 by the Emperor Hadrian, though, curiously, retaining Agrippa's original inscription on the pediment. Its history has been precarious ever since. In 609 the empty Pantheon was consecrated to Christianity as 'St Mary of the Martyrs'. Becoming a church is probably what saved it, though the Byzantines hauled away the gilded bronze roof tiles soon after, and for a while in the Middle Ages the portico saw use as a fish market. The Pantheon's greatest enemy, however, was Gian Lorenzo Bernini. He not only 'improved' it with a pair of baroque belfries over the porch (demolished in 1887), but he had Pope Urban VIII take down the bronze covering on the inside of the dome to use the metal for his *baldacchino* over the altar at St Peter's. Supposedly there was enough left over to make the Pope 60 cannons.

Looking at the outside you may notice the building seems perilously unsound. There is no way a simple vertical wall can support such a heavy, shallow dome (steep domes push downwards, shallow ones outwards). Obviously the walls will tumble at any moment. That is a little joke the Roman architects are playing on us, for here they are showing off their engineering virtuosity as shamelessly as in the Colosseum, or the aqueduct with four storeys of arches that used to run up to the Palatine Hill. The wall that looks so fragile is really 25ft thick and the dome on top isn't a dome at all; the real, hemispherical dome lies underneath, resting easily on the walls inside. The ridges you see on the upper dome are courses of cantilevered bricks, effectively almost weightless.

The real surprise, however, lies behind the enormous original bronze doors, an interior of precious marbles and finely sculpted details, the grandest and best-preserved building to have survived from the ancient world (*open Mon–Sat 9–6.30 and Sun 9–1*). The movie directors who made all those Roman epics in the 1950s and '60s certainly took many of their settings from this High Imperial creation of Hadrian's time, just as architects from the early Middle Ages onwards have tried to equal it. Brunelleschi learned enough from it to build his dome in Florence, and a visit here will show you at a glance what Michelangelo and his contemporaries were trying so hard to outdo. The coffered dome, the biggest cast-concrete construction ever made before the 20th century, is the crowning audacity, even without its bronze plate. At 140ft in diameter it is probably the largest in the world (St Peter's dome is almost 7ft less, though much taller). Standing in the centre and looking at the clouds through the 30ft *oculus*, the hole at the top, is an odd sensation you can experience nowhere else.

Inside, the niches around the perimeter were devoted to statues of the Pantheon's 12 gods, plus those of Augustus and Hadrian; in the centre, illuminated by a direct sunbeam at midsummer noon, stood Jove. All these are gone, of course, and the interior decoration is limited to an *Annunciation*, to the right of the door, attributed to Melozzo da Forlì, and the tombs of eminent Italians such as Kings Vittorio Emanuele II and Umberto I, as well as those of Raphael and other artists. The Pantheon simply stands open, with no admission charges, probably fulfilling the same purpose as in Hadrian's day—no purpose at all, save that of an unequalled monument to art and the builder's skill. The Cult of the Twelve Gods, a Greek import from Augustus' time, never attracted many followers in Rome—even though many of the individual gods were present in Roman religion from the earliest times.

Via del Corso

Campus Martius, the plain between Rome's hills and the Tiber, was the training ground for soldiers in the early days of the Republic. Eventually the city swallowed it up and the path towards the Via Flaminia became one of the most important thoroughfares, Via Lata ('Broad Street'). Not entirely by coincidence, the popes of the 14th and 15th centuries laid out a grand new boulevard almost in the same place. **Via del Corso**, or simply the Corso, has been the main axis of Roman society ever since. Goethe recorded a fascinating account of the

Carnival festivities held here in Rome's benignly decadent 18th century; the horse races that were held as the climax of the Carnival gave the street its name. Much of it is taken up by the overdone palaces of the age, such as the Palazzo Doria (1780), where the **Galleria Doria Pamphili** (*open Fri–Wed 10–5; visits to the apartments at 10.30 and 12.30; adm*), still owned by the Pamphili, has a fine painting collection with Velázquez' *Portrait of Innocent X*, Caravaggio's *Flight into Egypt*, and works by Rubens, Titian, Brueghel and more.

Continuing northwards, the palaces have come down in the world somewhat, tired-looking blocks that now house banks and offices. Look on the side streets for some hidden attractions: **Sant'Ignazio**, on Via del Seminario, is another Jesuit church with spectacular *trompe l'œil* frescoes on the ceiling; a block north, columns of the ancient **Temple of Hadrian** are incorporated into the north side of the city's tiny Stock Exchange (Milan is Italy's financial capital). **Piazza Colonna** takes its name from the column of Marcus Aurelius, whose great military victories are remembered in a column (just like those of Trajan); atop this column is a statue of St Paul. The obelisk in adjacent Piazza di Montecitorio once marked the hours on a gigantic sundial in Emperor Augustus' garden; **Palazzo Montecitorio**, begun by Bernini, now houses the Italian Chamber of Deputies.

A little way east of Piazza Colonna is the **Trevi Fountain**, into which you can throw your coins to guarantee your return trip to Rome. The fountain, completed in 1762, was originally planned to commemorate the restoration of Agrippa's aqueduct by Nicholas V in 1453. The source was called the 'Virgin Water' after Virgo, a young girl who had showed thirsty Roman soldiers the hidden spring. It makes a grand sight—enough to make you want to come back; not many fountains have an entire palace (the Palazzo Poli) for a stage backdrop. The big fellow in the centre is Oceanus, drawn by horses and tritons through cascades of travertine and blue water. Across from the fountain, the little church of **SS. Vicenzo and Anastasio** has the distinction of caring for the pickled hearts and entrails of several dozen popes; an odd custom. They're kept down in the crypt.

Piazza di Spagna

The shuffling crowds of tourists who congregate here at all hours of the day are not a recent phenomenon; this irregular but supremely sophisticated piazza has been a favourite with foreigners ever since it was laid out in the early 16th century. The Spaniards came first, as their embassy to the popes was established here in 1646, giving the square and the steps their name. Later, the English Romantic poets made it their headquarters in Italy; typical Romantic mementoes—locks of hair, fond remembrances, mortal remains, death masks—are awaiting your inspired contemplation at the **Keats-Shelley Memorial House** at No.26 (*open April–Sept Mon–Fri 9–1 and 3–6; Oct–Mar Mon–Fri 9–1 and 2.30–5.30; adm*). Almost every artist, writer or musician of the last century spent some time in the neighbourhood, but today the piazza often finds itself bursting at the seams with refreshingly philistine gawkers and wayward youth from all over Europe, America and Japan, caught between the charms of McDonald's (the first one built in Rome) and the fancy shops on and around nearby Via Condotti.

All these visitors need somewhere to sit, and the popes obliged them in 1725 with the construction of the **Spanish Steps**, an exceptionally beautiful and exceptionally baroque ornament about which it is hard to be cynical. The youth of today who loll about here are taking the place of the hopeful artists' models of the more picturesque centuries, who once crowded the steps, striking poses of antique heroes and Madonnas, waiting for some easy money. At the top of the stairs the simple but equally effective church of **Trinità dei Monti** by Carlo Maderno (early 16th century) was paid for by the King of France. At the southern end of Piazza di Spagna a Borromini palace housed the papal office called the *Propaganda Fide*, whose job was just what the name implies. The column in front (1856) celebrates the proclamation of the Dogma of the Immaculate Conception, one of their hardest tasks. Via del Babuino, a street named after a siren on a fountain so ugly that Romans called her the 'baboon', connects Piazza di Spagna with Piazza del Popolo. Besides its very impressive and equally expensive antique shops, the street carries on the English connection, with All Saints' Church, a sleepy neo-pub and an English bookshop just off it.

Piazza del Popolo

If you have a choice of how you enter Rome, this is the way to do it, through the gate in the old Aurelian wall and into one of the most successful of all Roman piazzas, copied on a smaller scale all over Italy. Valadier, the Pope's architect after the Napoleonic occupation, gave the piazza the form it has today, but the big obelisk of Pharaoh Ramses II punctuating the view down the boulevards arrived in the 1580s. It is 3,200 years old but, like all obelisks, it looks mysteriously brand-new; Augustus brought it to Rome from Heliopolis and planted it in the Circus Maximus, and it was transferred here by Pope Sixtus V. The two domed churches designed by Rainaldi, set like bookends at the entrance to the three boulevards, are from the 1670s, part of the original plan for the piazza.

Emperor Nero's ashes were interred in a mausoleum here, at the foot of the Monte Pincio. The site was planted with walnut trees and soon everyone in Rome knew the stories of how Nero's ghost haunted the grove, sending out demons—in the forms of flocks of ravens that nested there—to perform deeds of evil. About 1100 Pope Paschal II destroyed the grove and scattered the ashes; to complete the exorcism he built a church on the site, **Santa Maria del Popolo**. Rebuilt in the 1470s, it contains some of the best painting in Rome: Caravaggio's stunning *Crucifixion of St Peter* and *Crucifixion of St Paul* (in the left transept), and frescoes by Pinturicchio around the altar. Raphael designed the Chigi Chapel, off the left aisle, and contributed the designs for its mosaics.

Villa Borghese

From Piazza del Popolo a winding ramp leads up to Rome's great complex of parks. Just by coincidence this was mostly parkland in ancient times. The **Monte Pincio** once formed part of Augustus' Imperial gardens, and the adjacent **Villa Medici** occupies the site of the Villa of Lucullus, the 2nd-century BC philosopher and general who conquered northern Anatolia and first brought cherries to Europe. Now the home of the French Academy, the Villa Medici was a posh jail of sorts for Galileo during his Inquisitorial trials. The Pincio, redesigned by Valadier as a lovely formal garden, offers rare views over Rome. It is separated from the **Villa Borghese** proper by the Aurelian wall and the modern sunken highway that borders it; its name, Viale del Muro Torto, means 'crooked wall', and refers to a section of the Roman wall that collapsed in the 6th century and was left as it was because it was believed to be protected by St Peter.

Exploring the vast spaces of Villa Borghese, you will come across charming vales, woods and a pond (rowing boats for rent), an imitation Roman temple or two, rococo avenues where the bewigged dandies and powdered tarts of the 1700s came to promenade, bits of ancient aqueduct and the dated **Zoological Garden** (*open daily 8–two hours before sunset; adm*). On the northern edge of the park is a ponderous boulevard called **Viale delle Belle Arti**, setting for several academies, each set up by a foreign government to stimulate cultural exchange. The **National Gallery of Modern Art** (*open Tues–Sun 9–7; adm exp*) makes its home here in one of Rome's biggest and most inexcusable buildings (1913), but the collection includes some of the best works of Modigliani and the Futurists, as well as a fair sampling of 19th- and 20th-century artists from the rest of Europe.

From there, skirting the Romanian Academy, you come to the **Villa Giulia Museum** (*open Tues–Sat 9–7, Sun 9–2; adm exp*). If you can't make it to Tarquinia, this is the best place to get to know the Etruscans. Some of their best art has been collected here, as well as laboriously reconstructed terracotta façades to give you some idea of how an Etruscan temple looked. The compelling attraction of the art here is the Etruscans' effortless, endearing talent for portraiture: expressive faces that help bridge the gap between the centuries can be seen in terracotta *ex votos* (some of children), sarcophagi and even architectural decoration. The museum building and its courts and gardens are attractions in themselves.

The Borghese family collected an impressive hoard of ancient and modern art. Much of it was shipped off to the Louvre in the 1800s, to please Napoleon, but later generations did their best to rebuild the collection, and the **Museo and Galleria Borghese** (*open Tues–Sun 9–7; adm; tickets by reservation, call © 06 328 101, Mon–Fri 9.30–6*) today offers an intriguing mix of great art and Roman preciosity.

Via Veneto and the Quirinale

This chain of gardens was once much bigger, but at the end of the last century many of the old villas that hemmed in Rome were lost to the inevitable expansion of the city. Perhaps the greatest loss was the Villa Ludovisi, praised by many as the most beautiful of all Rome's parks. Now the choice 'Ludovisi' quarter, it has given the city one of its most famous streets, Via Veneto, the long winding boulevard of grand hotels, cafés and boutiques that stretches down from Villa Borghese to Piazza Barberini. A promenade for the smart set in the 1950s, it wears something of the forlorn air of a jilted beau now that fashion has moved on. Pull your-self away from the passing show on the boulevard to take in the unique spectacle of the **Convento dei Cappuccini** at the southern end of the street, just up from Piazza Barberini (*entrance halfway up the stairs of Santa Maria della Concezione; open Fri–Wed 9–12 and 3–6; adm*). Unique, that is, outside Palermo, for, much like the Capuchin convent there, the Roman brethren have created a loving tribute to Death. In the cellars 4,000 dead monks team up for an unforgettable *danse macabre* of bones and grinning skulls, carefully arranged by serious-minded Capuchins long ago to remind us of something we know only too well.

On the other side of Piazza Barberini, up a gloomy baroque avenue called Via delle Quattro Fontane, you'll find the Palazzo Barberini, one of the showier places in Rome, decorated everywhere with the bees from the family arms. Maderno, Borromini and Bernini all worked on it, with financing made possible by the election of a Barberini as Pope Urban VIII in 1623. Currently it houses the **National Museum of Ancient Art** (*open Tues–Sun 9–7; adm*)—a misleading title, since this is a gallery devoted to Italian works of the 12th–18th centuries.

San Carlino (*currently closed for restoration*), on the corner of Via delle Quattro Fontane and Via Quirinale, is one of Borromini's best works—and his first one (1638), a purposely eccentric little flight of fancy built exactly the size of one of the four massive pillars that hold up the dome in St Peter's. Follow **Via Quirinale** to reach the summit of that hill, covered with villas and gardens in ancient times, and abandoned in the Middle Ages. Then even the name Quirinale had been forgotten, and the Romans called the place 'Montecavallo' after the two big horses' heads projecting above the ground. During the reign of Sixtus V they were excavated to reveal monumental Roman statues of the **Dioscuri** (Castor and Pollux), prob-ably copied from Phidias or Praxiteles. Together with a huge basin found in the Forum, they make a centrepiece for Piazza del Quirinale. Behind it, stretching for a dreary half-kilometre along the street, is the **Palazzo del Quirinale** (*open 8.30–1.30 on the second and fourth Sun of each month; adm exp*), built in 1574 to symbolize the political domination of the popes, later occupied by the kings of Italy, and now the official residence of the president.

Further along the Via XX Settembre, the **Santa Maria della Vittoria**, on Piazza San Bernardo, is home to one of the essential works of baroque sculpture, the disconcertingly erotic *St Teresa in Ecstasy* by Bernini (in a chapel off the left aisle).

The Patriarchal Basilicas: Santa Maria Maggiore

Besides St Peter's there are three patriarchal basilicas, ancient and revered churches under the care of the Pope that have always been a part of the Roman pilgrimage. Santa Maria Maggiore, St Paul's outside the Walls and St John Lateran are all on the edges of the city, away from the political and commercial centre; by the Middle Ages they stood in open coun-tryside, and only recently has the city grown outwards to swallow them once more.

Santa Maria Maggiore, on the Monte Esquilino, was probably begun about 352, when a rich Christian saw a vision of the Virgin Mary directing him to build a church; Pope Liberius had received the same vision at the same time, and the two supposedly found the site marked out for them by a miraculous August snowfall. With various rebuildings over the centuries the church took its current form in the 1740s, with a perfectly elegant façade by Fernando Fuga and an equally impressive rear elevation by other architects; the obelisk behind it came from the Mausoleum of Augustus. Above everything rises the tallest and fairest **campanile** in Rome, an incongruous survival from the 1380s. Inside, the most conspicuous feature is the coffered ceiling by Renaissance architect Giuliano da Sangallo, gilded with the first gold brought back from the New World by Columbus, a gift from King Ferdinand and Queen Isabella of Spain. In the apse are splendid but faded mosaics from 1295 of the *Coronation of the Virgin*. Mosaics from the 5th century can be seen in the nave and in the triumphal arch in front of the apse. Santa Maria has a prize relic— nothing less than the genuine manger from Bethlehem, preserved in a sunken shrine in front of the altar; in front, kneeling in prayer, is a colossal, rather grotesque statue of Pope Pius IV added in the 1880s.

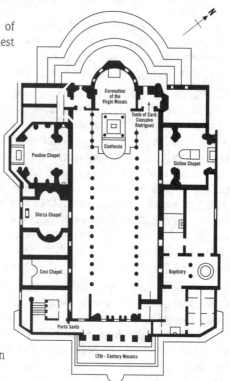

St John Lateran

Where is Rome's cathedral? It isn't St Peter's, and never has been. The true seat of the Bishop of Rome, and the end of a Roman pilgrimage, is here in the shadow of the Aurelian wall, a church believed to have been established by Constantine himself. The family of Plautius Lateranus, according to ancient records, had their property here confiscated after a failed coup against Nero in AD 66. It became part of the imperial real estate and Constantine and his wife Fausta (whom he later executed) once kept house in the Lateran Palace. Later he donated it to Pope Miltiades as a cult centre for the Christians of Rome. Almost nothing remains of the original basilica; the sacks of the Vandals and Normans, two earthquakes and several fires have resulted in a jigsaw of bits and pieces from each of the last 16 centuries.

Like Santa Maria Maggiore, this church has an 18th-century exterior that is almost miraculously good, considering other Italian buildings from that age, with a west front by Alessandro Galilei (1736) that confidently and competently reuses the High Renaissance architectural vernacular. The equally fine north façade is older, done by Domenico Fontana in 1586, and incorporating the twin medieval bell towers into the design. Entering at the west front you pass an ancient statue of Constantine, found at the baths he built on the Quirinale; the bronze doors in the central portal once graced the entrance to the Senate House in the Forum. Inside, the nave is dominated by giant, impressive statues of the Apostles (*c.* 1720), glaring down like Roman emperors of old. There is some carefree and glorious baroque work in the side chapels—also remains of a fresco by Giotto, behind the first column on the right. Near the apse, decorated with 13th-century mosaics (of a reindeer worshipping the cross, an odd conceit probably adapted from older mosaics in Ravenna), the Papal Altar supposedly contains the heads of Peter and Paul. Below floor level is the tomb of Pope Martin V; pilgrims drop flowers and telephone tokens on him for good luck.

Rome in the later Middle Ages had evolved an architectural style entirely its own, strangely uninterested in Gothic or reviving classicism, or, for that matter, anything else that was going on in the rest of Italy. Sadly, almost all of it disappeared in the Renaissance and baroque rebuildings. The towers of Santa Maria in Cosmedin and Santa Maria Maggiore are good examples of it, as well as the expressive mosaics of Pietro Cavallini and his school and the intricate, geometrical Cosmatesque pavements in this church and so many others. Perhaps the most striking survival of this lost chapter in art is the Lateran **Cloister** (*open daily 9–6, until 5 in winter; adm exp*), with its pairs of spiral columns and 13th-century Cosmatesque mosaics; it completely upstages everything else in the church. All around the cloister walls, fragments from the earlier incarnations of the basilica have been assembled, a hoard of broken pretty things that includes an interesting tomb of a 13th-century bishop, which may be the work of Arnolfo di Cambio.

The Lateran's **Baptistry** is no ordinary baptistry—nothing less than the first one in Christendom, converted from an older temple by Constantine; its octagonal form has been copied in other baptistries all over Italy. Fortunately the damage done by a Mafia bombing in 1993 has been restored. Inside there are unusual pairs of bronze doors on either side: one from 1196 with scenes of how the Lateran basilica appeared at that time, and the other from the Terme di Caracalla, 'singing' doors that make a low, harmonic sound when you open them slowly. Built around the baptistry are three venerable chapels with more mosaics from the early Middle Ages. The entrance to the baptistry is in Piazza San Giovanni in Laterano, behind the **Lateran Palace**, rebuilt in 1588 over the original building that had served as home of the popes for a thousand years (4th–14th centuries).

Across the piazza, with the obligatory obelisk at its centre, you will see the **Scala Santa** (*open daily 6.30–12 and 3–6.30*), supposedly the stairs of Pilate's palace in Jerusalem, ascended by Christ on his way to Judgement and brought to Rome by Constantine's mother, St Helena. The more serious pilgrims ascend them on their knees. The Chapel of San Lorenzo at the top of the stairs, a part of the medieval Papal Palace, contains two miraculous portraits of Jesus, painted by angels.

While you're here, you have a good opportunity to explore the Aurelian wall. The stretch of it behind the Lateran probably looks much as it did originally, and the nearby **Porta Asinara** (next to Porta San Giovanni) is one of the best-preserved monumental ancient gateways.

The Via Appia: Rome's Catacombs

Rome's 'Queen of Roads', the path of trade and conquest to Campania, Brindisi and the East, was begun in 312 BC by Consul Appius Claudius. Like most of the consular roads outside Rome, over the centuries it became lined with cemeteries and the elaborate mausolea of the wealthy: ancient Roman practice, inherited from the Etruscans, prohibited any burials within the *pomerium*, the sacred ground of the city itself. Later the early Christian community built some of its most extensive catacombs here—the word itself comes from the location, *ad catacumbas*, referring to the dip in the Via Appia near the suburban Circus of Maxentius. The Via Appia Antica (as distinguished from the modern Via Appia Nuova to the east) makes a pleasant excursion outside the city, especially on Sundays when the road is closed to traffic all the way back to Piazza Venezia.

The road passes under the Aurelian wall at **Porta San Sebastiano**, one of the best-preserved of the old gates. It houses the **Museum of the Walls** (*open Tues–Sun 9–one hour before sunset; adm*), a very thorough exhibition on the history of Rome's walls, admission to which also gives you access to a well-preserved section of the 4th-century wall alongside it. Continuing along the road, after about ½km, with some ruins of tombs along the way, there is the famous church of **Domine Quo Vadis**, on the spot where Peter, fleeing from the dangers of Rome, met Christ coming the other way. 'Where goest thou, Lord?' Peter asked. 'I am going to be crucified once more,' was the reply. As the vision departed the shamed apostle turned back, soon to face his own crucifixion in Rome.

Another kilometre or so takes you to the **Catacombs of St Calixtus**, off on a side road to the right (*open 8.30–12 and 2.30–5; closed Wed and Nov; guided tours only; adm*). Here the biggest attraction is the Crypt of the Popes, burial places of 3rd- and 4th-century pontiffs with some well-executed frescoes and inscriptions. A word about catacombs: popular romance and modern cinema notwithstanding, these were never places of refuge from persecution or anything else, but simply burial grounds. The word 'catacombs' was only used after the 5th century; before that the Christians simply called them 'cemeteries'. The burrowing instinct is harder to explain. Few other Mediterranean cities have catacombs (Naples, Syracuse, Malta and the Greek island of Milos are among those that do). One of the requirements for catacombs seems to be tufa, or some other stone that can be easily excavated. Even so, the work involved was tremendous, and not explainable by any reasons of necessity. Christians were still digging them after they had become a power in Rome, in Constantine's time. No one knows for certain what sort of funeral rites were celebrated in them, just as no one knows much about any of the prayers or rituals of the early Christians; we can only suspect that a Christian of the 4th century and one of the 16th would have had considerable difficulty recognizing each other as brothers in the faith.

Most catacombs began small, as private family cemeteries; over generations some grew into enormous termitaries extending for miles beneath the surface. Inside, most of the tombs you see will be simple *loculi*, walled-up niches with only a symbol or short inscription scratched in to identify the deceased. Others, especially the tombs of popes or the wealthy, may have paintings of scriptural scenes, usually very poor work that reflects more on the dire state of the late Roman imagination than on the Christians.

Monte Aventino

Every now and then, whenever left-wing parties walk out on negotiations or talks to establish a government coalition, Italian newspapers may call it an 'Aventine Secession', an off-the-cuff reference to events in Rome 2,500 years ago. Under the Roman Republic the Monte Aventino was the most solidly plebeian quarter of the city. On several occasions, when legislation proposed by the Senate and consuls seriously threatened the rights or interests of the people, they retired *en masse* to the Aventino and stayed there until the plan was dropped. Rome's unionists today often keep the city tied up in knots, but most are probably unaware that their ancestors had the honour of inventing the general strike.

The Aventino had another distinction in those times. In its uninhabited regions—the steep, cave-ridden slopes and parks towards the south—Greek immigrants and returning soldiers introduced the midnight rituals of Dionysus and Bacchus. Though secret, such goings-on soon came to the attention of the Senate, which saw the orgies quite rightly as a danger to the state and banned them in 146 BC. However, they cannot have died out completely and, in the Middle Ages, the Aventino had a reputation as a haunt of witches. The early Christian community also prospered here, and some of their churches are the oldest relics on the Aventino today.

Coming up from the Circus Maximus along Via Santa Sabina, the church of **Santa Sabina** is a simple, rare example of a 5th-century basilica, with an atrium at its entrance like a Roman secular basilica, and an original cypress door carved with scriptural scenes. This has been the head church of the Dominicans ever since a 13th-century pope gave it to St Dominic. Both S. Sabina and the church of **Sant'Alessio** down the street have good Cosmatesque cloisters.

At the end of this street, one of the oddities only Rome can offer stands on its quiet square, oblivious of the centuries: the **Priory of the Sovereign Order of Malta**, a fancy rococo complex designed by Giambattista Piranesi. The Knights of Malta—or more properly, the Knights Hospitallers of St John—no longer wait for the popes to unleash them against Saracen and Turk. Mostly this social club for old nobles bestirs itself to assist hospitals, its original job during the Crusades. The headquarters is presently at a fancier address in Rome, but the order's ambassadors to Italy and the Vatican live here.

St Paul's Outside the Walls

Paul was beheaded on a spot near the Ostia road; according to legend the head bounced three times, and at each place where it hit a fountain sprang up. The Abbazia delle Tre Fontane, near EUR, occupies the site today. Later, Constantine built a basilica alongside the road as a fitting resting place for the saint. Of the five patriarchal basilicas, this one has had the worst luck. Today it sits in the middle of the unprepossessing neighbourhood of Ostiense, full of factories, gasworks and concrete flats. Once it was the grandest of them all; 9th-century chroniclers speak of the separate walled city of 'Giovannipolis' that had grown up around St Paul's, connected to the Aurelian wall by a 1½km-long colonnade built by Pope John VIII in the 870s.

The Norman sack of 1084, a few good earthquakes, and finally a catastrophic fire in 1823 wiped Giovannipolis off the map, and left us with a St Paul's that for the most part is barely more than a century old. Still, the façade of golden mosaics and sturdy Corinthian columns is pleasant to look at, and some older features survive—the 11th-century door made in Constantinople, a Gothic *baldacchino* over Paul's tomb by Arnolfo di Cambio, a beautiful 13th-century Cosmatesque cloister (almost a double of the one in the Lateran), and 5th-century mosaics over the triumphal arch in front of the apse, the restored remains of the original mosaics from the façade, contributed by Empress Galla Placidia. Art Deco is not what you would expect from those times, but Americans at least will have a hard time believing these mosaics were not done by President Roosevelt's WPA. The apse itself has some more conventional mosaics from the 13th-century Roman school, and the nave is lined with the portraits of all 263 popes. According to Roman tradition, when the remaining eight spaces are filled, the world will end.

Castel Sant'Angelo

Though intended as a resting place for a most serene emperor, this building has seen more blood, treachery and turmoil than any in Rome. Hadrian, it seems, designed his own mausoleum three years before his death in 138, on an eccentric plan consisting of a huge marble cylinder surmounted by a conical hill planted with cypresses. The marble, the obelisks and the gold and bronze decorations did not survive the 5th-century sacks, but in about 590, during a plague, Pope Gregory the Great saw a vision of St Michael over the mausoleum, ostensibly announcing the end of the plague, but perhaps also mentioning discreetly that here, if anyone cared to use it, was the most valuable fortress in Europe.

There might not be a papacy without this castle—at least not in its present form. Hadrian's great cylinder is high, steep and almost solid—impregnable even after the invention of artillery. With rebellions of some sort occurring on average every two years before 1400, the popes often had recourse to this place of safety. It last saw action in the sack of 1527, when Clement VII withstood a siege of several months while his city went up in flames around him. The popes also used Castel Sant'Angelo as a prison; famous inmates included Giordano Bruno, Cellini and Beatrice Cenci (better known to the English than the Italians, thanks to Shelley's verse drama). Tosca throws herself off the top at the end of Puccini's opera.

Inside the castle (*open daily 9–7; closed the second and fourth Tues of each month; adm*), the recently restored spiral ramp leads up to the **Papal Apartments**, decorated as lavishly by 16th-century artists as anything in the Vatican. The **Sala Paolina** has frescoes by Perin del Vaga depicting events in the history of Rome, and the **Sala di Apollo** is frescoed with grotesques attempting to reproduce the wall decorations of the ancient palaces, perhaps like Nero's Golden House. Above everything, a mighty statue of Michael commemorates Pope Gregory's vision.

The three central arches of the **Ponte Sant'Angelo** were built by Hadrian, although the statues added in 1688 steal the show; at once dubbed Bernini's Breezy Maniacs, they battle a never-ending baroque hurricane to display the symbols of Christ's Passion.

The Vatican

Vatican Practicalities

The **museums** are open Nov–Feb Mon–Sat 8.45–1.45 (last admission 12.45); the rest of the year Mon–Sat 8.45–4.45 (last admission 3.45); adm; closed Sun, except the last Sun of each month and religious holidays 8.45–1.45 (last admission 12.45); free. The entrance is rather far from St Peter's Square, to the north on Viale Vaticano. **St Peter's** is open daily 7–7; Oct–Mar till 6; the basilica is closed when there are official ceremonies in the piazza—although visitors are allowed during Mass. The dress code—no shorts, short skirts or sleeveless dresses—is strictly controlled by the papal gendarmes.

The **Vatican Information Office**, ✆ 06 6988 4466, in St Peter's Square (*open daily 8–7*) is very helpful, and there are Vatican post offices on the opposite side of the square and inside the Vatican Museums for distinctive postcards home (it is rumoured to be a much more reliable mail service than that offered by the Italian post). The information office arranges 2hr-long morning tours of the **Vatican Gardens**, easily Rome's most beautiful park, with a remarkable Renaissance jewel of a villa inside, the **Casino of Pius IV** by Pietro Ligorio and Peruzzi (1558–62) (*open May–Sept Mon–Sat; Oct–April once a week; L18,000 per person; reserve in advance through the information office*). Underneath the crypt of St Peter's, archaeologists in the 1940s discovered a **street of Roman tombs**, perfectly preserved with many beautiful paintings and mosaics (*open Mon–Sat 9–5; adm; tours can be arranged through the Uffizio degli Scavi, just to the left of St Peter's; in summer book early as fragile conditions permit only 15 people at a time*). The rest of the Vatican is strictly off limits, patrolled by genuine Swiss Guards (still recruited from the three Catholic cantons).

Michelangelo also designed the **defensive wall** that since 1929 has marked the Vatican boundaries. Behind them are things most of us will never see: several small old churches, a printing press, the headquarters of *L'Osservatore Romano* and Vatican Radio (run, of course, by the Jesuits), a motor garage, a *palazzo di giustizia* and even a big shop—everything the world's smallest nation could ever need. Modern popes, in glaring contrast to their predecessors, do not take up much space. The current Papal Apartments are in a corner of the Vatican Palace overlooking Piazza San Pietro; John Paul II usually appears to say a few electrically amplified words from his window at noon on Sundays. For tickets to the Wednesday morning **papal audience**, usually held at 11am in the piazza (*May–Sept*) or in the Nervi Auditorium (*Oct–April*), apply in advance at the Papal Prefecture—through the bronze door in the right-hand colonnade of Piazza San Pietro (*open Mon and Tues 9–1, ✆ 06 6988 3217*).

St Peter's

Along Borgo Sant'Angelo, leading towards the Vatican, you can see the famous **covered passageway**, used by the popes since 1277 to escape to the castle when things became dangerous. The customary route, however, leads up **Via della Conciliazione**, a broad boulevard laid out under Mussolini over a tangled web of medieval streets. Critics have said it spoils the surprise, but no arrangement of streets and buildings could really prepare you for Bernini's Brobdingnagian **Piazza San Pietro**. Someone has calculated there is room for about 300,000 people in the piazza, with no crowding. Few have ever noticed Bernini's little joke on antiquity; the open space almost exactly meets the size and dimensions of the Colosseum. Bernini's **Colonnade** (1656), with 284 massive columns and statues of 140 saints, stretches around it like 'the arms of the Church embracing the world'—perhaps the biggest cliché in Christendom by now, but exactly what Bernini had in mind. Stand on either of the two dark stones at the foci of the elliptical piazza and you will see Bernini's forest of columns resolve into neat rows, a subtly impressive optical effect like the hole in the top of the Pantheon. Flanked by two lovely fountains, the work of Maderno and Fontana, the

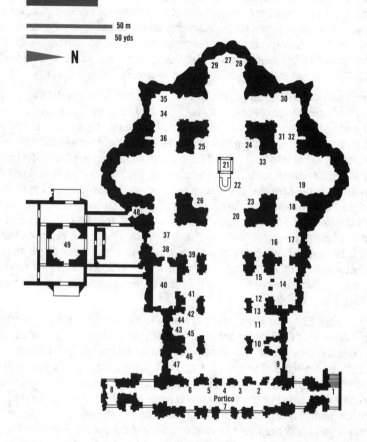

St Peter's

50 m
50 yds

N

1 Statue of Constantine / Scala Regia
2 Holy Door
3 Crocetti's Door
4 Filarete's Door
5 Manzù Door
6 Minguzzi's Door
7 Giotto's Navicella
8 Statue of Charlemagne
9 Michelangelo's Pietà
10 Queen Christina Monument
11 Cappella di S. Sebastiano
12 Countess Matilda Monument
13 Innocent XII Monument
14 Cappella del Smo. Sacramento
15 Gregory XIII Monument
16 Cappella Gregoriana
17 Madonna del Soccorso
18 Lift up to Dome

19 Altar of St Wenceslas
20 Statue of St Peter
21 High Altar / Bernini's
   Baldacchino
22 Confessio
23 St Longinus / Entrance
   to Grottoes
24 St Helen
25 St Veronica
26 St Andrew
27 Tribune / Cathedra of St Peter
28 Urban VIII Monument
29 Paul III Monument
30 Guercino's St Petronilla
31 Altar of the Navicella
32 Clement XIII Monument
33 St Bruno
34 Cappella della Colonna

35 Leo the Great's Tomb
36 Alexander VII Monument
37 Cappella Clementina
38 Pius VII Monument
39 Leo XI Monument
40 Cappella del Coro
41 Innocent VIII Monument
42 Pius X Monument
43 Cappella della Presentazione
44 John XXIII Monument
45 Clementina Sobieska Monument / stairs
   and down lift from dome
46 Monument to the Last Stuarts
47 Baptistry
48 Pius VIII Monument / entrance to
   St Peter's Treasury
49 Sacristy

Vatican **obelisk** seems nothing special as obelisks go, but is actually one of the most fantastical relics in all Rome. This obelisk comes from Heliopolis, the Egyptian city founded as a capital and cult centre by Akhenaton, the half-legendary pharaoh and religious reformer who, according to Sigmund Freud and others, founded the first monotheistic religion, influencing Moses and all who came after. Caligula brought it over to Rome in AD 37 to decorate the now-disappeared Circus Vaticanus (later referred to as the Circus of Nero) where it would have overlooked Peter's martyrdom. In the Middle Ages it was placed to the side of the basilica, but Sixtus V moved it to where it now stands in 1586.

It may be irreverent to say so, but the original St Peter's, begun over the apostle's tomb by Constantine in 324, may well have been a more interesting building, a richly decorated basilica full of gold and mosaics with a vast porch of marble and bronze in front and a lofty campanile, topped by the famous golden cockerel that everyone believed would some day crow to announce the end of the world. This St Peter's, where Charlemagne and Frederick II received their imperial crowns, was falling to pieces by the 1400s, conveniently in time for the popes and artists of the Renaissance to plan a replacement. Pope Nicholas V, in about 1450, conceived an almost Neronian building programme for the Vatican, ten times as large as anything his ancestors could have contemplated. It was not until the time of Pope Julius II, however, that Bramante was commissioned to demolish the old church and begin work on the new edifice. His original plan called for a great dome over a centralized Greek cross. Michelangelo, who took over the work in 1546, agreed, and if he had had his way St Peter's might indeed have become the crowning achievement of Renaissance art that everyone hoped it would be.

Unfortunately over the 120 years of construction too many popes and too many artists got their hand in—Rossellino, Giuliano da Sangallo, Raphael, Antonio da Sangallo, Vignola, Ligorio, della Porta, Fontana, Bernini and Maderno all contributed something to the tremendous hotchpotch we see today. The most substantial tinkering came in the early 17th century, when a committee of cardinals decided that a Latin cross was desired, resulting in the huge extension of the nave that blocks the view of Michelangelo's dome from the piazza. Baroque architects, mistaking size and virtuosity for art, found perfect patrons in the baroque popes, less interested in faith than the power and majesty of the papacy. Passing though Maderno's gigantic façade seems like entering a Grand Central Station full of stone saints and angels, keeping an eye on the big clocks overhead as they wait for trains to Paradise. All along the nave, markers showing the length of other proud cathedrals prove how each fails miserably to measure up to the Biggest Church in the World. This being Rome, not even the markers are honest—Milan's cathedral is actually 65ft longer.

The best is on the right: Michelangelo's *Pietà*, now restored and kept behind glass to protect it from future madmen. This work, sculpted when he was only 25, helped make Michelangelo's reputation. Its smooth and elegant figures, with the realities of death and grief sublimated on to some ethereal plane known only to saints and artists, were a turning point in religious art. From here the beautiful, unreal art of the religious baroque was the logical next step. Note how Michelangelo has carved his name in small letters on the band around the Virgin's garment; he added this after overhearing a group of tourists from Milan who thought the *Pietà* the work of a fellow Milanese. Not much else in St Peter's really stands out. In its vast spaces scores of popes and saints are remembered in assembly-line baroque, and the paintings over most of the altars have been replaced by mosaic copies. The famous bronze statute of St Peter, its foot worn away by the touch of millions of pilgrims, is by the right front pier. Stealing the show, just as he knew it would, is Bernini's great, garish **baldacchino** over the high altar, cast out of bronze looted from the Pantheon roof.

Many visitors head straight for Michelangelo's **dome** (*open May–Sept daily 8–6; Oct–April daily 8–5; adm*). To be in the middle of such a spectacular construction is worth the climb in itself. You can walk out on the roof for a view over Rome, but even more startling is the chance to look down from the interior balcony over the vast church 250ft below. In the **Sacristy** (*open April–Sept daily 9–6; Oct–Mar daily 9–5; adm exp*), built in the 18th century, there are a number of treasures—those that neither the Saracens, the imperial soldiers of 1527, nor Napoleon could steal. The ancient bronze cockerel from the old St Peter's is kept here, along with ancient relics, baroque extravaganzas and a gown that once belonged to Charlemagne.

Do not pass up a descent to the **Sacred Grottoes**, the foundation of the earlier St Peter's converted into a crypt. Dozens of popes are buried here, along with distinguished friends of the Church like Queen Christina of Sweden and James III, the Stuart pretender. Perhaps the greatest work of art here is the bronze tomb of Sixtus IV, a definitive Renaissance confection by Pollaiuolo, though the most visited is undoubtedly the simple monument to John XXIII.

The Vatican Museums

The admission (*currently L15,000*) may be the most expensive in Italy, but for that you get about 10 museums in one, with the Sistine Chapel and the Raphael rooms thrown in free. Altogether almost 7km of exhibits fill the halls of the Vatican Palace, and unfortunately for you there isn't much dull museum clutter that can be passed over lightly. Seeing this infinite, exasperating hoard properly would be the work of a lifetime. On the bright side, the Pope sees to it that his museum is managed more intelligently and thoughtfully than anything run by the Italian state. A choice of colour-coded itineraries, depending on the amount of time you have to spend, will get you through the labyrinth in 90 minutes, or five hours.

Near the entrance (with a branch of the Vatican Post Office), the first big challenge is a large **Egyptian Museum**—one of Europe's best collections—and then some rooms of antiquities from the Holy Land and Syria, before the **Museo Chiaramonti**, full of Roman statuary (including famous busts of Caesar, Mark Antony and Augustus) and inscriptions. The **Pio Clementino Museum** contains some of the best-known statues of antiquity: the dramatic *Laocoön*, dug up in Nero's Golden House and mentioned in the works of many classical authors, and the *Apollo Belvedere*. No other ancient works recovered during the Renaissance had a greater influence on sculptors than these two. A 'room of animals' captures the more fanciful side of antiquity, and the 2nd-century baroque tendency in Roman art comes out clearly in a giant group called *The Nile*, complete with sphinxes and crocodiles—it came from a Roman temple of Isis. The bronze papal fig-leaves that protect the modesty of hundreds of nude statues are a good joke at first—it was the same spirit that put breeches on the saints in Michelangelo's *Last Judgement*, a move ordered, in Michelangelo's absence, by Pius IV.

The best things in the **Etruscan Museum** (*open Tues*) are Greek, a truly excellent collection of vases imported by discriminating Etruscan nobles that includes the famous picture of *Oedipus and the Sphinx*. Beyond that, there is a hall hung with beautiful high-medieval tapestries from Tournai (15th century), and the long, long **Map Room**, lined with carefully painted town views and maps of every corner of Italy; note the long scene of the 1566 Great Siege of Malta at the entrance. Anywhere else, with no Michelangelos to offer competition, Raphael's celebrated frescoes (*recently restored*) in the **Stanze della Segnatura** would be the prime destination on anyone's itinerary. The *School of Athens* is too well known to require much of an introduction, but here is a guide to some of the figures: on Aristotle's side, Archimedes and Euclid are surrounded by their disciples (Euclid, drawing plane figures on a slate, is supposedly a portrait of Bramante); off to the right, Ptolemy and Zoroaster hold the terrestrial and celestial globes. Raphael includes himself among the Aristotelians, standing between Zoroaster and the painter Il Sodoma. Behind Plato stand Socrates and Alcibiades, among others, and to the left, Zeno and Epicurus. In the foreground, a crouching Pythagoras writes while Empedocles and the Arab Averroes look on. Diogenes sprawls philosophically on the steps, while isolated near the front is Heraclitus—really Michelangelo, according to legend; Raphael put him in at the last minute after seeing the work in progress in the Sistine Chapel.

Across from this apotheosis of philosophy, Raphael painted a triumph of theology to keep the clerics happy, the *Dispute of the Holy Sacrament*. The other frescoes include the *Parnassus*, a vision of the ancient Greek and Latin poets, the *Miracle of Bolsena*, the *Expulsion of Heliodorus*, an allegory of the triumphs of the Counter-Reformation papacy, the *Meeting of Leo I and Attila* and, best of all, the solemn, spectacularly lit *Liberation of St Peter*. Nearby, there is the **Loggia** of Bramante, also with decoration designed by Raphael, though executed by other artists (*only visitable with written permission*), and the **Chapel of Nicholas V**, with frescoes by Fra Angelico. The **Borgia Apartments**, a luxurious suite built for Pope Alexander VI, have walls decorated with saints, myths and sibyls by Pinturicchio. These run into the **Gallery of Modern Religious Art**, a game attempt by the Vatican to prove that such a thing really exists.

The Sistine Chapel

To the sophisticated Sixtus IV, building this ungainly barn of a chapel may have seemed a mistake in the first place. When the pushy, despotic Julius II sent Michelangelo up, against his will, to paint the vast ceiling, it might have turned out to be a project as hopeless as the tomb Julius had already commissioned. Michelangelo spent four years of his life on the Sistine Ceiling. No one can say what drove him to turn his surly patron's whim into a masterpiece: the fear of wasting those years, the challenge of an impossible task, or maybe just to spite Julius—he exasperated the Pope by making him wait, and refused all demands that he hire some assistants. Everywhere on the Sistine Ceiling you will note the austere blankness of the backgrounds. Michelangelo always eschewed stage props; one of the tenets of his art was that complex ideas could be expressed in the portrayal of the human body alone. With sculpture, that takes time. Perhaps the inspiration that kept Michelangelo on the ceiling so long was the chance of distilling out of the Book of Genesis and his own genius an entirely new vocabulary of images, Christian and intellectual. Like most Renaissance patrons, Julius

The Vatican Museums

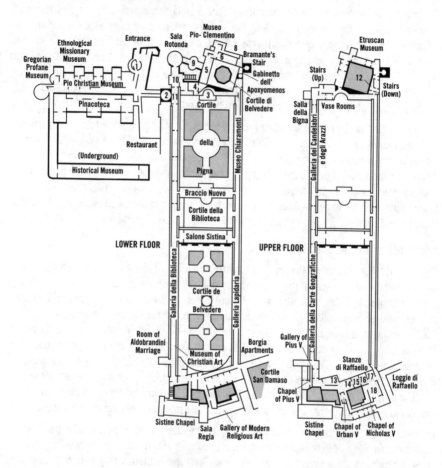

LOWER FLOOR

Gregorian Profane Museum

Ethnological Missionary Museum

Entrance

Sala Rotonda

Museo Pio-Clementino

Etruscan Museum

Pio Christian Museum

Pinacoteca

Restaurant

(Underground)

Historical Museum

Bramante's Stair

Gabinetto dell' Apoxyomenos

Cortile di Belvedere

Cortile della Pigna

Braccio Nuovo

Cortile della Biblioteca

Salone Sistina

Museo Chiaramonti

Cortile de Belvedere

Room of Aldobrandini Marriage

Museum of Christian Art

Borgia Apartments

Cortile San Damaso

Sistine Chapel

Sala Regia

Gallery of Modern Religious Art

Galleria della Biblioteca

Galleria Lapidaria

UPPER FLOOR

Stairs (Up)

Stairs (Down)

Sala della Bigna

Vase Rooms

Galleria dei Candelabri e degli Arazzi

Galleria della Carte Geografiche

Gallery of Pius V

Stanze di Raffaello

Loggie di Raffaello

Chapel of Pius V

Sistine Chapel

Chapel of Urban V

Chapel of Nicholas V

1 Spiral
2 Quattro Cancelli
3 La Pigna
4 Egyptian Museum
5 Animal Room
6 Gallery of Statues
7 Mask Room
8 Gallery of Busts
9 Hall of the Muses

10 Hall of the Greek Cross
11 Museum of Pagan Antiquities
12 Rooms of Greek Originals
13 Hall of Immaculate Conception
14 Stanza dell'Incendio
15 Stanza della Segnatura
16 Stanza di Eliodoro
17 Sala di Costantino
18 Sala dei Chiaro Scuri

merely asked for virtuoso interior decoration. What he got were not simple illustrations from Scripture; this is the way the Old Testament looks in the deepest recesses of the imagination.

The fascination of the Sistine Ceiling, and the equally compelling **Last Judgement** on the rear wall, done much later (1534–41), is that while we may recognize the individual figures we still have not captured their secret meanings. Hordes of tourists stare up at the heroic Adam, the mysterious *ignudi* in the corners, the Russian masseuse sibyls with their long-shoremen's arms, the six-toed prophets, the strange vision of Noah's deluge. They wonder what they're looking at, a question that would take years of inspired wondering to answer. Mostly they direct their attention to the all-too-famous scene of the Creation, with perhaps the only representation of God the Father ever painted that escapes being merely ridiculous. One might suspect that the figure is really some ageing Florentine artist, and that Michelangelo only forgot to paint the brush in his hand.

The restoration of the ceiling and *Last Judgement*, paid for by a Japanese television network, have accurately revealed Michelangelo's true colours—jarring, surprise colours that no interior decorator would ever choose, plenty of sea-green, with splashes of yellow and purple and dramatic shadows. No new paint is being applied, only solvents to clear off the grime. Most visitors overlook the earlier frescoes on the lower walls, great works of art that would have made the Sistine Chapel famous by themselves: scenes from the *Exodus* by Botticelli, Perugino's *Donation of the Keys*, and Signorelli's *Moses Consigning his Staff to Joshua*.

More Miles in the Big Museum

There's still the **Vatican Library** to go, with its endless halls and precious manuscripts tucked neatly away in cabinets. The brightly painted rooms contain every sort of oddity: thousands of reliquaries, an entire wall of monstrances, a memorable collection of medieval ivories, gold-glass medallions from the catacombs, every sort of globe, orrery and astronomical instrument. If you survive, the next hurdle is the new and beautifully laid out **Museo Gregoriano**, with a hoard of excellent classical statuary, mosaics and inscriptions collected by Pope Gregory XVI. Then comes a **Carriage Museum** (*currently closed for restoration*), the **Pius Christian Museum** of early Christian art and, finally, one of the most interesting of all, though no one has time for it: the **Ethnological Museum**, with wonderful art from peoples of every continent, brought home by Catholic missionaries over the centuries.

By itself the Vatican **Pinacoteca** would be by far the finest picture gallery in Rome, a representative sampling of Renaissance art from its beginnings, with some fine works of Giotto (*Il Redentore* and the *Martyrdoms of Peter and Paul*) and contemporary Sienese painters, as well as Gentile da Fabriano, Sano di Pietro and Filippo Lippi. Don't overlook the tiny but electrically surreal masterpiece of Fra Angelico, the *Story of St Nicolas at Bari*, or the *Angelic Musicians* of Melozzo da Forlì, set next to Melozzo's famous painting of Platina being nominated by Sixtus IV to head the Vatican Library—a rare snapshot of Renaissance humanism. Venetian artists are not well represented, but there is a *Pietà* by Bellini and a *Madonna* by the fastidious Carlo Crivelli. Perhaps the best-known paintings are the recently restored *Transfiguration of Christ*, Raphael's last work, and the *St Jerome* of Da Vinci.

Rome on the whole isn't as exciting for big-game shoppers as Milan, though when it comes to clothing you will find all the major designers and labels well represented. Rome is not famous for any particular artisanal craft, save the religious items and priestly garb sold near the Vatican and along Via dei Cestari near the Pantheon. There is no shortage of shops selling **antiques**, a great number of them clustered together between the Tiber and Piazza Navona; look especially off Via Monserrato, Via dei Coronari and Via dell'Anima. For old prints, generally inexpensive, try **Casali**, Piazza Rotonda 81A; **Alinari**, Via Alibert 16/a is a good address for artistic black and white pictures of old Rome. **L'Art Nouveau**, Via dei Coronari 221, offers just what its name implies. Antiques also show up in Rome's large and celebrated Sunday morning flea market at **Porta Portese**, as well as anything else you can imagine, all lumped together in often surreal displays. It starts just after dawn and closes gradually around noon; beware the pickpockets.

The most **fashionable shopping** is on the streets between Piazza di Spagna and the Corso. Some special items: **Massoni**, Largo Goldoni 48, near Via Condotti, much frequented by film stars, sells some of Rome's finest jewellery; for menswear, **Testa,** Via Borgognona 13 and Via Frattina 42, or **Valentino Uomo**, Via Condotti 13, or for custom tailoring, **Battistoni**, Via Condotti 61/a; for womenswear try Rome's outlets of the great designers like **Missoni**, Via del Babuino 96, **Giorgio Armani**, Via Condotti 77 and Via del Babuino 102, **Mila Schöen**, Via Condotti 51, or the Rome-based **Fendi**, Via Borgognona 8, 10, 12 and 39. For leather, the **Gucci** outlet is at Via Condotti 8, and do not miss **Fausto Santini**, Via Frattina 120.

For a special bottle of **wine**, try **Enoteca Costantini**, Piazza Cavour 16, for a wide selection. If you wish to stock up on Italian **coffee**, **Tazza d'Oro**, Via degli Orfani 84, has special bags of the city's best, the 'Aroma di Roma'.

Rome ✉ *00100*   **Where to Stay**

For a city that has been entertaining crowds of visitors for the last 2,000 years, Rome does not seem to have acquired any special flair for accommodating them. From *belle époque* palaces on Via Veneto to grimy hovels on the wrong side of Stazione Termini, there will always be something for you to come home to after a hard day's sightseeing, although places with a history, a famous view or quiet gardens to shut out the city noise are rare; on the whole, this is not the place to make the big splurge.

In the 1890s when the Stazione Termini district was the newest and choicest part of Rome, the streets around the station spawned hundreds of hotels, some quite elegant. Today a great part of the city's accommodation is still here. Unfortunately it has gone the way of all such 19th-century toadstool neighbourhoods: overbuilt, dingy and down-at-heel, and not at all the place to savour the real Rome. It's also inconvenient for most of the sights.

Rooms can be difficult to find on short notice, but the free Hotel Reservation Service, ℂ 06 699 1000, will do the looking for you.

★★★★★**Hassler-Villa Medici**, Piazza Trinità dei Monti 6, ✆ 06 699 340, 🖷 06 678 9991, is one of Rome's best hotels, with a fine location at the top of the Spanish Steps and wonderful views over the city for those who book far enough in advance. Around for over a century, it has a beautiful garden courtyard, deferential service and large wood-panelled rooms.

★★★★★**Excelsior**, Via V. Veneto 125, ✆ 06 47081, 🖷 06 482 6205, is also located in a choice area, though lacking the aura of glamour it had in the 1950s. The reception areas have thicker carpets, bigger chandeliers and more gilded plaster than anywhere in Italy, and most of the rooms are just as good—don't let them give you one of the modernized ones. There are saunas, boutiques, a famous bar and as much personal attention as you could ask for.

★★★★**D'Inghilterra**, Via Bocca di Leone 14, ✆ 06 69981, 🖷 06 6992 2243, is another favourite in the Piazza di Spagna area. Parts of this building date from the 15th century, when it served as a prince's guesthouse; in its career as a hotel, since 1850, it has played host to most of the literati and artists of Europe and America. Recent restorations have left it looking more palatial than ever, although some rooms are a bit on the small side. ★★★★**Forum**, Via Tor de' Conti 25, ✆ 06 679 2446, 🖷 06 678 6479, is the only real luxury establishment near the ancient Forum, a somewhat worn hotel, but with unbeatable views from the roof terrace.

★★★★**Cardinal**, Via Giulia 62, ✆ 06 6880 2719, 🖷 06 678 6376, in the heart of the *centro storico*, is perhaps the best place to experience Renaissance Rome—in a building attributed to Bramante and completely restored, without spoiling the atmosphere. ★★★**Carriage**, Via delle Carrozze 36, ✆ 06 699 0124, 🖷 06 678 8279, almost at the foot of the Spanish Steps, is a sleepy but well-run place with air conditioning. ★★★**Columbus**, Via della Conciliazione 33, ✆ 06 686 5435, 🖷 06 686 4874, is staid but reliable with nice rooms, some with views over St Peter's; prices are a bit high. ★★★**Fontana**, Piazza di Trevi 96, ✆ 06 678 6113, 🖷 06 679 0024, would be a good hotel anywhere; it is also right across the street from the Trevi Fountain—something to look at out of your window that will guarantee nice dreams.

★★★**Gregoriana**, Via Gregoriana 18, ✆ 06 679 4269, 🖷 06 678 4258, close to the Spanish Steps but reasonably priced, is small, tasteful and gratifyingly friendly, with a devoted regular clientele—there are only 19 rooms, so book early. ★★★**La Residenza**, Via Emilia 22, ✆ 06 488 0789, 🖷 06 485 721, near the Via Veneto, stands out as a very pleasant base, with beautifully appointed rooms in an old town house, and some luxuries more common to the most expensive hotels.

★★★**Teatro di Pompeo**, Largo del Pallaro 8, ✆ 06 6830 0170, 🖷 06 6880 5531, is a small hotel built on Teatro di Pompeo by Campo de' Fiori, perfect for peace and quiet. ★★★**Villa Florence**, Via Nomentana 28, ✆ 06 440 3036, 🖷 06 440 2709, near the Porta Pia, is a very well-run and friendly hotel in a refurbished 19th-century villa with a garden. **★★★Villa del Parco**, Via Nomentana 110, ℂ 06 4423 7773, ◍ 06 4423 7572, is similar, but slightly more expensive.

moderate

★★★Hotel Sant'Anselmo, Piazza Sant'Anselmo 2, ℂ 06 578 3214, ◍ 06 578 3604, up on the Monte Aventino, is a very peaceful hotel with a garden and comfortable rooms. **★★★Villa San Pio**, Via Sant'Anselmo 19, ℂ 06 574 5232, ◍ 06 574 3547, run by the same management, is just as peaceful. Prices are reasonable. **★★Campo de' Fiori**, Via del Biscione 6, ℂ 06 6880 6865, ◍ 06 687 6003, has small comfortable rooms and a roof terrace overlooking Campo de' Fiori.

★★Margutta, Via Laurina 34, ℂ 06 322 3674, ◍ 06 320 0395, in a quiet street off Via del Babuino, has simple accommodation. **★★Sole**, Via del Biscione 76, ℂ 06 6880 6873, ◍ 06 689 3787, is a large old hotel with lots of character, just off the Campo de' Fiori market. **★★Abruzzi**, Piazza della Rotonda 69, ℂ 06 679 2021, has views over the Pantheon, but none of the rooms have private bath. **★Primavera**, Via San Pantaleo 3, ℂ 06 6880 3109, ◍ 06 6880 3109, is a slightly cheaper hotel just west of Piazza Navona.

cheap

★Campo Marzio, Piazza Campo Marzio 7, ℂ 06 6880 1486, is just north of the Pantheon; none of the rooms has private bath. **★Fiorella**, Via del Babuino 196, ℂ 06 361 0597, in a good location just off Piazza del Popolo, has simple rooms, none with private bath. The area around Stazione Termini offers a wide choice of cheap hotels; **Via Principe Amedeo** is also a good place to look, particularly at Nos.62, 76, 82 and 79. **★Tony**, Via Principe Amedeo 79, ℂ 06 446 6887, ◍ 06 485 721, is a friendly above-average-quality budget hotel. **★Katty**, Via Palestro 35, ℂ 06 444 1216, ◍ 06 444 1261, is simple and clean, on a street on the east side of the station which has a number of other cheap hotels.

Rome ✉ *00100*   **Eating Out**

Unlike many other Italian peoples, the Romans aren't afraid to try something new and you should find plenty of choice. Lately, for example, Chinese restaurants have been appearing in numbers that culinary conservatives find alarming, not to mention Arab, Korean and macrobiotic places and the occasional hamburger stand.

Of course, there is also a grand old tradition of Roman cooking, with such specialities as *saltimbocca* (literally 'jump in the mouth'), tender veal *scalope* cooked with ham, *stracciatella* (a soup with eggs, parmesan cheese and parsley), fried artichokes called *carciofi alla giudia* and veal *involtini*. On a genuine Roman menu in the less expensive places you are likely to encounter such favourites as *baccalà* (salt cod), *bucatini all' amatriciana* (in a tomato and bacon sauce) or *alla carbonara* (with egg and bacon), tripe and *gnocchi*. Unless you ask for something different, the wine will probably come from the Castelli Romani—light, fruity whites of which the best come from Frascati and Velletri.

Perched high above the city is **La Pergola dell'Hotel Hilton**, Via Cadlolo 4, ℰ 06 3509 2211, currently Rome's most celebrated restaurant for first-rate *alta cucina* served in elegant surroundings with all of Rome at your feet. *Closed Sun and Mon; open for dinner only; reserve well ahead.* For fish, head to **La Rosetta**, Via della Rosetta 8, near the Pantheon, ℰ 06 686 1002, Rome's best fish-only restaurant. If the menu posted outside the door seems too expensive, step in anyway just to admire the heap of shiny, coloured fish, oysters and sea urchins arranged on the marble slab in the hall. *Closed Sun; reserve well ahead.*

There is no better place to try *carciofi alla giudia* than right on the edge of the old ghetto at **Piperno**, Via Monte de' Cenci 9, ℰ 06 6880 6629, Rome's most famous purveyor of Roman-Jewish cooking—simple dishes on the whole, but prepared and served with refinement. *Closed Sun eve and Mon.*

Across the river, Trastevere, with its attractive piazzas with space for tables outside, has long been one of the most popular corners of the city for dining. Many of its restaurants specialize in fish, most notably **Alberto Ciarla**, Piazza San Cosimato 40, ℰ 06 581 8668, some way south of Santa Maria in Trastevere. The French-trained owner, proud enough to put his name on the sign, sees to it that everything is delicately and perfectly done, and graciously served: oysters, seafood ravioli and quite a few adventurous styles of *pesce crudo* (raw fish) are among the most asked for. *Dinner only; closed Sun.* Not far away, **Sabatini**, Piazza Santa Maria in Trastevere 13, ℰ 06 581 2026, has been a Roman tradition for many a year, as much for the cuisine (again, lots of seafood) as for the tables outside, which face the lovely piazza and its church. *Closed Tues in winter, Wed in summer.*

If you find yourself anywhere around Porta San Paolo and the Testaccio district at dinner time, don't pass up a chance to dine at the acknowledged temple of old Roman cooking, **Checchino dal 1887**, Via di Monte Testaccio 30, ℰ 06 574 6318, which has been owned by the same family for 107 years—the longest family record in Rome. Both the fancy and humble sides of Roman food are well represented, with plenty of the powerful offal dishes that Romans have been eating since ancient times, and the setting is unique—on the edge of Monte Testaccio, with one of Rome's best cellars excavated underneath the hill. *Closed Sun eve and Mon.*

Dal Toscano, Via Germanico 58, ℰ 06 397 25717, is perhaps your best option in the tourist-trap Vatican area: family-run and very popular with Roman families, this restaurant offers well-prepared Tuscan specialities like *pici* (rough, fresh spaghetti rolled by hand) in game sauce and *fiorentina* steak—save room for the good homemade desserts. Reserve. *Closed Mon.* Another Tuscan place off the Via Veneto, also family-run but slightly fancier and more expensive, is **Papà Baccus**, Via Toscana 33, ℰ 06 4274 2808, which has remarkably good *prosciutto* sliced by hand, delicious potato ravioli and, in winter, baked fish (called *rombo* in Italian) with artichokes, along with the more strictly regional soups and *fiorentina*. Reserve. *Closed Sat lunch and Sun.*

Only in Rome would you find a good French restaurant run by a Catholic lay missionary society—*sole meunière* and onion soup in the well-scrubbed and righteous atmosphere of **L'Eau Vive**, Via Monterone 85, © 06 6880 1095, not far from the Pantheon. A nourishing meal at a modest price, served with serenity, will have you joining in a prayer to the Virgin Mary before dessert; the fixed lunch menu at L25,000 is a great bargain. *Closed Sun.* Also near the Pantheon, **Myosotis**, Vicolo della Vaccarella 3, © 06 686 5554, is a great family-run restaurant with an ample menu of traditional and creative meat and fish dishes. *Closed Sun.*

The Piazza di Spagna area is not as promising for restaurants as it is for hotels, but there are a few, of which the best, perhaps, is **Nino**, Via Borgognona 11, © 06 678 6752, with an attractive flask full of cannellini beans simmering in the window, the signpost for true, well-prepared Tuscan cuisine. *Closed Sun.* In the vicinity, a few steps from the Trevi Fountain, one safe option is **Al Presidente**, Via in Arcione 95, © 06 679 7342, offering fish in all manners. **Dal Bolognese**, Piazza del Popolo 1, © 06 361 11426, with tables outside on the grand piazza and a view of the Pincio, is the place to go to sample Emilian specialties—don't miss the tortellini or any other fresh pasta dish, and finish with *fruttini*, a selection of real fruit shells each filled with its own sorbet flavour. *Closed Mon.*

At **Paris**, Piazza San Calisto 7/a, © 06 581 5378, just beyond Piazza Santa Maria in Trastevere, you get classic Roman-Jewish cuisine; particularly good is the *minestra di arzilla* (skate soup). *Closed Sun eve and Mon.* **Antico Arco**, Piazzale Aurelio 7, © 06 581 5274, is well worth the climb up the Monte Gianicolo; it is a reliable, informal restaurant for no-nonsense creative Italian cuisine. Reserve. *Closed Mon.*

The quarters just outside the Aurelian wall and north and east of the Villa Borghese are more good places to look for restaurants. **Le Coppedè**, Via Taro 28/a, between Via Nomentana and Villa Ada, © 06 841 1772, is a pleasant neighbourhood restaurant totally devoted to Pugliese cuisine, which is lighter than typical Roman fare. **Semidivino**, Via Alessandria 230, © 06 4425 0795, is a classy and intimate wine bar which is also good for a first-rate meal based on excellent salads, an interesting selection of cheese and *salumi* (cured meats) and comforting soups at reasonable prices. *Closed Sat lunch and Sun.*

cheap

Roman Lounge de l'Hotel d'Inghilterra, Via Bocca di Leone 14, © 06 699 81500, is an elegant retreat in the heart of the shopping district at the foot of the Spanish Steps, which at lunchtime offers an interesting *piatto unico* (one-dish menu) for L35,000; if you like their style you can return for a very expensive dinner. The **Grappolo d'Oro**, Piazza della Cancelleria 80, © 06 686 4118, near Campo de' Fiori, offers exceptionally good value traditional Roman cooking. *Closed Sun.* **Il Collegio**, Via Pie' di Marmo 36, © 06 679 2570, not far from the Pantheon, has tables outside and a few Roman first courses along with more imaginative dishes and a good chocolate soufflé. *Closed Sat lunch and Sun.* Nearby, **Armando al Pantheon**, Salita de' Crescenzi 31, © 06 6880 3034, not far from the Pantheon, is an authentic Roman trattoria famous for spaghetti *cacio e pepe* (with pecorino cheese and black pepper) or *all'amatriciana, saltimbocca* (veal topped with sage and prosciutto) and a delicious ricotta tart. *Closed Sat eve and Sun.*

In Trastevere there's a small family trattoria, **Da Lucia**, Vicolo del Mattonato, © 06 580 3601, two streets north of Piazza Santa Maria, that offers local cooking in a typical setting. If you are near the Vatican, an area with little more than forgettable tourist restaurants, venture a little way north to the **Antico Falcone**, Via Trionfale 60, © 06 3974 3385, a simple place housed in what's left of a 15th-century farmhouse, for tasty *rigatoni alla nasona* (pasta with melted cheese and tomato sauce), *melanzane alla parmigiana* (baked eggplants topped with mozzarella, tomato and parmesan) and, in season, well-fried *carciofi alla giudia. Closed Tues.* An excellent budget trattoria in the centre is **Gino in Vicolo Rosini**, Vicolo Rosini 4, off Piazza del Parlamento, © 06 687 3434, near the parliament, and often crammed with civil servants and the occasional deputy. *Closed Sun.*

pizzerias

Roman pizza tends to be crisp and thin; most traditional wood-oven pizzerias have tables outside and are open only for dinner, often until 2am.
Da Baffetto, Via del Governo Vecchio 11, © 06 686 1617, is a beloved institution not far from Piazza Navona, as is **Panattoni**, Viale Trastevere 53, © 06 580 0919, perhaps the best place to see *pizzaioli* at work, *closed Wed.* Nearby **Dar Poeta**, Vicolo del Bologna 45, © 06 588 0516, is more on the verge of Neapolitan pizza, and perhaps the only pizzeria in town with a pizza dessert, the *calzone di ricotta* (filled with ricotta and chocolate), and a non-smoking room. *Closed Mon.* For strictly Neapolitan pizza, head to pricey **Al Forno della Soffitta**, Via dei Villini 1/e, off the Via Nomentana, © 06 440 4692, where they also have delicious pastry delivered daily from Naples. *Closed Sun.*

Entertainment and Nightlife

The best entertainment in Rome is often in the passing cosmopolitan spectacle of its streets; as nightlife goes, the capital can be a real snoozer compared with other European cities, though if you don't expect too much you'll have a good time.

To keep up with any area of entertainment in Rome you would do well to buy a copy of *Romac'e'* (from news-stands) which has comprehensive listings and a small section at the back in English. Another source is the weekly *Time Out*, with listings and articles (in Italian).

opera, classical music, theatre and film

From November until May you can take in a performance at the **Teatro dell'Opera di Roma**, Via Firenze 72 (box office, © 06 4816 0255, information, © 06 481 601). Other concerts and chamber music are performed at and by the **Accademia Nazionale di Santa Cecilia**, in the auditorium on Via della Conciliazione 4 (box office, ℧ 06 6880 1044, information, ℧ 06 361 1064), and by the **Accademia Filarmonica** at the **Teatro Olimpico**, Piazza Gentile da Fabriano 17 (box office, ℧ 06 323 4936, information, ℧ 06 323 4890). Medieval music, baroque music, chamber music and choral music are frequently performed at the **Oratorio del Gonfalone**, Via del Gonfalone 32/a, ℧ 06 687 5952.

If you want to go to any concerts in Rome, try to get tickets as soon as possible to avoid disappointment. **Orbis**, Piazza Esquilino 37, ℧ 06 474 4776, is a reliable concert and theatre ticket agency (*open Mon–Sat 9.30–1 and 4–7.30*).

Despite the Italian tendency to dub all foreign films, you can find films in *versione originale* at the **Alcazar**, Via Cardinal Merry del Val 14 (*Mon*), at the **Nuovo Sacher**, Largo Ascianghi 1 (*Mon and Tues*), at the **Majestic**, Via SS. Apostoli 20 (*Tues*), and at the **Pasquino**, on Piazza Sant'Egidio, near Piazza Santa Maria in Trastevere, ℧ 06 580 3622 (*daily*).

cafés and bars

When you're tired of window-shopping you can rest your legs at Rome's oldest café, the **Antico Caffè Greco**, Via Condotti 86 (1760), and fantasize that you are sitting perhaps in the very place where Keats or Casanova once sat. The headquarters for visiting poets in the Romantic era, the Greco is now the average tourist's cheapest chance for a 20-minute dose of *ancien régime* luxury in Rome. Another of the city's *grand cafés* is the **Caffè Rosati**, in Piazza del Popolo, an elegant place founded in 1922, and traditionally popular with the Roman intelligentsia, no doubt attracted by its extravagant ice-creams. Other cafés can be dignified, historic or crazily expensive—for example, the 150-year-old **Babington's Tea Rooms**, on Piazza di Spagna, for scones and tea or a full lunch in the proper Victorian atmosphere. At trendy **Sant'Eustachio**, Piazza Sant'Eustachio, near Piazza Navona, tell them to mind the sugar.

Another kind of Roman bar is represented by the ultra-hip **Bar della Pace**, Via della Pace 3, supposedly much frequented by celebrities and a place for serious posing. A more funky and friendly atmosphere can be found most evenings at **La Vineria**, Campo de' Fiori 15, a relaxed traditional wine bar/shop with tables outside.

It's not hard to find *gelato* on nearly every corner in Rome, but hold out for the best the city has to offer, at the celebrated **Il Gelato di San Crispino**, Via della Panetteria 42, near the Trevi Fountain. Another novelty in Rome are sweets from **Il Forno del Ghetto** (*closed Sat*), the Jewish bakery at the west end of Via del Portico d'Ottavia (note the incredible building it's in—a recycled ancient structure covered with reliefs and inscriptions).

rock, jazz and clubs

Rome has a select band of clubs with live music almost every night—*Romac'e'* will have details of current programmes at the folk-oriented **Folkstudio**, Via Frangipane 42, ℧ 06 487 1063, the mainly-rock venues such as **Big Mama**, Vicolo San Francesco a Ripa 18, in Trastevere, ℧ 06 581 2551, and a blues club, **Alpheus**, Via del Commercio 36–38, in Ostiense, ℧ 06 574 9826. Also for jazz venues—which have a strong Roman following—like the suave **Alexanderplatz**, Via Ostia 9, in Prati, ☎ 06 3974 2971, and the **New Mississippi Jazz Club**, Borgo Angelico 18/a, near San Pietro, ☎ 06 6880 6348.

For serious dancing try **Alien**, Via Velletri 13, near Piazza Fiume, ☎ 06 841 2212, **Alpheus**, Via del Commercio 36, off Via Ostiense, ☎ 06 574 7826, or the less juvenile (jacket required) **Gilda**, Via Mario de' Fiori 97, close to the Spanish Steps, ☎ 06 678 4838.

Sports and Activities

Participating in sports is virtually impossible in Rome without paying a hefty fee to become a member of a club. You can, of course, jog or cycle most pleasantly in one of the parks, and swim gratis on some beaches and at Lake Bracciano. The **Gruppo Escursionisti Verdi**, Via Nomentana 939, ☎ 822 733, **La Montagna Iniziative**, Via Mercantonio Colonna 44, ☎ 320 3443, and **Club Alpino Italiano**, Piazza S. Andrea della Valle 3, ☎ 861 0111 or 683 2684, organize hikes, treks, bike and cross-country skiing excursions outside Rome.

Of the main sports complexes, **Foro Italico**, Viale dei Gladiatori, built by Mussolini, is reserved for football, swimming competitions and water polo, and host to the prestigious **international tennis championships** in May. **Flaminio**, just across the bridge from Foro Italico, has another Palazzetto dello Sport, at Piazza Apollodoro 10, for tennis, basketball, skating, gymnastics, etc. The **Stadio Flaminio** on Viale Pilsudski is also used for football and big events.

EUR's **Palazzo dello Sport** at Viale del Umanismo, is used for basketball, boxing, indoor tennis, and rock concerts; it also has an Olympic velodrome, field hockey ground, and a pool. You can also watch competitions and championships at two private sports complexes, the **Complesso Sportivo Tre Fontane**, Via delle Tre Fontane 1, ☎ 592 2485, in EUR, with running tracks and a covered gym, and, up beyond Villa Ada, the **Acqua Acetosa**, Via dei Campi Sportivi 48, with fields for rugby, polo, football, etc.

Naples

The most loathsome nest of human caterpillars I was ever forced to stay in—a hell with all the devils imbecile in it.

John Ruskin

...it reveals itself only to the simpatici.

Peter Gunn

For many, Naples is the true homeland of a particular Italian fantasy, the last bastion of singing waiters and red-checked tablecloths, operatic passion and colourful poverty, balanced precariously between Love's own coastline and the menace of Vesuvius. But mention Naples or the Neapolitans to any modern, respectable north Italian, and as they gesticulate and roll their eyes to heaven you will get a first-hand lesson in the dynamics of Italy's 'Problem of the South'. Many Italians simply cannot accept that such an outlandish place can be in the same country with them, a sentiment that probably contains as much envy as contempt. Naples, the city that has given the world Enrico Caruso, Sophia Loren, pizza and syphilis (the disease appeared here in 1495, and was immediately blamed on the French garrison), may also be the first city to make social disorder into an art form.

Degradation, Italian Style

On Naples' Piazza Garibaldi you can buy a boiled pig's organ on a stick, served with a slice of lemon, and watch eight-year-old *scugnizzi* (street children) puff contraband Marlboros while casually tossing firecrackers into traffic. Fireworks, along with slamming doors, impromptu arias, screams, ambulance sirens and howling cats, are an essential part of the Neapolitan ambience. This anarchic symphony is harder to catch these days, unfortunately, drowned as it is under the roar of Italy's worst traffic problem. In central Naples, three-quarters of a million rude drivers chase each other around a street plan that hasn't changed much since Roman times. Meanwhile, the nation's worst air pollution keeps the hospitals full, in spite of occasional half-hearted attempts to solve the problem by only allowing drivers to take their cars out on alternate days, and every few weeks some old lady on a back street burns to a crisp while the firemen, just down the block, gamely push illegally parked cars out of their way.

Another chronic problem is housing, enough of a nightmare even before the earthquake of 1980; on the outskirts of the city, you may see Napoletani living in stolen ship cargo containers, with windows cut in the sides, in shacks made of sheet metal and old doors, or in abandoned buses. In the city centre, thousands of earthquake refugees are still camping in hotels. One bizarre side-effect of this housing shortage—found all over Italy, but particularly visible here—is the 'quivering car' phenomenon. You'll see them everywhere, especially up on Posillipo hill, cars parked nose to tail, their windows blacked out with newspaper, turned into temporary bedrooms by courting couples or even married couples who have no privacy at home. A cruel but popular prank with Neapolitan kids is to sneak up on the cars and set fire to the newspaper.

Reform has been the buzz word in recent years but the city still has to deal with the spectre of the Camorra, a loose term for the crime syndicates that keep Naples as securely strung up as any mountain village in Sicily. Crime is so well organized here that, to give one example, seagoing smugglers have formed a trade union to protect their interests against the police.

In the 18th century, when the city and its spectacular setting were a highlight of the Grand Tour, the saying was 'See Naples and die...'. Nowadays you usually can't see much of anything through the smog, and you'll probably survive if you're careful crossing streets. Don't let Naples' current degradation spoil your visit, though; you haven't seen Italy—no, you haven't seen the Mediterranean—until you have spent some time in this fascinating metropolis. The only thing subtle about Naples is its charm, and the city will probably win your heart at the same time as it is deranging your senses.

On the Other Hand...

If Naples immediately repels you, however, it means you are probably a sticky sort, and will miss all the fun. The city has an incomparable setting, and much of it is still admittedly beautiful, but its real attraction is a priceless insight into humanity, at the hands of a population of 2.2 million dangerous anarchists. The Napoletani may be numbered among the few peoples of Europe who realize they are alive, and try to enjoy it as best they can. Their history being what it is, this manifests itself in diverse ways.

The Napoletani do not stand in lines, or fill out forms, or stop for traffic signals; they will talk your ears off, run you over in their ancient Fiats, criticize the way you dress, whisper alarming propositions, give you sweets, try to pick your pockets with engaging artlessness, offer surprising kindnesses, and with a reassuring smile they will always, always give you the wrong directions. In an official capacity, they will either break the rules for you or invent new ones; in shops and restaurants, they will either charge you too much or too little. The former is much more common, but whichever it is, they will undoubtedly do it with a flourish.

If the accounts of long-ago travellers are to be believed, Naples has always been like this. Too much sunshine, and living under such a large and ill-mannered volcano, must contribute much to the effect. It would be somewhat harder to explain some of Naples' ancient distinctions. First and foremost, Naples is Italy's city of philosophers. Her greatest, Giambattista Vico, was a Neapolitan, and others such as St Thomas Aquinas and Benedetto Croce spent much of their time here.

Naples can also claim to be first in music. Among native composers are Gesualdo, Scarlatti and Leoncavallo, and the conservatory is claimed to be the oldest in Europe. Even today, members of the opera company at San Carlo look down on their colleagues at Milan's La Scala as a band of promising upstarts who could stand to take their jobs a little more seriously. Neapolitan popular song, expressive and intense, is an unchained Italian stereotype; the Napoletani maintain its traditions as jealously as they do their impenetrable dialect, one of the most widely spoken and robust in modern Italy.

History

Naples' rise to become the metropolis of Campania was largely the result of the lucky elimination of her rivals over the centuries. Capua, Cumae and Benevento rose and fell, Pompeii and Herculaneum disappeared under volcanic ash, but fortune has always seemed to protect Naples from the really big disasters. As a Greek colony founded by Cumae in 750 BC, the city began with the name Neapolis (*new city*), and prospered moderately throughout the periods of Greek, Samnite and Roman rule. Belisarius, Justinian's famous general, seized the region for Byzantium in 536, after invasions of the Goths and Vandals, but a duke of Naples declared the city independent in 763, acknowledging only the authority of the pope.

The chronicles are understandably slim for this period; early medieval Naples offers us more fairy-tales than facts. Many of its early legends deal with none other than the poet Virgil; somehow, folklore in the dark ages had transformed the greatest Latin poet into Master Virgil, a mighty magician who was given credit for many of the unexplainable engineering feats of the ancient Romans. Naples claimed him for its founder, and its legends told of how he built the Castel dell'Ovo, balancing it on an egg at the bottom of the harbour. Master Virgil also built a talking statue that warned the city of enemies, earthquakes or plagues, and medieval chroniclers mention the bronze horses and bronze fly he built over two of the city's gates, still to be seen in those days, and said to be magical charms on which the fortune of the city depended.

Naples lost its independence to the Normans in 1139, later passing under the rule of the Hohenstaufen emperors along with the rest of southern Italy. Charles of Anjou took over in 1266, and lopped off the head of the last Hohenstaufen, Conradin, in what is now Naples' Piazza del Mercato. Under the Angevins, Naples for the first time assumed the status and architectural embellishments of a capital. The Angevin kings of Naples, however, did little to develop their new realm, expending most of their energy in futile attempts to recapture Sicily, lost to them after the Sicilian Vespers revolution of 1282. After their line expired in 1435, with the death of Giovanni II, the kingdom fell to Alfonso V of Aragon—a fateful event, marking Spain's first foothold on the Italian mainland.

Habsburgs and Bourbons

Aragonese rule seemed promising at first, under the enlightened Alfonso. In later decades, though, it became clear that the Spaniards were mainly interested in milking Italy for taxes with which to finance further conquests. The city itself, as the seat of the viceregal court, prospered greatly; by 1600 its population of 280,000 made it perhaps the largest city on the Mediterranean. The long period of Spanish control did much to give Naples its distinct character, especially during the 17th and 18th centuries, when the city participated almost joyfully in the decadence and decay of the Spanish Empire. This period saw the construction of the scores of frilly, gloomy baroque churches—now half-abandoned, with bushes growing out of the cornices—that add so much to the Neapolitan scene. In manners especially, the imperial Spanish influence was felt. 'Nothing', in the words of one observer, 'is cheaper here than human life.'

In 1707, during the War of the Spanish Succession, Naples passed under the rule of Archduke Charles of Austria. Prince Charles of Bourbon, however, snatched it away from him in 1734, and mouldering, picturesque Naples for the next century and a half made the perfect backdrop for the rococo shenanigans of the new Bourbon kingdom. The new rulers were little improvement over the Spaniards, but immigrants from all over the south poured into the city, chasing the thousands of ducats dropped by a free-spending court. Naples became the most densely populated city in Europe (a distinction it still holds today) and crime and epidemics became widespread.

Nevertheless, this was the Naples that became a major attraction for thousands of northern aesthetes doing the Grand Tour in the 18th and 19th centuries. Goethe flirted with contessas here, while the English poets were flirting with dread diseases and Lord Nelson was making eyes at Lady Hamilton. The Neapolitans are frank about it; Naples owed its prominence on the Grand Tour less to Vesuvius and the ruins of Pompeii than to good old-fashioned sex. Naples at the time was incontestably the easiest place in Europe to find some, and everyone knew it—saving Goethe and the rest the trouble of ever mentioning the subject in their travel accounts and letters home.

War and Politics

Garibaldi's army entered Naples in February 1861. As the new Italy's biggest basket case, the city has since received considerable assistance with its planning and social problems—though unfortunately not nearly enough to make up for the centuries of neglect. The Second World War didn't help; for four days in late September 1944, the city staged a heroic though unsuccessful revolt against the Germans. Even more damage was done by Allied bombing, not forgetting the destruction of the city's port and utilities by the retreating Nazis.

While the post-war period saw considerable rebuilding, it also brought new calamities. Illegal and speculative building projects grabbed most of the already-crowded city's open space (you'll notice the almost total absence of parks) and turned the fringe areas and much of the once-beautiful Bay of Naples shore into a nightmare of human detritus, one of the eeriest industrial wastelands of Europe. At the moment there seems to be a common realization that Naples has reached a point of no return. It has either to clean itself up or perish; discussions of the city's problems in the press are often conducted in alarmingly apocalyptic tones. Leave some room for exaggeration—the Napoletani probably couldn't enjoy life properly without a permanent state of crisis.

In the political turmoil that has taken over Italy since the beginning of the nineties, with the collapse of the old parties, Naples has become one of the major bases of support for the neo-Fascist MSI party, in yet another twist to the city's history. It has, however, marked up one genuine accomplishment in the last few years, though not one that will have much effect on the most serious problems—the *Centro Direzionale*, a huge modernistic development on the lines of a Neapolitan Manhattan built over the wastelands around Corso Malta, north of the Central Station. In spite of a few hiccups, most notably when the new palace of justice was mysteriously burnt to the ground (no prizes for guessing by whom), the project is currently nearing completion, its aim being to provide a new centre for the regional economy.

Bassolino, the anti-Mafia mayor who in 1994 narrowly beat Alessandra Mussolini, Benito's granddaughter and Sophia Loren's niece, is nearing the end of his second term. In his first term, the worst of the ghettos around the port went, tourist trails across Spaccanapoli were encouraged, and churches and sites long closed were reopened. Most spectacularly of all, the Piazza del Plebiscito, for a long time choked by traffic and fated to remain the city's parking lot, was emptied and cleaned up. But the excitement has fizzled out—Camorra families are still bombing each other right in the middle of town and Bassolino has lost his halo. He is now accused of addressing only the outer layer of Naples' problems rather than tackling major issues and, even worse, of anointing his successor before his term ends.

Art and Architecture

Greek and Roman

With the arrival of the Greeks and Etruscans in the mid-8th century BC, Italy joined the wider Mediterranean world, artistically as well as politically. The wealthy cities of Magna Graecia imported classical Greek art and artists wholesale, and even though many of the cities themselves have disappeared, the archaeological museum of Naples has huge stores of sculpture, painted vases, architectural decoration, figurines and lovely terracotta *ex votos*. Native artists also made endless copies of painted Greek ceramics, many of them excellent. There are Greek ruins at **Cumae**, west of Naples.

The art and architecture of the Roman world is out on display in Naples' museum and at the matchless sites of **Pompeii** and **Herculaneum**. There are plenty of other ruins of Roman buildings to see: at **Pozzuoli**, **Baia** and other sites around the western bay, including some grandiose survivals of Roman engineering, such as the reservoirs and canals of the great naval base at Cape Misenum and the Fuorigrotta road tunnel, the longest ever built in antiquity, in Naples. What's left of one of the largest amphitheatres of the Roman world can be seen at **Pozzuoli**. Most of these spectacular works came in the confident, self-assured age of the Flavian and Antonine emperors (late 1st–2nd centuries), a time that also saw important progress in sculpture. Until then, Roman work had been closely bound to Hellenistic styles, or was expressed in outright copies of classical Greek sculpture.

Painting and mosaic work were both present from at least the 1st century BC, though Romans always considered them as little more than decoration, and only rarely entrusted to them any serious subjects. Both are a legacy from the Greeks, and both found their way to Rome by way of talented, half-Greek Campania. Painting, in the days of Caesar and Augustus, usually meant wall frescoes in the homes of the wealthy (*see* pp.155–6), with large scenes of gardens in the form of window views, making small Roman rooms look brighter and bigger; also mythological scenes, paintings of battles and, occasionally, portraits (the best, courtesy of Vesuvius, are at Pompeii and Herculaneum, also in the museum of Naples). Mosaics had their greatest centre at Antioch, in Hellenized Syria, and only became a significant medium in Italy as painting was declining. As with the other arts, mosaics were done better in cultured Campania. If Rome, too, had been buried under volcanic lava, at whatever period, it is unlikely that much would be found to surpass the 2nd- and 1st-century paintings and mosaics discovered at Pompeii.

Byzantine and Medieval

So much from every age has been lost due to earthquakes and neglect, it is not surprising that even the most rudimentary structure from the Dark Ages is a rarity, though Naples' cathedral retains its 5th-century baptistry. Further south, Byzantine influence predominated until the late Middle Ages, especially in areas that remained Greek in religion and culture. In the 10th–12th centuries cultural revival was made possible by a number of factors: the trade and overseas contacts of Amalfi and Naples not only creating wealth but bringing in influences from Byzantium and the Muslim world; the ascent of the Normans, bringing the blessings of political stability and a sophisticated court; and, artistically, the work of Abbot Desiderius at the great Abbey of Montecassino, between Naples and Rome, importing artists and architects from Constantinople, and helping to spread their advanced styles and techniques across the south—one good example being finely incised bronze church doors, a Greek speciality. Painting too, in this age, was largely a matter of importing styles and artists from Greece, and Byzantine art, so unfairly disparaged by the Renaissance, would continue to influence all of Italy until the fall of Constantinople.

Gothic churches are more common than in most parts of Italy; the style was brought down by the French under the rule of Charles of Anjou after 1266 (San Domenico Maggiore in Naples is one of the best examples). Survivals of painting and sculpture are sadly few. Giotto came down to Naples to work for Robert the Wise, and he painted a series of frescoes for the Castel dell'Ovo, now completely lost.

An Imported Renaissance

In the 15th and 16th centuries, while the rest of Italy made a revolution in western art and culture, the south unfortunately was not often able to take part. With the economic decline of the southern cities, there was little opportunity for artistic advance. Northern artists, especially Tuscans, still came to Naples in the 1400s, but like the Gothic masons and sculptors of 200 years before they must have found themselves acting as cultural missionaries. They left some fine works behind but, for reasons that are difficult to see clearly, they never seemed to make a strong impression on the southern sensibility. Notable visitors at Naples include Donatello and Michelozzo (tomb in S. Angelo a Nilo); Antonio Rossellino (tombs at Monteoliveto); and Giuliano da Maiano (the Capua gate). Many important early Renaissance painters are represented at Naples's Capodimonte museum.

There are a few exceptions, unexpected little candles in the prevailing gloom. Giovanni da Nola, a first-rate sculptor, though little known, decorated many churches in Naples. That city also contributed some fine and original work, such as Romolo Balsimelli's Santa Caterina a Formiello. The most important Renaissance achievement in Naples was the Castel Nuovo (1454–67), and especially its triumphal arch. Built for Alfonso I, this was a Renaissance landmark, a mythological rendering of statesman-like virtue entirely equal to the arches and columns of antiquity. Local talent, such as Tommaso Malvito's Cappella Carafa at the Duomo, tried to carry the trend onwards, but in Naples the ideals of the Renaissance would never really take hold.

Baroque and Neoclassicism

If the baroque began in Rome, it soon found a warm welcome throughout the south. With its escapism, emotionalism and excess, the new style proved an inspiration to a troubled and long somnolent region, and the concentration of wealth in the hands of the court and the Church ensured a lavish patronage.

In Naples the greatest exponent of the baroque was a brilliant, tortured soul named Cosimo Fanzago (1591–1678), sculptor, architect and decorative artist who designed the great cloister of San Martino, the *guglia* in Piazza San Domenico and a little masterpiece of a church, Santa Maria Egiziaca, at Pizzofalcone (a *guglia* is a tall, elaborately decorated religious monument for a piazza, a Neapolitan speciality). Fanzago is known for his love of *pietra dura* work, exquisite floral patterns in brightly coloured marble inlay (as in S. Domenico Maggiore), an art from late Renaissance Florence; it set the trend for the lush interiors of Neapolitan churches over the next century. Another Neapolitan worthy of mention is Ferdinando Sanfelice, a light-hearted pastry chef of churches (the Nunziatella) and palaces, famous for his fascinating, geometrically complex grand staircases (Palazzi Sanfelice, Bartolomeo di Maio, Serra di Cassano).

In sculpture, the best Neapolitan works are also the most eccentric—the spectacular virtuosity of Francesco Queirolo, Antonio Corradini and Giuseppe Sammartino in the Sansevero Chapel; art historians always damn these to the lowest circles of the inferno, but you might enjoy them. Almost all the Neapolitan sculptors devoted much effort to figures for *presepi*—Christmas cribs (*see* p.124); the San Martino museum has a delightful collection. In painting, Naples and the south began the baroque era under the spell of Caravaggio, who arrived in Naples in 1607 (there are paintings at Capodimonte). Among his followers, adapting the dark and dramatic realism of the master to different ends, were the Spaniard José Ribera (San Martino) and the Calabrian Mattia Preti, one of the most talented of all southern artists, who did much of his best work for the Knights of Malta. (He also worked at Capodimonte and S. Pietro a Maiella in Naples, and in his home town of Taverna.) Another important painter, at his best in unusual, highly original landscapes, was the native Neapolitan Salvator Rosa (1615–73).

Later Neapolitan painting, frivolous and colourful, with little to challenge the intellect or the imagination, was just right for the times and enjoyed a widespread influence. Luca Giordano, the mercurial and speedy *Luca fa presto* (1634–1705), painted all over Italy, spent ten years at the court in Madrid, and still found time to cover acres of Neapolitan ceilings with clouds and *putti*, tumbling horses and pastel-robed floating maidens (as at the Duomo and San Martino). His greatest follower, in his time perhaps the most popular painter in Italy, was Francesco Solimena (1657–1747; S. Paolo Maggiore, Gesù Nuovo).

A more modern, sober turn in Neapolitan art came with the reforming King Charles III, in 1750. That year saw the death of Ferdinando Sanfelice, and the arrival of two architects from the north who brought the neoclassical manner to Naples. Ferdinando Fuga was for a time court architect to the Bourbons (his work includes the *Albergo dei Poveri* on Via Foria, the biggest and fanciest poorhouse in the world). The 18th century, though, belonged to Luigi Vanvitelli (1700–73), son of the Italianized Dutch painter Gaspar van Wittel and favourite architect of King Charles III, the most assiduous builder among the Bourbon kings. Most of Vanvitelli's energies were expended on the huge Royal Palace at **Caserta**, fully in line with the international neoclassicism of the time with its tastefully unimaginative façades, grand stairways and axis-planned gardens. Neoclassicism in Naples, a surprising reaction against the city's long-standing love affair with the baroque and the bizarre, dominated the 1700s and indeed the remainder of the Bourbon period, as seen in such buildings as the Capodimonte palace and the San Carlo opera house (both by G.A. Medrano, in the 1730s) and the grandiose domed San Francesco di Paola (1817).

Naples' **Capodichino airport** is on the north side of the city, relatively close to the centre. It has frequent direct services to and from all major Italian destinations and to many foreign cities, including London (several flights daily). For airport information, call ✆ 081 789 6111. From 6am to midnight there is a bus service every 50 minutes (a blue bus run by Sepsa), between the airport and Piazza Municipio near the ferry harbour. For the Stazione Centrale there is the half-hourly city bus (no.14) which does not run as late. The journey takes 20–45 mins, depending on the time of day. As on all city buses, tickets should be bought at a news-stand or ticket booth before boarding. Lastly, Curreri (✆ 081 801 5420) runs four daily buses (*at 9, 2, 4.30 and 7*) to Sorrento departing from the stop outside the Arrivals hall (on the right).

If you opt for a taxi from the airport, remember that on top of the fare on the meter you will officially be charged extra supplements for the airport trip and for luggage—plus, very possibly, additional unexplained 'extras' as well (*see* below). If in doubt, ask to see the list of prices, which should be displayed in the cab, or try to agree on the fare to your destination before getting into the cab. If traffic is not too heavy—and this is a big if—the fare to the centre should not exceed L40,000.

by sea

Naples' port has more ship and hydrofoil connections than anywhere else in the Mediterranean, so you can choose to arrive by sea from—or flee to—a wide variety of places, among them the islands in the Bay of Naples, Sicily and the Aeolian Islands. Generally, ferries are cheaper than hydrofoils, but take approximately twice as long. One of the loveliest of the possible sea excursions is the night ferry to the Aeolian Islands, which arrives as the sun is rising over Vulcano.

Ferries and hydrofoils leave from three different points in Naples, but most longer-distance ferries operate from the **Stazione Marittima**, in the centre of the port near the Castel Nuovo. Consult the individual companies for timetables, otherwise look in the daily newspaper *Il Mattino* or in *Qui Napoli*. The main companies operating from Stazione Marittima are **Tirrenia**, ✆ 081 720 1111, for Palermo and Cagliari; and **Siremar**, ✆ 081 720 1595, for the Aeolian Islands and Milazzo in Sicily. In addition, one company, **SNAV**, ✆ 081 761 2348, operates a twice-a-day long-distance hydro-foil service from Mergellina quay to the Aeolian Islands.

For more information on boat services from Naples and hydrofoil services to the islands and ports around the bay, *see* p.163 and p.169.

by rail

Most visitors arrive by train at the modern **Stazione Centrale** on Piazza Garibaldi, which is also a junction for city buses and the local *Circumvesuviana* railway. Trains along the coast towards Rome or Reggio di Calabria pass through Naples every half-hour on average. In addition, many trains also stop at **Napoli Mergellina** and

Napoli Campi Flegrei, on the western side of the city, and at some other local stations. There are also good rail connections from Naples to Palermo (4–8 hours, depending on the train) via Messina.

As well as the state FS lines, three local railway lines serve the Bay of Naples area. The **Ferrovia Circumvesuviana**, ✆ 081 772 2444, runs trains to Herculaneum, Pompeii and Sorrento from the **Stazione Circumvesuviana** in Corso Garibaldi, and from the Stazione Centrale. The **Ferrovia Cumana**, ✆ 081 551 3328, runs regular trains to the Campi Flegrei area, including Pozzuoli and Baia, from the station at Piazza Montesanto. The **Ferrovia Circumflegrea**, also ✆ 081 551 3328, runs from the same station at Piazza Montesanto to points west, including Licola and Cuma. For more information on the regional rail lines *see* pp.144–5 and p.150.

by long-distance bus

Most services to destinations within the province and the Campania region operate from Piazza Garibaldi, in front of the FS Stazione Centrale. An exception is the bus service to Salerno along the coast, which runs from Via Pisanelli, near Piazza Municipio (*see* p.162).

by road

The A2 *autostrada* from Rome approaches Naples from due north, via Caserta, and in the outskirts of the city, just east of Capodichino airport, meets up with a series of massive road junctions: the A16 turns off east for Avellino, Bari and the Adriatic, and then two roads head off to the west, the P1 for the coast and the Naples inner ring road, the *tangenziale*, which leads around the back of the city towards Pozzuoli and the Campi Flegrei. Using the *tangenziale* makes it possible to reach most areas of the city without going through the centre. Traffic going further south should stay on the A2 until it meets the A3, so avoiding the city entirely.

Once you arrive at wherever you are staying in Naples, you are categorically advised to park your car in a safe place (such as a hotel garage) and not attempt to use it anywhere within the city (*see* p.114).

Tourist Information

The best place to go for information about Naples itself is the well-run and friendly information booth run by the city's **Azienda Autonoma di Soggiorno** on Piazza del Gesù Nuovo, ✆ 081 552 3328/✆ 081 551 2701, in the old town (*open Mon–Sat 8.30–7.30, Sun 8.30–3.30, hols 9–2*). Their main office is in the Royal Palace, ✆ 081 252 5711, 🖷 081 418 619. In summer they open offices in the Castel dell'Ovo, ✆ 081 764 5688.

Information about excursions outside the city and so on is only available from the less helpful provincial tourist office **EPT**, Piazza dei Martiri 58, ✆ 081 405 311. The EPT has another office at the Stazione Centrale, ✆ 081 268 779, which may be some help in finding a hotel. Two others are to be found at the airport, ✆ 081 780 5761, and the Stazione Mergellina, ✆ 081 761 2102.

Look out for the excellent free monthly handbook *Qui Napoli*, available at tourist offices and some hotels, which carries a great deal of useful information, timetables, listings and calendars of events. The **EPT** produce good maps of the city centre and the bay itself (both free of charge).

In an attempt to draw visitors into the old city, Naples has set up designated walks and keeps the points of interest along them open for longer hours. Information on accompanied walks is available from the **AAST** at Piazza del Gesù Nuovo. For a fascinating trip around subterranean Naples, **Laes** (Libera Associazione Escursionisti Sottosuolo, © 081 400 256) operate guided tours from Piazza Trieste e Trento (next to Piazza del Plebiscito) (*weekends at 10am*).

Getting Around

Transport around the city is a fascinating subject. Such is the state of most public transport and so impenetrable is the traffic that walking is often by far the most practical way of getting anywhere, apart from up to the heights by the *funicolari.*

Orientation is a little difficult. If you arrive by sea—the only proper way to do it—you'll get a good idea of the layout. Naples' dominant landmarks, visible from almost anywhere in town, are Castel Sant'Elmo and the huge, fortress-like monastery of San Martino. They are neighbours on the steep hill that slopes down to the sea near the port, neatly dividing the city into its old and new quarters. Modern Naples is on the western side, the busy, pleasant districts of Mergellina, Vomero and Fuorigrotta, to which middle-class Napoletani escape from the city centre at the end of each day, on their creaking old funicular railways. To the east, towards Vesuvius, lies the centre, along Via Toledo, and beyond it the oldest neighbourhoods, tall tenements jammed into a grid of narrow streets, reaching a climax in the oriental bazaar atmosphere around the Piazza Mercato and the Piazza Garibaldi.

One benefit of reforms aimed at cleaning up the city's image and attracting tourists is the introduction of the new-style 'Giranapoli' ('Around Naples') bus tickets. There are two types, one lasting 90 minutes for L1,500, and a day ticket for L4,500. If you plan on staying for more than nine days, invest in a monthly pass (L45,000), enabling you to travel on buses, the funiculars and the Metropolitana throughout the city.

by bus

Given the problems involved in using cars and even taxis in Naples, visitors often find themselves left with the buses, which is small cheer, since the city has the worst bus system in Italy. Buses will be slow and usually indecently crowded. There are no schedules, no maps, and nowhere you can get accurate information; even the drivers rarely have the faintest idea what is happening. The ultimate Neapolitan experience is waiting an hour for a bus after being misinformed by line employees, and then finding out that the right bus is the one marked 'out of service'.

The confusion is compounded by the recent division of services run by the old bus company Atam under its successor ANM and other smaller companies. Most bus lines start at Piazza Garibaldi or Piazza del Plebiscito. Some that might be useful are **R2**, from Piazza Garibaldi to Corso Umberto and Piazza Municipio; **R3**, from Piazza

Municipio to Riviera di Chiaia and Mergellina; **110, 127,** from Piazza Garibaldi to Piazza Cavour and Capodimonte; **152,** from Piazza Garibaldi to Pozzuoli. The relatively new Artebus service runs through the most interesting areas of town and can be used for short hops between sights. It departs from Mergellina and must be arranged through your hotel (*Fri–Sun; free*).

by metro and funicolare

Naples also has a sort of underground. The **Metropolitana FS,** a single line from Gianturco to Pozzuoli, is really a part of the state railway, and uses the same underground tracks as the long-distance trains. The FS runs it as anarchically as the buses, but it will be helpful for reaching the station (Piazza Garibaldi), the archaeological museum, points in Vomero and Fuorigrotta, and Solafatara. As on the buses, few people ever buy tickets.

A much more agreeable way to travel, though you can't go very far, is on the three *funicolari*, or inclined railways, up to Vomero. The longest—one of the longest in the world, in fact—is the **Funicolare Centrale,** from Via Toledo, just behind the Galleria, up to Via Cimarosa. The **Funicolare di Chiaia** also ends nearby in the same street, having started from Piazza Amedeo in Chiaia. Finally, the **Funicolare di Montesanto** runs to Via Morghen from Montesanto Station, the start of the suburban Circumflegrea and Cumana rail lines. All three *funicolari* bring you out near the San Martino Museum and the Castel Sant'Elmo and all run daily until about 10pm.

by taxi

Neapolitan taxi drivers are uniformly dishonest, and try out any number of scams involving fixed meters, turning the meter on before you get in the car, imaginary 'surcharges' and so on. Also, the traffic is frequently so thick that relatively short journeys can take so long (and cost so much) that they're really not worth it. If you want to take a taxi to a specific destination, always try to agree on the fare in advance, whether there is a meter or not.

by car

The first thing to get straight is simply—*leave your car elsewhere*. Cars disappear in Naples with alarming frequency, and foreign numberplates are especially prized. Even if you get to keep your wheels, you'll be sorry. Driving in Naples is a unique experience. Motorists studiously disregard all traffic signals and warnings, and the city has given up trying to coerce them. There are no rules, except to get there first, and fatalities are common. Even if this sounds exciting, note that the novelty soon wears off, even for the most boorish motorhead. For scant sympathy about stolen cars, call the city police on © 081 794 1435.

Several **car hire** firms have offices in Naples, mainly on Via Partenope (near the port), at the airport, and/or at the Stazione Centrale. For the most convenient office for you try: **Avis,** Via Partenope 32, © 081 764 5600; **Europcar,** Via Partenope 38, © 081 780 5643; **Hertz,** Via Sauro 21, © 081 764 5323; **ItalRent,** Via S. Lucia, © 081 764 5423. Be warned, however, that as car theft is rife in Naples some companies will not rent certain models in the city, so you may find your choice restricted. The most basic models start from L85,000 per day.

Check with hotels if they have secure parking (*parcheggio custodito*). If not, you might want to use the private car parks. Overnight stays can cost L20,000 and more: **Grilli**, Via Ferraris 40, close to the Stazione Centrale, ✆ 081 264 344; **Mergellina**, Via Mergellina 112, ✆ 081 761 3470; **Sannazaro**, Piazza Sannazaro 142, close to Stazione Mergellina, ✆ 081 681 437.

Around the City

Piazza del Plebiscito

After years as a parking lot this immense and elegant square, the centre of modern Naples, has been rescued and restored to the city. Children now come here at sundown to kick a football, under the eyes of adoring parents. The recent shows staged here by the city for the benefit of national television have even forced some northern Italians to revise their opinions of Naples and admit that it may not be all that bad after all.

The huge domed church, embracing the piazza in its curving colonnades as does St Peter's in Rome, is **San Francesco di Paola**. King Ferdinand IV, after the British restored him to power in 1815, made a vow to construct it; the great dome and classical portico were modelled after the Pantheon in Rome. There's little to see in the austere interior, and anyone with a little understanding of Naples will not be surprised to find the colonnades given over to light manufacturing and warehouse space.

Across the square rises the equally imposing bulk of the **Palazzo Reale** (Royal Palace) (*✆ 081 580 8111, open Mon–Sat 9.30am–10pm, Sun and hols 9.30–8; closed Wed; adm*), begun by the Spanish viceroys in 1600, expanded by the Bourbons and finished by the kings of Italy. Umberto I, a good friend of the Neapolitans, added the eight giant figures on the façade, representing the eight houses that have ruled at Naples. It seems the 19th-century sculptors had trouble taking some of them seriously; note the preposterous figures of Charles of Anjou, whom the Neapolitans never liked, and Vittorio Emanuele II, the latter probably an accurate portrayal.

There are Ruritanian stone sentry boxes and stone peacocks in the courtyard to recall the Bourbons, and a number of rooms inside that can be visited—the ones that escaped the bombings in the Second World War, including a suitably grand staircase, a theatre, and several chambers in 18th-century style. The theatre saw the premieres of many of the works of Alessandro Scarlatti. The rear of the palace, now the home of Naples' important **Biblioteca Nazionale**, faces a pretty, little-visited garden across from the Castel Nuovo.

The Bourbons were great opera buffs, and they built Italy's largest opera house, the **San Carlo**, right next to their palace. Begun in 1737, making it older than La Scala, the theatre was sumptuously restored after a fire in 1816, during the period when Naples was the unquestioned capital of opera; so important was the theatre to the people of Naples that King Ferdinand made sure the workmen got the job done in record time—300 days.

Today the San Carlo is still among the most prestigious opera houses in the world (the Neapolitans of course would place it first), and its productions are certainly among the most polished and professional, and occasionally among the most adventurous. Each season at least one lesser-known Neapolitan opera is performed. Tickets are as expensive as anywhere

1 S. Lorenzo Maggiore
2 S. Gregorio Armeno
3 San Severo
4 S. Giuseppe
5 S. Domenico Maggiore
6 Monastero di S. Chiara
7 Palazzo Gravina
8 Palazzo Penna
9 S. Anna dei Lombardi
10 Poste e Telegrafi

(up to L500,000 on an opening night). Brief tours of the theatre are possible for considerably less (*for information, call© 081 797 2111*).

Opposite the San Carlo is the grandest interior of Southern Italy, the **Galleria Umberto I**. This great glass-roofed arcade, perhaps the largest in the world, was begun in 1887, nine years after the Galleria Vittorio Emanuele in Milan. The arcade is cross-shaped, with a mosaic of the zodiac on the floor at the centre, and its dome is 184ft tall; surprisingly, the Neapolitans do not seem to like it as much as they once did; even at high noon, you are likely to find its vast spaces deserted but for a few small clouds of grey-suited men arguing politics around the entrances.

Castel Nuovo

Offices open Mon–Fri 8–1, © 081 795 2003; museums Mon–Sat 9–7; adm.

The port of Naples has been protected by this odd, beautiful castle, looming over the harbour behind the Palazzo Reale and San Carlo, for some 700 years now. Charles of Anjou built it in 1279; many Napoletani still call it by the curious name of *Maschio* (male) *Angioino*. Most of what you see today, however, including the eccentric, ponderous round towers, is the work of Guillermo Sagrera, the great Catalan architect who built the famous Exchange in Palma de Mallorca. Between two of these towers at the entrance, the conquering Aragonese hired the finest sculptors from all over Italy to build Alfonso's **Triumphal Arch**, a unique masterpiece of Renaissance sculpture and design inspired by the triumphal arches of the ancient Romans. The symbolism, as in the Roman arches, may be a little confusing. The figure at the top is St Michael; below him are a matched pair of sea gods, and further down are allegorical virtues and relief panels portraying Alfonso's victories and wise governance.

Inside, the castle currently houses parts of the Naples city administration and some cultural societies. If you come during office hours, someone will probably be around to show you the **Sala dei Baroni**, where the city council meets; it has a cupola with an unusual Moorish vaulting, an eight-pointed star made of interlocking arches. King Ferrante used this as his dining hall, and it takes its name from the evening when he invited a score of the kingdom's leading barons to a ball, and then arrested the lot. There are also two museums: one, housed in the Gothic **Cappella Palatina**, next to the council hall, contains 14th- and 15th-century frescoes; the other, in the south wing, has paintings, and a good collection of silver and bronzes, from the 15th century to the present day.

King Ferrante's Dungeons

Guillermo Sagrera was the Frank Lloyd Wright of the Renaissance, a brilliant, iconoclastic architect who dreamt up shapes and forms never seen before. In his rebuilding of the Castel Nuovo, with its arch and its massive and eccentric towers, he and his intelligent patron, King Alfonso, must have been fully aware of the revolutionary design statement (as we might call it today) they were making—a castle meant to be not only a royal residence and stronghold, but a landmark and symbol for Naples.

Even before the arrival of the Spaniards and the rebuilding, the Castel Nuovo had witnessed a good deal of history. Here, when the castle was brand new, Charles of Anjou had received the news of the Sicilian Vespers, and reportedly cried out: 'Lord God, since it has pleased you to ruin me, let me only go down by small steps!' 1294 saw the visit of Pope Celestine V, who had been a simple and slow-witted hermit in the Abruzzo before his surprise election. The church bosses, who wanted a stronger hand on the papal throne, meant to get rid of him as soon as possible, and in this castle they tricked him into abdicating by whispering into his room through a hidden tube, claiming to be the voice of God and commanding him to quit. King Robert the Wise kept his great library here, and graciously received Petrarch and Boccaccio in his royal apartments.

Poor Sagrera would be sad to hear that the Castel Nuovo seems somewhat dark and sinister to many visitors today. It isn't his fault; perhaps it isn't even a matter of changing architectural tastes. Most of the credit must surely go to the ruler who stamped his own personality on the castle more than anyone else, the monstrous King Ferrante. Illegitimate son of Alfonso the Magnanimous (or just as likely, people whispered, of a certain Moor of Valencia), Ferrante took the throne of Naples in 1458; he was a devious and capable ruler, just the sort of man the state needed among the dangerous intrigues and ever-shifting political fortunes of Renaissance Italy. He is better remembered for his calculated cruelty.

On one occasion he invited an enemy back to Naples, professing great affection, and treated him to a month of parties before suddenly arresting him and sending him off to the torture room. An invitation to the King's table for dinner was often as good as a death warrant. Ferrante was known to keep a 'museum of mummies' of executed foes and rebellious barons at the castle, each dressed in his own clothes. And stories went round that he kept a crocodile in the castle's dungeons, which was fed only on live prisoners.

Via Toledo

From the landward side of Piazza del Plebiscito and the Palace, Naples' most imposing street, the Via Toledo, runs northwards past the Galleria to Piazza Carita where it becomes Via Roma. Its name commemorates its builder, Don Pedro de Toledo, the Spanish viceroy at the beginning of the 16th century, and a great benefactor of Naples. Stendhal, in 1817, rightly called this 'the most populous and gayest street in the world', and it is still the city's main business and shopping street, leading up to Capodimonte and the northern suburbs. Don Pedro's elegant Renaissance tomb, among others, can be seen in the little church of **San Giacomo degli Spagnuoli**, now swallowed up by the 19th-century Palazzo Municipale complex, originally home to the Bourbon royal bureaucracy.

Going north along Via Toledo, any street on your left can be the entrance to the dense, crumbling, slightly sinister inner sanctum of the Neapolitan soul, the vast slum called the *Quartieri Spagnuoli*. It can be a fascinating place to walk around, in daytime at least. Lately though, thanks to battling factions of the Camorra, the *Quartieri* has achieved even more than its accustomed share of notoriety; for a while the hoods were bumping each other off at the rate of one per week. Though the *Quartieri* covers almost all the area sloping up to San Martino and Vomero, the most populous and colourful part is that immediately adjoining Via Toledo, a strict grid of narrow streets laid out by Don Pedro de Toledo and now called the *Tavoliere*, or chessboard.

Four Days in Naples

The contempt that many northern Italians often show for this city and its accomplishments can look a bit silly when compared with the facts. Just for the record, note that in September 1944 Naples did more than its part in redeeming Italian honour by becoming the first city to liberate itself, and the only one to do so until the German collapse at the end of the war.

At the time of the Allied landings in Salerno, the city was in a bad way. Rations of everything were short, sometimes nonexistent, and the Germans were preparing to dynamite all the important facilities in case the Allied advance should reach Naples. Worst of all, SS units were combing every quarter for able-bodied males to ship off to forced labour in the north or in Germany.

No one knows exactly what incident touched off the great revolt. In the excellent 1960s film account, *Quattro Giornate a Napoli*, a group of men who escaped from the Germans here in the *Quartieri Spagnuoli* are recaptured and lined up against a wall to be shot. A basket on a string suddenly appears among them, of the type old women would send down from their windows in the tall tenements to buy tomatoes or chestnuts from street vendors; this time, though, the basket contained a gun—unexpected aid from heaven has always been a common theme in Neapolitan mythology.

However it started, the uprising spread like a prairie fire through the city. Pistols and old rifles came out from their hiding places, and the police arsenals were broken into for more. *Scugnizzi* (street children) waited in doorways with stolen grenades, ready to try and tip one into a passing Nazi truck or tank. The prisons were thrown open, and while many of their inmates scuttered off into the shadows, plenty of others took what arms they could find and joined in the fight. Not long after, the rebels surrounded the heavily defended football stadium in Vomero, full of captured Neapolitans waiting to be sent to Germany; they took it, despite heavy casualties, and freed the lot.

At the beginning the rebels carried on without any leadership whatsoever—except of course among the Communists. The totally anarchic, overwhelming, totally spontaneous movement of the city's people was something that few cities but Naples could ever produce. The Germans found it the ultimate Neapolitan experience; it was as if they had kicked over a beehive. They responded with customary brutality—massacres of prisoners and tanks firing point-blank into apartment blocks—but stung and pestered on every side, they could not endure long. A hastily formed committee went to negotiate terms with the exasperated German commander, and a deal was cut: the troops would depart immediately, and attacks on them would cease. An eerie silence fell over the city and indifferent faces watched from their windows as the German columns filed out. And then Naples went back to being Naples.

To the right of Via Toledo, the confusion of Naples' half-crumbling, half-modern business centre conceals a few buildings worth a look. The **Palazzo Gravina**, on Via Monteoliveto, is a fine palace in the northern Renaissance style, built between 1513 and 1549. It now houses Naples University's Faculty of Architecture. Almost directly across the street, the church of **Monteoliveto** (*open Tues–Sat 8.30–12.30*) is a little treasure house of late Renaissance sculpture and painting, with tombs and altars in the chapels by southern artists like Giovanni da Nola and Antonio Rosellino, as well as some frescoes by Vasari.

Spaccanapoli

This street's familiar name means 'Split-Naples', and that is exactly what it has done for the last 2,600 years. On the map it changes its name with alarming frequency—Via Benedetto Croce and Via San Biagio dei Librai are two of the most prominent—but in Roman times you would have called it the *decumanus inferior*, the name for the second east–west street in any planned Roman city. No large city in all the lands conquered by Rome has maintained its ancient street plan as completely as Naples (the Greeks laid out these streets, of course, but the Romans learned their planning from them). It is easier to imagine the atmosphere of a big ancient city here than in Rome itself, or even in Pompeii. The narrow, straight streets and tall *insulae* cannot have changed much; only the forum and temples are missing.

This is the heart of old Naples—and what a street it is, lined with grocery barrows and scholarly bookshops, shops that sell old violins, plaster saints, pizza, or used clothes pegs. Drama is supplied by the arch-Neapolitan characters who live here, haunting the street-corners and entertaining wan hopes of dodging the manic motorists; the colour comes from the district's laundry—down any of the long alleys of impossibly tall tenements you may see as many as a hundred full clothes-lines, swelling bravely in the breeze and hoping for a glint of southern sun.

It has always been a poor neighbourhood, though even now it is not a desperate one. As always, its people live much of their life on the streets, carrying on whatever is their business from makeshift benches on the kerbs. The visitor will probably find that claustrophobia is right around the corner, but anyone born and raised here would never feel at home anywhere else.

Santa Chiara and the Gesù Nuovo

Your introduction to this world, just off Via Toledo, is the cramped, disorderly, most characteristic of Neapolitan squares: **Piazza del Gesù Nuovo**, decorated by the gaudiest and most random of Neapolitan decorations, the **Guglia della Immacolata**. A *guglia* (pinnacle), in Naples, is a kind of rococo obelisk dripping with frills, saints and *putti*; there are three of these in this area.

The unsightly, unfinished façade behind the Guglia, covered with pyramidal extrusions in dark basalt, belongs to the church of **Gesù Nuovo**. As strange as it is, the façade, which was originally part of a late 15th-century palace, has become one of the landmarks of Naples. The interior is typically lavish Neapolitan baroque, gloriously overdone in acres of coloured marbles and frescoes, some by Solimena. One of his best works (dated 1725) is here above the main door inside, depicting three angels driving the Syrian minister Eliodorus out of the Temple of Jerusalem. In the second chapel on the right you will see a bronze statue of Naples' newest saint. St Giuseppe Moscati was a doctor who lectured at Naples University and otherwise devoted himself to caring for the poor. He died after a normal day of do-gooding on 12 April 1927.

Santa Chiara, just across the piazza, dates from the early 14th century, though it once had a baroque interior as good as the Gesù; Allied bombers remodelled it to suit modern tastes in 1943, and only a few of the original Angevin tombs have survived. To get some idea of what the interior must have been like, stop in and see the adjacent **Majolica Cloister** (*open April–Sept Mon–Sat 8.30–12.30 and 4–6.30; Oct–Mar Mon–Sat 8.30–12.30 and 4–6; under restoration but it can still be visited*), nothing less than the loveliest and most peaceful spot in Naples—especially in contrast to the neighbourhood outside. So much in Naples shows the Spanish influence—like the use of the title 'Don', now largely limited to Camorra bosses—and here someone in the 1740s transplanted the Andalucian love of pictures done in painted *azulejo* tiles, turning a simple monkish cloister into a little fairyland of gaily coloured arbours, benches and columns, shaded by the only trees in the whole district. Recently, during the restoration of a vestibule off the cloister, it was discovered that underneath the indifferent 17th-century frescoes (reached via the back of the church) there were some earlier, highly original paintings of the Last Judgement. They have since been uncovered and restored, revealing an inspired 16th-century vision of the event, in a style utterly unlike the slick virtuosity of the time, with plenty of novel tortures for the damned and angels welcoming some cute naked nuns among the elect.

The **Museo dell'Opera di S. Chiara** (*© 081 797 12 56; open Thurs–Tues 9.30–1 and 3.30–5.30, Sat and Sun 9.30–1; adm*), at the rear of the cloister, houses the church treasures, marbles and an area of archaeological excavations on the Roman period.

The Sansevero Chapel

A few streets further down Via Benedetto Croce is tiny Piazza San Domenico, which has monuments from Naples' three most creative periods. **San Domenico Maggiore** (*under restoration*) built between 1283 and 1324, was the Dominican church in Naples. St Thomas Aquinas lived in the adjacent monastery. Later this became the favourite church of the Spanish, and it contains some interesting Renaissance funerary monuments; a better one, though, is across the Piazza in the church of **Sant'Angelo a Nilo** (*open daily 8–1 and 4–7.15*)—the tomb of Cardinal Brancaccio, designed by Michelozzo, with a relief of the *Assumption of the Virgin* by Donatello (the two artists had collaborated before on the Baptistry in Siena). The second of the baroque pinnacles decorates the Piazza, the **Guglia di San Domenico**, begun after a plague in 1650. Best of all, just around the corner on Via F. de Sanctis, you can inspect Neapolitan rococo at its very queerest in the **Sansevero Chapel** (*open Nov–June Mon–Sat 10–5; July–Oct Mon–Sat 10–6, Sun 10–1.30; adm*).

Prince Raimondo di Sangro (b. 1701), who was responsible for the final form of this, his family's private chapel, was a strange bird, a sort of aristocratic dilettante mystic. Supposedly there some grand allegorical scheme behind the arrangement of the sculptures and frescoes he commissioned, but a work like this, only 200 years old, seems as foreign to our sensibilities and understanding as some Mayan temple. The sculptures, by little-known Neapolitan artists like Giuseppe Sammartino and Antonio Corradini, are inscrutable allegories in themselves, often executed with a breathtakingly showy virtuosity. Francesco Queirolo's *Il Disinganno* (Disillusion) is an extreme case; nobody else, perhaps, has ever tried to carve a fishing-net, or the turning pages of a book, out of marble. Others, such as Sammartino's *Cristo Velato*, display a remarkable illusion of figures under transparent veils. There are a dozen or so of these large sculptural groups, all under a crazy heavenly vortex in the ceiling fresco, by Francesco Mario Russo. Down in the crypt are two complete human cardiovascular systems, removed from the bodies and preserved by Prince Raimondo in the course of his alchemical experiments.

Near San Domenico, a block south of the Spacca, is Naples' **University**, one of Europe's oldest and most distinguished. Emperor Frederick II founded it in 1224, as a 'Ghibelline' university to counter the pope's 'Guelph' university at Bologna, as well as to provide scholars and trained officials for the new state he was trying to build. It still occupies its ancient, woefully overcrowded quarters around Via Mezzocannone.

Around the Piazza del Duomo

Continuing down the Spaccanapoli (now Via San Biagio dei Librai), just around the corner on Via San Gregorio is the **San Gregorio Armeno** church (*chapels under restoration*), with another gaudy baroque interior. If the gilding and the painting by Luca Giordano of the *Arrival of Saint Basilio* are not your cup of tea, try the **cloister** (*open daily 9.30–12.30*). This is another oasis of tranquillity and a step back to the 16th century. Since the 1500s the cloister has served the convent of Benedictine nuns. At the centre of the cloister there is a fountain sculpted in 1733 depicting Christ meeting the Samaritan woman. On the way out note the revolving drums for communicating with the outside world pre-1922, when the monastic order was totally closed off from the profane. A caustic note by the nuns on one of them dismisses the popular misconception that they were for abandoned newborn babies.

In December, this street and others around it become Naples' famous Christmas Market, where everyone comes to buy figurines of the Holy Family, the Three Kings and all the other accessories required for their Christmas *presepi*, or manger scenes, one of the most devotedly followed of local traditions. For several weeks, hundreds of stands fill up the neighbourhood's narrow streets.

Presepi

It would not be easy to explain why the genius of Naples should have chosen Christmas cribs as a subject to elevate to an art form. After philosophy, pizza and music, it's what this city does best. Churches and private homes have always had a little competitive edge on when they begin their displays (some time in November, if not earlier).

The most extreme cases have been assembled inside the Museo Nazionale di San Martino. One is as big as a bus, and must have taken someone a lifetime; another is fitted inside an eggshell—still with over a hundred figures in it. The best parts are the large, finely carved individual wooden or ceramic figures. Most represent Neapolitans of two or three centuries ago from every walk of life; with their painstakingly detailed and expressive faces, each is a genuine portrait. To have them all here in one place is like old Bourbon Naples appearing before your eyes.

For do-it-yourself modern cribs, Via San Gregorio is the place to go. At Christmas time the whole street is taken over by the stalls of artisans who make and sell figurines for the crib scene, as well as little trees, sheep, donkeys, amphorae, cooking pots, Turks, salamis, dogs, chickens, angels, cheese wheels, and all the other items without which no Neapolitan *presepe* would be complete.

Convention requires that, quite apart from the Holy Family, certain things be present in every crib. Besides the usual angels, shepherds and animals, a Roman ruin is absolutely necessary, as are several Turks in Ottoman Empire dress (which come in handy if one of the Three Kings gets lost). A band of musicians is also expected, and all the better if they too are Turks. Beggars and dwarfs earn envy for the crib-maker—there is a whole display of figures called the 'deformities'—but above all there must be tons of food everywhere there is room for it.

The best cribs have the busiest cooks and the most bulging pantries, with tiny wooden roast pigs, sausages, eggs, plates of macaroni, cheeses and fancy cakes—even a pizza or two. Look out for the giant *presepe* in the Galleria Umberto at Christmas time, and watch Neapolitans throw money at it to pay for its upkeep for another year.

A little further north up Via San Gregorio is **San Lorenzo Maggiore** (late 12th century), one of Naples' finest medieval churches; Petrarch lived for a while in the adjacent monastery. In addition, recent excavations have uncovered a considerable area of Greek and Roman remains on the site. Entering via the cloister, where the base of a Roman *macellum* (market place) is being excavated, head down the stairs at the very back to see this fascinating piece of subterranean Naples. **San Paolo**, across the street, isn't much to see now but, before an earthquake wrecked it in the 17th century, its façade was the portico of an ancient Roman temple to Castor and Pollux. Andrea Palladio studied it closely, and it provided inspiration for his classical villas and churches in the Veneto.

After Spaccanapoli, **Via dei Tribunali** (the *decumanus maximus*) is the busiest street of old Naples, and has been for a long time. The arcades that line the street in places, a sort of continuous covered market, are a thousand years old or more. Here, at the otherwise unremarkable **Girolamini Church** (*open daily 9–1*), you may see the modest tomb (at present unapproachable due to conservation) of Naples' greatest philosopher, Giambattista Vico.

Northwest of the Girolamini, around Via Anticaglia, you'll find a few crooked streets, the only ones in old Naples that do not stick to the rectilinear Roman plan. These follow the outline of the **Roman Theatre**, much of which still survives, hidden among the tenements. A few arches are all that is visible from the street.

The Cathedral of San Gennaro

The wide **Via del Duomo** is a breath of fresh air in this crowded district—exactly what the city intended when they ploughed it through Old Naples after the cholera epidemic of 1884. The **Duomo** (*interior under restoration*) itself is another fine medieval building, though it is hidden behind an awful pseudo-Gothic façade pasted on in 1905. The best things are inside: the Renaissance **Cappella Minùtolo**, the tomb of Charles of Anjou and the **Cappella San Gennaro**, glittering with the gold and silver of the cathedral treasure, and with frescoes by Domenichino and Lanfranco, the latter a swirling *Paradiso* in the dome (1643).

The **Basilica Santa Restituta**, a sizeable church in its own right, is tacked on to the side of the cathedral. Its columns are thought to be from the temple of Apollo that once occupied the site. Begun in 324, though often rebuilt, this is the oldest building in Naples. The ceiling frescoes are by Luca Giordano.

Just off the basilica, the 5th-century **baptistry** contains a good Byzantine-style mosaic by the 14th-century artist Lello di Roma; the baptismal font itself probably comes from an ancient temple of Dionysus. From Santa Restituta's chapel you can access a collection of archaeological remains dating from the Greeks to the Middle Ages (*open daily 9–12 and 4.30–7, Sun and hols 9–12; adm*). The last and most elaborate of the *guglie*, the **Guglia San Gennaro**, designed by Cosimo Fanzago, can be seen just outside the south transept.

If the sacristan is around, you can visit the **Crypt of San Gennaro**, patron of Naples, with elaborate marble decoration from the Renaissance, and the tomb of Pope Innocent IV.

The Legend of San Gennaro

San Gennaro (St Januarius) was a bishop from Benevento who was executed along with other martyrs at the Solfatara in Pozzuoli in AD 305 during the persecution of Christians under Diocletian. Initially he was sentenced to death by being torn apart by wild animals in the amphitheatre at Pozzuoli, but because the Roman governor was not present this was commuted to being beheaded at the Solfatara. After the execution, his body was taken to the Catacombs of S. Gennaro (*see* p.129). It was moved in the beginning of the 5th century, and from this date on he became identified as the patron of Naples, protecting it from destruction by Vesuvius and other disasters.

The saint's head is now kept upstairs in the chapel named after him, along with two phials of his blood that miraculously 'liquefy' three times each year—the first Sunday in May, 19 September and 16 December—so as to prove that San Gennaro is still looking out for the Napoletani. The only time the miracle has ever failed, during the Napoleonic occupation, the people of the city became enormously excited and seemed ready to revolt. At this the French commander, a true son of the Enlightenment, announced that San Gennaro had 10 minutes to come through—or else he'd shoot the Archbishop. Somehow, just in time, the miracle occurred.

On a small piazza a block north of the Duomo, **Santa Maria Donnaregina** offers more overdone baroque, but off to the side of this 17th-century work is the smaller, original church, built in 1307 by Queen Mary of Hungary (who was none other than the wife of Charles of Anjou; her title only reflects a claim to the throne). Her elaborate tomb, and some good frescoes from the first half of the 12th century, are the sights of the church.

South of the cathedral in the Via del Duomo is the **Filangieri Museum** (*©* *081 203 175; open Tues–Sat 9.30–2 and 3.30–7, Sun and hols 9.30–1.30; adm*), a small collection of china, armour and curiosities housed in the 15th-century Palazzo Cuomo. Its pictures include works by some of Naples' favourite artists: Luca Giordano, Mattia Preti, Ribera and others. Almost all the collection was gathered in the last forty years. Count Filangieri's original collection was much larger, but the Nazis torched it before they left in 1944.

Piazza Garibaldi

In Italian, the word for a market stand is *bancarella*. In Naples they are as much a part of everyday life as they must have been in the Middle Ages; the city probably has as many of them as all the rest of Italy put together. The greatest concentration can be found in the Forcella market district, in the narrow streets east off the Via del Duomo, selling everything from stereos to light bulbs. According to the government's economists, at least one-third of Naples' economy is underground—outright illegal, or at the least not paying taxes or subject to any regulation.

Bootleg cassette tapes are one example; Naples is one of the world leaders in this thriving industry, and you'll have your choice of thousands of titles along these streets, though it might be a good idea to get them to play your tape before you part with any money. Hundreds of tired-looking folks sit in front of little tables, selling contraband American cigarettes. This is one of the easiest means for Naples' poor to make a living, and it is all controlled by the Camorra. As in New York, whenever it rains, shady characters crawl out of the woodwork selling umbrellas. You will see plenty of designer labels on the *bancarelle*—if they're real, don't ask where they came from.

Piazza del Mercato, south of Garibaldi, is one of the nodes of the Neapolitan bazaar and has been a market square perhaps since Roman times. In the old days this was always the site of major executions, most notably that of 16-year-old Conradin, the rightful heir to the throne, by Charles of Anjou in 1268, an act that shocked all Europe. Charles ordered him buried underneath the Piazza—he couldn't be laid in consecrated ground since he had just been excommunicated for political reasons by Charles's ally the pope.

In 1647 Masaniello's Revolt started here during the festival of Our Lady of Mount Carmel; Masaniello (Tommaso Aniello), a young fisherman of Amalfi, had been chosen by his fellow conspirators to step up in the middle of the ceremonies and proclaim to the people and the viceroy that the new tax the viceroy had introduced 'no longer existed'. As the plotters had hoped, a spontaneous rising followed, and for a week Masaniello ruled Naples while the frightened viceroy locked himself up in Castel Sant'Elmo.

In Naples, unfortunately, such risings can burn out as quickly as a match; the viceroy's spies first secretly drugged Masaniello, so that he appeared drunk or mad to the people, and then in an unguarded moment they murdered him and sent his head to the viceroy. That was the end for Naples, but the incident touched off a wave of revolts across the south that took the Spaniards three years to stamp out.

The Porta Capuana

Northwest of the Piazza Garibaldi, some of Naples' shabbiest streets lead towards the Piazza Enrico de Nicola, once the city's main gate. The **Porta Capuana**, built in 1484, seems a smaller version of the Castel Nuovo's triumphal arch, crowded in by the same squat round towers. The **Castel Capuano**, next to it, began its life as a castle-residence for the Hohenstaufen kings. Since its construction in the 13th century it has been reshaped so many times it doesn't even look like a castle any more; for four centuries it has served as Naples' law courts.

If anything makes wandering into this unlikely district worthwhile, though, it is **Santa Caterina a Formiella**, facing the Porta Capuana, a church by the obscure architect Romolo Balsimelli that is one of the masterpieces of 16th-century Italian architecture. Completed in 1593, the church's bulky, squarish form was a Renaissance eccentricity, but an important stepping-stone towards the baroque. Despite long neglect during which its dome seemed to tilt at a more precarious angle with each year, the church has reopened to the public and further projects are under way for the conservation of its interior.

Museo Archeologico Nazionale

Open Wed–Mon 9am–10pm, Sun and hols 9–8; adm.

Back on the western side of the old city, Via Toledo, after passing Spaccanapoli and changing its name to Via Roma, continues northwards through the **Piazza Dante**, one of the most delightful and animated corners of the city; beyond this, as Via Enrico Pessina, in an area of oversized tenements and busy streets, it opens to display the crumbling red palazzo that contains the National Archaeological Museum.

Naples has the most important collection of Roman-era art and antiquities in the world, due partly to Vesuvius, for burying Pompeii and Herculaneum, and partly to the sharp eyes and deep pockets of the Farnese family—many of the best works here come from the collection they built up over 300 years. Unfortunately, the place is run by Neapolitans; at any given time, half of the collections will be closed for 'restorations' that never seem to happen, and what they condescend to let you see may well be the worst-exhibited and worst-labelled major museum in Europe.

On the first floor, room after room is filled with ancient sculpture. Many of the pieces on view are the best existing Roman-era copies of lost Greek statues, including some by Phidias and Praxiteles; some are masterpieces in their own right, such as the huge, dramatic ensemble called the *Farnese Bull*, the *Tyrannicides* (with other statues' heads stuck on them), and the truly heroic *Farnese Hercules* that once decorated the Baths of Caracalla. Several provocative Aphrodites compete for your attention, along with a platoon of formidable Athenas, the famous *Doryphorus* (spear-bearer), and enough Greek and Roman busts to populate a Colosseum.

Upstairs, most of the rooms are given over to finds from Pompeii. The collection of **Roman mosaics**, mostly from Pompeii and Herculaneum, is one of the two best to be found anywhere (the other is in Antalya, Turkey); the insight it provides into the life and thought of the ancients is priceless. One feature it betrays clearly is a certain fond silliness—plenty of chickens, ducks and grinning cats, the famous *Cave canem* (beware of the dog) mosaic from the front of a house, comic scenes from the theatre, and especially one wonderful panel of crocodiles and hippopotami along the Nile. Some of the mosaics are very consciously 'art': including one showing a detailed scene of the Battle of Issus, where Alexander the Great defeated the Persian king Darius, and one with a view of the Academy of Athens that includes a portrait of Plato.

A recently opened addition is a section devoted entirely to the Temple of Isis at Pompeii. Five rooms display sculptures, frescoes and paintings taken from the temple, which was first discovered in 1765.

Besides the mosaics, nowhere in the world will you find a larger collection of **Roman mural painting** (*see* pp.155–6), and much of it is fascinatingly modern in theme and execution. Many of the walls of Pompeiian villas were decorated with architectural fantasias that seem strangely like those of the Renaissance. Other works show an almost baroque lack of respect for the gods—as in the *Wedding of Zeus and Hera*. Scholars in fact do denote a period of 'Roman baroque', beginning some time about the 2nd century. From it come paintings graced by genuine winged *putti*, called *amoretti* in Roman days. Among the most famous pictures are *The Astragal Players*—young girls shooting craps—and the beautiful *Portrait of an Unknown Woman*, a thoughtful lady holding her pen to her lips who has become one of the best-known images from Roman art.

Other attractions of the museum include large collections of jewellery, coins, fancy gladiators' armour, the famous *sezione pornografica* (*closed for years and unlikely*

to reopen in the foreseeable future), Greek vases, decorative bronzes and a highly detailed, room-sized **scale model** of all excavations up to the 1840s at Pompeii (lovingly restored since the memorable assault on it by the authors' baby boy, back in 1980). The Egyptian collection is not a large one, but it is fun, with a dog-headed Anubis in a Roman toga, some ancient feet under glass, and a mummified crocodile.

North Naples: Capodimonte

North of the museum, the neighbourhoods along Via Toledo—briefly named Via Santa Teresa degli Scalzi—begin to lose some of their Neapolitan intensity as they climb to the suburban heights. On the way, after changing its name again to Corso Amedeo di Savoia, the street passes an area that was full of cemeteries in Roman times. Three Christian underground burial vaults have been discovered here, with a total area of over 100,000 square metres, only part of which has been completely explored.

Two may be visited: the **Catacombe di San Gennaro** (entrance through the courtyard of the Basilica dell'Incoronata a Capodimonte; look for the yellow signs; tours daily at 9.30, 10.15, 11.00 and 11.45; adm) is the more interesting, with extensive early Christian mosaics and frescoes, some as early as the 2nd century. The **Catacombe di San Gaudioso** (tours Sun only at 9.45 and 11.45; adm), which include the 5th-century tomb of the saint of the same name, a martyred African bishop, were discovered under the baroque church of **Santa Maria della Sanità**, on Via Sanità.

The **Parco di Capodimonte**, a well-kept and exotically tropical park, began as a hunting preserve of the Bourbons in the 18th century. Charles III built a Royal Palace here in 1738 that now houses Naples' picture gallery, the **Museo Nazionale di Capodimonte** (open Tues–Sun 9–2; adm). The collection is the best in the south of Italy, and especially rich in works of the late Renaissance. Some of the works you shouldn't miss: an Annunciation by Filippino Lippi; a Botticelli Madonna; the mystical portrait of the mathematician Fra Luca Pacioli by an unknown quattrocento artist; two wry homilies by the elder Brueghel, The Misanthrope and The Blind; works by Masaccio and Mantegna, and a hilarious picture of St Peter Martyr by Lotto, showing that famous anti-Semitic rabble-rouser conversing nonchalantly with the Virgin Mary—with a hatchet sticking out of his head.

Five big, beautifully restored Caravaggios take up one room; others are devoted to important works by Titian. One entire wing of the museum is filled with delightfully frivolous 18th-century **porcelain figurines**; the Bourbons maintained a royal factory for making such things at Capodimonte, which is still in operation today. In another hall, there are scores of 19th-century watercolour scenes of Naples and the Campanian countryside (the best of them by Giacinto Gigante). Here, for the first time, you will see the Naples that so struck the 18th-century travellers. Not much has changed, really; if only all the traffic could magically disappear, it would still be almost the same spectacular city today.

The museum's collections are mostly up on the second floor; the first, the old piano nobile (royal apartments), is still much the way the Bourbons left it. Persevere through the score of overdecorated chambers; the Salotto di porcellana, a little room entirely lined with Capodimonte porcelain, makes the whole thing worthwhile.

The Certosa di San Martino

Up on the highest point overlooking Naples, the 17th-century **Castel Sant'Elmo** (*open Tues–Sun 9–2; adm*) is an impressive enough baroque fortification, partly built of the tufa rock on which it stands (the city now uses it to park the cars the police tow away). Next to it, hogging the best view in Naples, the Carthusians built their original modest, monastery of **San Martino**, some time in the early 14th century. Two centuries later, like most Carthusian branch offices, they were rolling embarrassingly in lucre; building the poshest monastery in all Italy was the only thing to do. The rebuilt **Certosa** (charterhouse) is only marginally smaller than Fort St Elmo. Built on the slope of the mountain, it is supported by a gargantuan platform, visible for miles out to sea and probably containing enough stone to construct a small pyramid.

Nobody knows exactly what is in the **Museo Nazionale di San Martino** (*open Tues–Sun 9–2; adm*), which now occupies the monastery. Intended as a museum specifically of Naples, its history, art and traditions, San Martino suffers from the same mismanagement as the Archaeological Museum; only parts are ever open, and the Grand Cloister, at the time of writing, has become a wilderness of weeds and scaffolding. Not that this should discourage you from taking the long ride up the Montesanto Funicular. The views and the architecture are marvellous, and at least they always keep open the collection of *presepi*—what the Neapolitans come here to see (*see* p.124).

Upon entering the complex, the first attraction is the **church**, another of the glories of Neapolitan baroque, with an excess of lovely coloured inlaid marble to complement the over-abundance of painting. The work over the altar, the *Descent from the Cross*, is one of the finest of José Ribera. This tormented artist, often called *Lo Spagnuolo* in Italy, has paintings all over Naples. His popularity does not owe everything to his artistic talent; apparently he formed a little cartel with two local artists and cornered the market by hiring a gang of thugs to harry all the other painters out of town.

The cloister, the **Chiostro Grande**, even in its present state, is a masterpiece of baroque, elegantly proportioned and gloriously original in its decoration. Also, thanks to a sculptural scheme by a pious, mad artist named Cosimo Fanzago, it is the creepiest cloister east of Seville. Fanzago (who was also one of the architects of San Martino) gives us eight figures of saints that seem more like vampires in priestly robes and mitres, a perfect background for his little enclosed garden, its wall topped with rows of gleaming marble skulls. Most of the collections are in the halls surrounding the Chiostro Grande—costume, painting, ship models and every sort of curiosity; at the corners are **belvederes** from which to look over Naples (outside the complex, a series of lovely terraced gardens offer a similar view). The *presepi* take up a few large rooms near the entrance.

West of the Piazza del Plebiscito

The hill called Pizzofalcone rises directly behind the Piazza del Plebiscito; around it was the site of Parthenope, the Greek town that antedated Neapolis and was eventually swallowed up by it (though Neapolitans still like to refer to themselves as Parthenopeans). Parthenope had a little harbour, formed by an island that is now almost completely covered by the ancient, strangely-shaped fortress of the **Castel dell'Ovo**—the one Master Virgil is said to have built balanced on an egg, hence the name. Most of it was really built by Frederick II, and expanded by the Angevins.

It is closed to the public, but the Egg Castle has been the scene of many unusual events in Italian history. Long before there was a castle, the island may have been part of the original Greek settlement of Parthenope. Later it contained the villa of the Roman general and philosopher Lucullus, victor over Mithridates in the Pontic Wars; Lucullus curried favour with the people by making his sumptuous gardens, and his famous library, open to the public. In the 5th century AD the villa became a home in exile for Romulus Augustulus, last of the western Roman emperors. The Goths spared him only because of his youth and simple-mindedness, and pensioned him off here.

Modern Naples: the Villa Comunale

Once past the Egg Castle, a handsome sweep of coastline opens up the districts of **Chiaia** and **Mergellina**, the most pleasant parts of the new city. Here the long, pretty **Villa Comunale**, central Naples' only park, follows the shore. In it, there is an **Aquarium** (*open winter Tues–Sat 9–5, Sun 9–2; summer Tues–Sat 9–6, Sun 10–6; adm*), built by the German naturalist Dr Anton Dohrn in the 1870s, and perhaps the oldest in the world. All the wide variety of fish, octopuses and other marine delicacies here are from the Bay of Naples; depending on the hour of day, you will either find them fascinating, or else overwhelmingly appetizing. When the Allied armies marched into town in 1943, the Neapolitans put on a big party for the officers. There being practically nothing decent to eat anywhere in Naples, they cleaned out the aquarium and managed an all-seafood menu. General Mark Clark, the commander, is said to have got the aquarium's prize specimen, a baby manatee, though how they prepared it is not recorded.

Ask to see the murals and you will be led upstairs to see Dohrn (who was, incidentally a friend and colleague of Charles Darwin) and some of his other buddies depicted by the German artist Hans von Marees. The wall opposite has local boys frolicking naked under the orange groves. Recently restored after the 1980 earthquake, the murals are an insight into the secret life of aquariums.

Behind the park, on the Riviera di Chiaia, the **Museo Principe di Aragona Pignatelli Cortes** (*open Tues–Sat 9–2, Sun 9–2; adm*) will show you more of the same kind of decorative porcelain as at Capodimonte, along with a score of 18th- and 19th-century noble carriages, furniture and art.

If you're still not tired of little smiling figurines, you can plunge deeper into Chiaia to see the greatest collection of all at the **Museo Nazionale della Ceramica**, also known as the Duca di Martina Museum, but familiar to Neapolitans only as the **Villa Floridiana** (*open Tues–Sun, 9–2; adm*), after the tasteful 18th-century estate it occupies, with one of the loveliest gardens in Naples and one of Italy's great hoards of bric-a-brac. The museum is on Via Cimarosa, near the Funicolare di Chiaia.

Virgil's Tomb

Beginning a few streets beyond the western end of the Villa Comunale, **Mergellina** is one of the brightest and most popular quarters of Naples, a good place for dinner or a *passeggiata* around the busy Piazza Sannazzaro. Its centre is the **Marina**, where besides small craft there are hydrofoils to Sorrento and the islands in the summer months, and excursion boats which do daily tours of the shore between the Egg Castle and Point Posillipo.

From the harbour, Mergellina rises steeply up the surrounding hills; there is a funicular up to the top (every 15 minutes). On the hillside, between the railway bridge and the tunnel that leads under the hill to Fuorigrotta, there is a Roman funerary monument that tradition has always held to be the **Tomb of Virgil** (*open Tues–Sun 9–1*). The poet died in Brindisi in 19 BC on his way back from a trip to Greece. Neapolis was a city dear to him—he wrote most of the *Aeneid* here—and Virgil was brought here for burial, though ancient authors attest that the tomb was closer to the Aquarium.

Just below it lies the entrance to one of the little-known wonders of the ancient world. The **Crypta Neapolitana** (*unfortunately not due to reopen in the foreseeable future*) is a 1,988ft road tunnel, built during the reign of Augustus to connect Neapolis with Puteoli and Baiae, the longest such work the Romans ever attempted.

Shopping

Surprisingly, no one ever thinks of Naples as one of the prime shopping destinations of Italy; this is a mistake, as there are as many pretty and unusual things to be bought here as anywhere else, and usually at lower prices. The back streets around Spaccanapoli and other old sections are still full of artisan workshops of all kinds. The Royal Factory at Capodimonte, founded by the Bourbons, still makes what may be the most beautiful **porcelain and ceramic figures** in Europe, sold at the fancier shops in the city centre. Another old Neapolitan tradition is the making of **cameos** from special seashells; you'll see them everywhere, but the shops outside the Certosa di San Martino have a good selection at relatively low prices.

Via San Biagio dei Librai, the middle of the Spaccanapoli, is as its name implies a street of **booksellers**—some of the best old-book dealers in Italy, conveniently near the University—but the street is also full of many more odd surprises for shoppers as well. Many of the religious goods shops have surprisingly good works in terracotta; the **Doll Hospital** at No.81, ℗ 081 203 067, is one of the most charming shops in Naples.

All around the back streets near the Archaeological Museum, there are antique and junk shops that won't overcharge you unless you let them. The swankiest antique shops tend to be along Via Merelli off Piazza dei Martiri. The city also has an immense twice-monthly antiques market, the **Fiera dell'Antiquariato**, held on alternate Saturday and Sunday mornings in the gardens of the Villa Comunale.

You can buy lovely old prints of Naples and beyond at **Bowinkel**, Piazza dei Martiri 24, ℗ 081 764 4344, and beautiful candles, including some sculpted to depict well-known Italian political and show-business personalities, from the **Antica Cereria**, Via C. Doria 6–8, ℗ 081 549 9745. For the once-in-a-lifetime souvenir, the

150-year-old **Fonderia Chiurazzi**, Via Ponti Rossi 271, ✆ 081 751 2685, makes artistic bronzes, specializing in reproductions of works in the Museo Archeologico; if you have billions of lire to spare, they'll do them life-size, or even bigger.

For **clothes and shoes** the best area is again off Piazza dei Martiri, in particular along the flashy Via Chiaia. You can find its other end just to the right of the central Piazza del Plebiscito.

Last of all do not miss the *bancarelle* and open street markets around Piazza Garibaldi. The daily catch of fish, live squid and octopus is a must, just to the right off Corso Garibaldi. Here you can also find fruit stalls that sell lemons from the Sorrentine peninsula which are too big to cup with both hands.

Naples ✉ *80100*   ***Where to Stay***

Naples can present real problems for the casual traveller who arrives expecting to pick up a reasonably priced room without difficulty, a situation that only gets worse as Naples becomes more popular. There are many options at either extreme of the price range but few good choices in between.

The best area to stay is undoubtedly down on the waterfront where you have easy access to shopping, museums and good restaurants. It's less claustrophobic too. The area around the station offers thousands of cheap rooms, but many of them are in horrible dives. Sticking to those selected here you shouldn't go too wrong and at least you'll be safe.

very expensive

Naples does have less than its share of top-quality hotels; the Germans, inexplicably, blew up a few of them before their retreat in 1944. Three of the best are located in a row along Via Partenope, overlooking the Castel dell'Ovo, where the views over the bay more than compensate for the traffic noise below.

Visiting sheiks, kings and rock stars favour the ★★★★**Excelsior**, Via Partenope 48, ✆ 081 764 0111, 🖷 081 764 9743, Naples' finest, with beautiful suites and a tradition of perfect service ever since 1909. You pay for space—elegant lounges, a beautiful rooftop solarium and restaurant, rooms with large beds and antique-style furniture. Above all, this is a place for those who think the hotel is the most important part of the holiday. Being on the right of the three, it faces Vesuvius.

That's annoying for the ★★★★**Vesuvio**, Via Partenope 45, ✆ 081 764 0044, 🖷 081 764 4483, which otherwise provides the same. However, it has a lovely roof garden for dining, important since none of these hotels' rooms have good balconies.

The ★★★★**Santa Lucia**, Via Partenope 46, ✆ 081 764 0666, 🖷 081 764 8580, a beautifully restored 18th-century *palazzo*, is sandwiched between the others. Rooms are less grand, with fussy floral curtains and a distinctly Laura Ashley feel. In face of the competition and its lack of roof garden, the management has clearly opted for the corporate crowd, offering extensive conference facilities.

Still on the seafront, the ★★★★**Miramare**, Via N. Sauro 24, ✆ 081 764 7589, ✉ 081 764 0775, is the find in this category. The manager Enzo Rosalino exudes the kind of old-world charm more often found outside cities. His infectious goodwill is apparent in the array of personal touches to each of his 31 rooms. The atmosphere is intimate. Some rooms are too small but the old lift and rooftop solarium (where he plans to reopen his restaurant) more than make up. The rooms that don't face the sea are quieter.

Other good bets are the ★★★★**Paradiso**, Via Catullo 11, ✆ 081 761 4161, ✉ 081 761 3449, with stunning views over the bay—make sure you book a sea-facing room. For a more old-fashioned atmosphere, but further inland (near the Cumana stop Corso V.E.), try the ★★★★**Parker's**, Corso Vittorio Emanuele 135, ✆ 081 761 2474, ✉ 081 663 527, which has ample charm, with plenty of polished wood, chandeliers and comfortable furniture.

Lastly the ★★★★**Angioino**, Via de Pretis 123, ✆ 081 552 9500, ✉ 081 552 9509, owned by the French Mercure hotel chain, offers 86 good-sized rooms in a central location (a minute from Piazza Municipio), with efficient service that makes it popular with the business crowd. The views are unspectacular, the furnishings functional—you feel you could be in any city— but all rooms are comfortable and sound proofed. It is a good base.

moderate

Near the Stazione Centrale, the ★★★**Cavour**, Piazza Garibaldi 32, ✆ 081 283 122, ✉ 081 287 488, is a well-run decent hotel in an otherwise desperate area. Book the top-floor suites for little more than a standard room. These enjoy ample terraces and good views over Vesuvius, and are a respite from the bustle below. Rooms are nicely decorated in the omnipresent Liberty style. Bathrooms are good in an area where the plumbing hasn't been overhauled since the Greeks. The restaurant gets two Michelin *fourchettes*. Otherwise near the pretty Mergellina esplanade the good-value ★★★**Canada**, Via Mergellina 43, ✆ 081 680 952, ✉ 081 681 594, offers 12 comfortable rooms where you won't want for TV, safe, minibar, hairdryer or ceiling fans. The hotel has no pretensions and a miserable excuse for a breakfast area. It is, however, well placed for the evening *passeggiata* here.

Back in the central S. Lucia districts the ★★★**Rex**, Via Palepoli 12, ✆ 081 764 9389, ✉ 081 764 9227, is slightly more expensive offering simple rooms with bare 70s-style furnishings. If you like lots of brown wood and breakfast in bed— there are no public areas in the hotel—then this is fine as a base in this good area.

Lastly the ★★**Ausonia**, Via Caracciolo 11, ✆/✉ 081 682 278, is a clean, comfortable *pensione* with 20 rooms and a nautical character to its decoration. There are portholes around the numbers and nautical theme bedspreads. The owner is kind and cheerful. The rooms are well-appointed, each with TV and video recorder (tapes are also available in English). Located within a *palazzo*, looking on to an interior courtyard, this is the quiet option for the Mergellina area.

Naples has a dearth of reasonable cheap hotels. The ****Fontane al Mare**, Via N. Tommaseo 14, ✆ 081 764 3811, is definitely worth booking in advance. There are only 21 rooms located on the last two floors of an old palazzo next to the Chiaia gardens. To take the lift, you will need to bring L100 coins! Ask for rooms without bathroom since they enjoy the great sea view and are better value. Breakfast is available and costs extra. This hotel has character, but bear in mind that it's well known and popular with the local *carabinieri* college.

As already mentioned, many of the cheap places are to be found around Piazza Garibaldi. It should be stressed that the hotels around here are invariably substandard. They are at best a place to sleep and certainly not a good holiday base.

Elsewhere in Italy you can visit good one-star hotels and feel you have had a bargain but not here. A good night's sleep in this area depends pretty much on your neighbours. Best in the category is the ***Zara**, Via Firenze 81, ✆ 081 287 125, with 10 rooms, two with baths. Here they operate a racist vetting procedure only admitting Poles and other Europeans in an area crowded with illegal immigrants from Africa.

The Polish-Italian ***Fiore**, Via Milano 109, ✆ 081 553 8798—once rumoured to have Naples' fattest cat, now replaced by Lilly the dog—is barely acceptable, but good for the area (remember to bring L50 coins for the lift). Next to the Porta Nolana, the ***Colombo**, Via Nolana 35, ✆ 081 269 254, offers grubby-looking rooms, each with TV—hence the reinforced steel doors—but noisy hookers arriving back late in the small hours can make sleeping difficult.

Another place to look for cheap accommodation is Via Mezzocannone, south of Spaccanapoli. This street borders the university, and many of the most pleasant cheap lodgings in Naples can be found here—though with so many students it may be hard to find a vacancy. Naples' **youth hostel** is the **Ostello Mergellina**, Salita della Grotta 23, ✆ 081 761 2346, ✆ 081 761 2391, near the Mergellina Metropolitana station. IYHF cards are required.

Naples ✉ *80100*   **Eating Out**

> *Now, everyone thinks of China as a ponderous, elephantine country; Naples, on the other hand we think of as something exciting, stimulating. Perhaps the Chinese invented slow, pacific fat macaronis, not the spaghetti that moves like the waves of the sea ...*
>
>   Domenico Rea

This local savant, writing in *Qui Napoli*, is carrying on one of Naples' grand old causes. Forget those old legends about Marco Polo—just imagine anyone brazen enough to say spaghetti doesn't originally come from Naples! This capital of cooking, this citadel of *Italianità*, can already claim pizza, and probably many other Italian specialities as well.

Neapolitans spend as much time worrying about what's for dinner as any people in the world, but like most other Italians they have a perfectly healthy attitude towards the subject. Neapolitan cuisine is simple—one of the most celebrated dishes is *spaghetti alle vongole*—and even in some of the more pretentious places you will see favourites of the Neapolitan *cucina povera* sneaking onto the menu, like *pasta e fagioli*. There are very few bad restaurants or tourist restaurants in the city, but an infinity of tiny, family-run *trattorie* or *pizzerie*; you will depart from most of them serene and satisfied.

For famous Neapolitan pizza, look for the genuine Neapolitan pizza oven, a built-in, bell-shaped affair made of stone with a broad, clean tile floor; the fire (only certain kinds of wood will do) is at the back, close to the pizza, not hidden underneath out of sight.

Watch out in restaurants for the house wines; in cheaper places this is likely to be Gragnano from nearby Monte Faito—detestable rough stuff. On the other hand you can find some real surprises from Campania; a dry white called Greco di Tufo, and Taurasi, a distinguished red—as well as Falerno, the descendant of the far-famed ancient *Falernian* that Latin poets never tired of praising. Some restaurants in Naples, you will find, are the cheapest in all Italy—as they cheat on their taxes. Others can be alarmingly expensive, especially if you order fish.

Restaurants in all price ranges are spread pretty evenly around central Naples. For romantic harbour-side dinners, it's difficult to beat the Borgo Marinara beside the Castel Dell'Ovo where you will find the whole marina area set aside for dining. The Mergellina area also does pretty well. Up nearer the historic centre you will find character; poky streets with poky restaurants whose chefs pop over to the local street sellers for their fresh veg. For those in the know, other less likely spots harbour one or two treats as well.

Many of the cheapest and homeliest places in Naples can be found on or around Via Speranzella, a block west of Via Toledo in the *Tavoliere*, where few tourists ever penetrate. As for the area around the railway station, restaurants here, more than elsewhere in Naples, have succumbed to opportunity and necessity; Piazza Garibaldi isn't nearly as much fun as it was a few years ago, and its hundreds of restaurants are neither keeping standards up nor prices down. But this area, and also Piazza Mercato, is an open bazaar, and you can get fat and happy just snacking from the bars and stands—slices of pizza, heavy *arancini*, and the flaky pastries called *sfogliatelle*, another Naples speciality.

expensive

La Cantinella, Via Nazario Sauro 23, ✆ 081 464 8684, near the Castel dell'Ovo on the esplanade, is believed by many to be Naples' finest restaurant—it's also the place to be seen for the Parthenopeans, with a telephone on each table, which they retain despite the invention of mobile phones. Their *linguine Santa Lucia*, made with home-made pasta, octopi, squid, prawns, clams and fresh baby tomatoes, takes some beating. The risotto is also excellent. Though it certainly isn't cheap, you can easily spend more in other establishments nearby. The atmosphere is smart but relaxed and the service friendly.

Close by, in an excellent location beneath the Castel dell'Ovo, lies **La Bersagliera**, Borgo Marinara 10, ℃ 081 764 6016. The large 1900s restaurant cuts an elegant image despite the tacked-on '80s extension, the fish is delicious and the wine good too, especially the white Fiano de Avellino. *Closed Tues.*

Closer to the civic centre is **Ciro**, Via Santa Brigida 71, ℃ 081 552 4072, near the Castel Nuovo. Go ahead and order *pasta e fagioli* or any other humble pasta dish; that's what the place is famous for, typical Naples cuisine at its best. They also do pizzas and are *numero uno* on the Vera Pizza trail. They have been around for decades but the restaurant is smartly refurbished and without the character that a place of its reputation might lead you to expect. *Closed Sun.*

On the heights at Mergellina is **La Sacrestia**, Via Orazio 116, ℃ 081 761 1051, run for generations by the Ponsiglione family and another temple of Neapolitan gastronomy, in a superb location overlooking the Bay of Naples. Try the risotto with baby squid (*risotto con neonati di seppietta*). *Closed Mon.*

Giuseppone a Mare, Via Ferdinando Russo 13, ℃ 081 575 6002, overlooking Cape Posillipo since 1889, is one of Naples' institutions, especially popular with wedding parties. The fish is excellent, the setting memorable, and you probably won't forget the bill either. *Closed Mon.*

On the Mergellina esplanade, **Don Salvatore**, Via Mergellina 5, ℃ 081 681 817, has been around for over 40 years, during which time it has built up a well-deserved reputation for turning out consistently fine Neapolitan dishes, accompanied by some of the area's best wines. There are set menus for those who want an introduction to Naples' best, and pizza for those who want to keep the bill down. *Closed Wed.*

Lastly, a nice surprise in the area at the end of Piazza Garibaldi is **Mimì alla Ferrovia**, Via Alfonso d'Aragona 19, ℃ 081 553 8525, popular with the local media posse. Again, you'll find no new-fangled concoctions, just honest-to-goodness dishes based on the freshest ingredients and recipes handed down for generations. The speciality here is *pasta e ceci*, a khaki-green soup of flat pasta and chick peas to be savoured with closed eyes. Don't worry about the brusque service but concentrate on the seafood and excellent mozzarella. *Closed Sun.*

moderate

Off the Villa Communale approaching Piazza Sannazzaro, **La Cantina di Triunfo**, Riviera di Chiaia 64, ℃ 081 668 101, offers Neapolitan *cucina povera* raised to an art form—wintry soups of chestnuts and lentils, or lighter versions of broad beans and fresh peas in spring, *polpette di baccalà*—small balls of minced salt-cod, fried or served in a fresh tomato sauce—and mouth-watering pasta dishes, all of which change according to the season. Desserts are as good as everything else. The *crostata d'arance e mandorle* (an orange and almond tart) is excellent. The wine list is also exceptional, and many of the grappas—there are 80 types to choose from— home-made. Be sure to book, as space is very limited. *Closed Sun.*

Back on the esplanade of Via Partenope beyond the Castel dell'Ovo but before the Villa Communale, track down the **Taverna e Zi Carmela**, Via Niccolò Tommaseo

11/12, ℗ 081 764 3581. Aunt Carmela runs a busy and well-kept ship, with excellent home cooking, much of it done by herself, and other members of the family waiting at table. The speciality here, once more, is seafood. *Closed Sun.*

Up near the Mergellina end, **O Sole Mio**, Via Tommaso Campanella 7, ℗ 081 761 2323, is run by a fisherman's family, and though you will find some meat on the menu, you will be better advised to go straight for the seafood, in all its many forms. Try the wonderfully tasty *cassuola di pesce* (fish casserole) but tuck your napkin into your collar, Neapolitan-style, before you start! *Closed Tues.*

cheap

Pizza is always the best friend of the budget-minded tourist (*see* below), and you can get two superb pizzas and lots of wine (for the price of a plate of pasta in some smarter places) at **Da Pasqualino**, Piazza Sannazzaro 78/9, ℗ 081 681 524, in Mergellina. If you need cigarettes, shout 'Gennaro!' to the balconies above and they will appear. Don't miss the old granny in the corner, whose job it is to make the superb but calorie-laden *crocchette*—potato croquettes spiked with mozzarella cheese, with which the locals invariably start their meal. Sitting out in the piazza this is as simple as it gets but not to be missed. *Closed Tues.*

For a quick snack, **Da Michele**, Via Sersale 1 ℗ 081 553 9204, is the place to go. Neapolitans cluster outside it and it might be the only place you'll ever see them queueing with their little tickets, in order to taste their superb massive pizzas. They only come in two models: *margherita* and *marinara*.

In the historic centre, the **Pizzeria Port'Alba**, Via Port'Alba 18, ℗ 081 459 713, founded in 1830, will do excellent pizzas for both lunch and dinner. You can also get full dinners, including the house speciality, *linguine al cartoccio*—seafood pasta made into a foil parcel and baked in the oven—for a reasonable sum (it is vast so go easy on the antipasti). You can choose either to sit outside under the Port'Alba itself or inside, in which case the upstairs area is more snug. Just across the road at the **Bellini**, Via Santa Maria di Costantinopoli 80, ℗ 081 459 774, you'll find more good pizza and pasta dishes, with a few outdoor tables for summer dining. Once more, *linguine al cartoccio* are on offer, or opt for *pesce alla griglia. Closed Sun.*

Slightly more upmarket, but only slightly, the **Lombardi a Santa Chiara**, Via Benedetto Croce 59, ℗ 081 552 0780, just off Piazza del Gesù Nuovo, offers memorable *antipasti* of fried courgettes, baby mozzarella and artichokes, before you ever get to eat your pizza, wonderfully cooked in the classic wood oven. Noisy but friendly, this place fills up quickly, so book ahead or be prepared to wait. *Closed Sun.*

Brandi, Salita Sant'Anna di Palazzo 1/2, ℗ 081 416 928, a pretty, lively pizzeria, claims to have invented the *margherita*, Naples' most famous pizza, with mozzarella, tomatoes and fresh basil, in honour of the 19th-century queen whose favourite dish it apparently was. She would pick up up pizza on the way back from balls, to eat cold in the morning. They have two floors and a small terrace. The seafood pizza includes octopi cooked with their ink sacks intact!

Cheap and homely, but occupying a million-dollar position down on the Borgo Marinara next to the Castel dell'Ovo, **Patrizia**, Via Luculliano 24, has barely seven tables and no menu. They serve you wine in plastic cups and tell you their daily fare, as you relax next door to far more prestigious establishments. The food is delicious and the prices downright ridiculous. *Spaghetti alle cozze* made with fresh *pomodorini* is one of their staples. The grilled *scamorza* cheese and aubergine is likewise delectable.

An amazing bargain, the **Trattoria Nennella**, Vico Lungo Teatro Nuovo 103–105, in the *Quartieri Spagnuoli*, offers true Neapolitan food and spirit in a simple setting (paper cups and tablecloths and photocopied hand-written menus); while signora Nennella plots your meal in the kitchen, her son runs the show. Don't be surprised to see lots of men in suits having their lunch break—local businessmen discovered it long ago. You are likely to be the only foreigner. *Open weekdays at lunch time only.*

Finally, we offer you an honest breakfast—bacon and eggs, if you like—at the **Ristorante California**, Via Santa Lucia 101, ✆ 081 764 9752, Italy's greatest rendez-vous for homesick Americans and a longtime Naples landmark. For dinner, the menu is split between Italian and Gringo dishes, and the roast turkey isn't bad. *Closed Sun.*

Pizza Paradise

Its origins are almost certainly Arab. Some people claim its name is derived from *pitta*, the unleavened bread eaten throughout Greece, Turkey and the Middle East. But wherever it hails from, pizza as we know it is an invention of Naples. Neapolitans are fiercely proud of this versatile dish, and haughtily disdainful of imitations and the variations made by others on the formula—the thin-crusted affair served in Roman *pizzerie* is enough to make a Neapolitan cry. And as for the deep-pan version invented in Chicago and served up in many British and American pizza parlours—the less said the better.

For Neapolitans, a real pizza must have an uneven base and be cooked in a real wood-fired oven. Some say the secret is in the flour, others in the water. But all agree the technique for flattening the dough is crucial. Not for the Neapolitans the pedantic practice of stretching out the dough with a rolling pin. In Naples, the *pizzaiolo* is a flamboyant character, flinging the dough up into the air, smashing it down on the marble table and swinging it round his head until it reaches the required shape and thickness. The best *pizzaioli* are much in demand, and take home very respectable pay. As for the topping, the most authentic is *pomodoro fresco*—fresh tomatoes chopped over a bed of mozzarella, sprinkled with fresh basil and liberally doused with olive oil. Another Neapolitan favourite is the *ripieno*, a gut-buster of a pizza folded in two, and stuffed with fresh ricotta, mozzarella, pieces of salami and cooked ham.

However you order it, pizza should really be eaten with beer rather than wine. Many pizzerias only serve fizzy, bottled wine, which is much more expensive and best left alone. Pizza is usually eaten as a meal in itself, sometimes for lunch but more often in the evening, preceded by an *antipasto* of *bruschetta*—slices of thick toasted bread soused in olive oil and garlic and topped with tomatoes and basil, or fried bite-sized chunks of mozzarella and vegetables.

For anyone on a tight budget—Neapolitans or tourists—the pizzeria is a lifeline. The bill for a pizza and a beer comes to about half that of a meal in a normal restaurant. In Naples, particularly good pizzerias are rewarded by a *vera pizza* (real pizza) emblem to hang up outside. Some of the best are the **Lombardi a Santa Chiara** and the exceptional **Da Pasqualino**, now in its fourth generation (for details *see* above).

---

cafés and gelaterie

As well as being the inventors of the pizza, Neapolitans are, it is generally recognized, Italy's most dedicated and punctilious coffee consumers (*see* p.50), and the city accordingly has its crop of elegant, ornate (though now often faded) 19th-century *gran caffè*, mostly not too far from the Galleria and the Piazza del Plebiscito (*see* above).

The best location is occupied by **Gambrinus**, Piazza Trieste e Trento, ✆ 081 417 582, overlooking the Teatro San Carlo and Piazza Plebiscito, but as you would expect it's not cheap. Other fine places to take coffee can be found along the waterfront, particularly out towards Mergellina; look out for **Ciro**, generally considered the best.

Naples also, naturally, produces some great ice cream and pastries. *Gelaterie* can be found all over town, but **Scimmia**, Piazza della Carità 4, just off the Via Toledo not far from Spaccanapoli, has long been regarded as one of the city's best. For an ice cream with a view **Bilancione**, via Posillipo, will supply both. Last of all, for *sfogliatelle*, **Scaturchio**, Piazza San Domenico Maggiore, is acclaimed as the great *pasticceria* of Naples.

Entertainment and Nightlife

For concerts, shows, and other cultural events—Naples always has plenty—the best information on programmes and times will be found in the newspaper *Il Mattino*, or in the free monthly guide *Qui Napoli*.

opera, classical music and theatre

For opera-lovers one of the ultimate experiences is a night at the **San Carlo** (box office ✆ 081 797 2370/081 797 2111), but tickets are extremely hard to come by, and very pricey. Hotels may be able to get them most easily. Otherwise you must go to the box office in person. If you do manage to get a ticket, dress your best.

You may have more luck catching a **concert** at the **Auditorium RAI-TV**, Via Guglielmo Marconi (Fuorigrotta), ✆ 081 725 1111, at the **Conservatorio San Pietro a Maiella**, Via San Pietro a Maiella, ✆ 081 459 255, or at the **Associazione Alessandro Scarlatti**, Piazza dei Martiri 58, ✆ 081 406 011, which holds concerts for jazz, chamber music and a bit of everything.

Check with the tourist office or in *Qui Napoli* for programmes, and don't forget also that many, often free, concerts are staged in the city's churches. Look out for street billboards with details of coming events. Tickets for major events may be obtainable at the ticket offices in the **Box Office**, Galleria Umberto I 15–16, ✆ 081 551 9188 and **Concerteria**, Via Schipa 23, ✆ 081 761 1221.

Unless your Italian is fluent, **theatre** will probably be a frustrating experience, and if you go for one of the superbly executed dialect plays, you may not understand a word. If that doesn't put you off, the best theatres to try are the **Politeama**, Via Monte di Dio, ✆ 081 764 5016, the **Cilea**, Via S. Domenico, ✆ 081 714 3110, the **Bracco**, Via Tarsia 40, ✆ 081 549 5904, and the **Sannazaro**, Via Chiaia 157, ✆ 081 411 723.

clubs, bars and discos

Neapolitans are night-owls, probably thanks to their Spanish heritage, and many, especially in summer, don't even think about going out to dinner until 10pm. That doesn't leave too much time for partying, once the 2–3 hour ritual of eating is over, but there are some reasonable clubs and late-night bars (as well as some terrible ones). The thing to remember is that some areas are best left alone after midnight, most notably the Piazza Garibaldi area near the station, and the so-called *quartiere*, the narrow side streets that run off the Via Toledo. And if the vampish hookers to be seen at every street corner after dark should take your fancy, remember to take a second look—those girls could well be boys. Naples is famous even in drag-obsessed Italy for its transvestites, and some of them are positively remarkable. The genuine female prostitutes tend to be the crones on the other side of the street.

It's worth checking with the locals where their most popular night spots are since the popularity of haunts can change with the current fads. Neapolitans tend to bop the weekends away, so very few open during the week. You will rarely pay over L30,000 to get in—the fairer sex often get in for less or even for free—which normally includes a drink. Remember that things never kick off until after midnight, so if you turn up before bring your own crowd.

A list of clubs can be found in *Qui Napoli* but for a start we include **La Mela**, Via dei Mille 41, ✆ 081 413 881, which has good reports from the young and beautiful crowd. The **Madison Street**, Via Sgambati 47, ✆ 081 546 6566, Naples' biggest disco, is an institution, with different theme nights (Saturday is gay night) and an affluent young crowd. **My Way**, Via Cappella Vecchia 30/c, ✆ 081 764 4735, is another popular nightspot, where Neapolitans have been dancing into the small hours for as long as anyone can remember. **Velvet**, Via Cisterna dell'Olio, in the historic centre, is an alternative disco with a rougher edge.

At the **Otto Jazz Club**, Piazzetta Cariati 23, ✆ 081 552 4373, you'll get **jazz** which looks for inspiration as much to the famous Neapolitan folk songs as to New Orleans. It also serves plates of pasta and light meals, and has a well-stocked bar serving 200 cocktails (their specials are beer-based!). Don't take too much cash with you, as this otherwise very pleasant club is in a pretty hard area—when you leave it's best to get a taxi rather than walk around much outside. *Open Thurs–Sun.* The **Virgilio Sporting Club**, Via Tito Lucrezio Caro 6, © 081 769 5261, up on Posillipo Hill, is a much more tranquil nightclub, set in its own parkland, with tables outside in fine weather. *Open Fri–Sun midnight–4am.*

The bars of **Via Paladino** are where it all happens (*movida*, Napoli-style). **Piazza Bellini**, especially in summer, is the spot where the young and trendy come to see and be seen; it is also one of the few piazzas in Naples whose cafés have outside tables. Try to get a table at **Intra Moenia,** the literary café-cum-publishing house, © 081 200 720.

Ferdinandstrasse, Piazza Porta Nova 8, © 081 207 390, is a gay disco-bar, particularly crowded on Sundays.

Sports and Activities

The best sources of information on forthcoming events of all kinds are the local newspaper *Il Mattino* and the free multilingual monthly guide *Qui Napoli.* Many of the city's permanent attractions are concentrated in the Fuorigrotta district, west of Mergellina. **Edenlandia**, © 081 239 1182, is the big amusement park there, on Viale Kennedy in the Mostra d'Oltremare, Naples' big trade fair site (take the Ferrovia Cumana to the station of the same name). There is also a **dog-racing** track and a small but fun **zoo** (*open daily 9–5; adm*) in the same area (bus route 152 from the Stazione Centrale passes the gates).

Nearby on Via Fuorigrotta, just past the tunnel, there's **jai-alai** (Basque Pelota) every night at 8pm. Anything a Neapolitan can bet on flourishes here; the **race-track**, the *Ippodromo di Agnano*, with both thoroughbred and trotting races throughout most of the year, is out west in Agnano, 10km from the city centre along the *tangenziale*.

And of course there's always **football**. With the help of Diego Armando Maradona, Napoli won its first-ever league title in 1987; since his departure the club has fallen on harder times, but every significant victory still calls forth a spontaneous celebration all over town that seems like Carnival in Rio de Janeiro, and any match is likely to prove an unforgettable experience with the Neapolitans to make up the crowd. Matches are played at the **Stadio San Paolo**, Piazzale Vincenzo Tecchio, © 081 239 5623. To get there, take the Ferrovia Cumana to Mostra or the Metropolitana to Campi Flegrei.

However tempting the sea off Naples might look on a scorching summer day, it's worth waiting until you get to one of the islands before taking a plunge. There is a public **swimming pool**, the **Piscina Scandone**, Via Giochi del Mediterraneo, also in the Fuorigrotta area of town, © 081 570 2636.

Tennis can be played at **Tennis Club Napoli**, Viale Dohrn, © 081 761 4656, in the Villa Comunale, **Tennis Club Vomero**, Via Rossini 8, © 081 658 912, and the **Virgilio Sporting Club**, Via Tito Lucrezio Caro 6, © 081 769 5261.

Vesuvius and the Ancient Cities

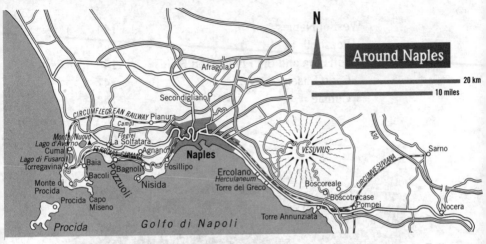

20 km
10 miles

In Roman days, the land around the Bay of Naples was *Campania Felix*—fortunate Campania, the richest and most beautiful province of Italy, its seaside villas the chosen abodes of the Roman élite. The Campanian shore was nothing less than the California of the ancient world: lined with glittering resort towns full of refugees from the Roman rat-race, as favoured by artists and poets as by rich patricians. As with California, though, the perfume hid a little whiff of danger.

Despite its fearsome reputation, and its formidable appearance looming over Naples, Mount Vesuvius is a midget as volcanoes go—only 4,202ft. No one even suspected it was a volcano until it surprised the people of Pompeii, Herculaneum, and Stabiae on 24 August AD 79. That titanic eruption did not include much lava, but it buried Herculaneum under mud and the other two cities under cinders and ash, while coating most of Italy with a thin layer of dust. After that explosion Roman writers noted that the plume of smoke and ash over the volcano looked like a young pine tree; observers have noted the same sinister shape in many eruptions in more recent years.

West of Naples

Here, where Rome's prosperous élite once kept their marble pleasure palaces (*see* pp.46–7), are eternally rising and sinking landscapes, sulphurous pools, thermal springs and even a baby volcano—altogether, perhaps the most unstable corner of the broad earth's crust.

Getting Around

by rail

Naples' own **Metropolitana FS** goes as far as Pozzuoli-Solfatara (there are trains every eight minutes). The two other regional lines both have trains about every half-hour from Piazza Montesanto Station, near the Piazza Dante.

The **Ferrovia Cumana** (© 081 551 3328) runs along the shore, through Fuorigrotta, Bagnoli, Pozzuoli and Baia to Torregaveta (trains every 10 minutes).

The remarkable **Circumflegrea** (also © 081 551 3328) also finishes at Torregáveta, after passing through plenty of places you probably won't want to visit (trains every 20 minutes) but usually only as far as Licola. For the stop at the archaeological site of Cumae it runs six trains daily, three in the morning and three in the afternoon. The Circumflegrea is easily the most macabre railway in the western world: the trip begins by passing a neon shrine to the Virgin Mary in the middle of the Montesanto Tunnel, and then passes through stations that are metal sheds or bombed-out ruins, with smashed and derailed cars lying alongside the tracks to give passengers something to think about. The station at Cumae is gutted and abandoned; those dodging the entrance fee can head up towards the acropolis through the thorn bushes and dense adder-haunted forests.

by bus

Naples city bus no.152, from Piazza Garibaldi and Via Mergellina, travels to Solfatara and Pozzuoli. There is a blue bus run by Sepsa departing from Piazza Garibaldi and calling at Solfatara, Pozzuoli and Baia. From the bus stop in the centre of Baia, there are connecting buses to Cumae, Bacoli and Cape Misenum.

by road

Drivers heading for the west bay area and wishing to arrive quite quickly should get on to the *tangenziale* out of Naples and stay on it until past Pozzuoli, before turning off on to the (by then) more tranquil SS7qu, which runs around the Miseno peninsula. Alternately, they can take the SS7qu all the way from the harbourside in Naples, via the Mergellina tunnel, or the pretty but slow coastal road—initially the Via Posillipo—around Cape Posillipo.

Tourist Information

Pozzuoli: Via Campi Flegrei 9, © 081 526 1481.

Pozzuoli

The very pretty coastal road leaving the city, with views of Vesuvius all through the suburb of Posillipo, passes the little island of Nisida; this was a favoured spot in ancient times, and legend has it that Brutus and Cassius planned Caesar's murder here in the villa of one of their fellow conspirators. Naples' suburbs continue through **Agnano**, a town of spas and hot springs set around a mile-wide extinct crater, and stretch as far as Pozzuoli.

Pozzuoli, Sophia Loren's home town, today is a modest little city, with only its ruins to remind it of the time when Roman Puteoli, and not Naples, was the metropolis of the bay. In the time of Caesar and Augustus it was the main port of Italy; at one point the Senate actually considered the bizarre idea of digging a 160-mile-long canal to Rome to make shipping safer. The city's decline began in the 2nd century with the emperor Trajan's expansion of the port of Ostia, closer to Rome. During the 5th-century invasions, most of Puteoli's citizens took refuge in better-defended Naples.

The **Amphitheatre** (*open daily 9am–one hour before sunset; adm*), on Via Domiziana, near the railway station, was the third largest in the Roman world (after those in Rome and Capua), with 60 gates for letting the wild beasts in. It is remarkable for the preservation of its subterranean structure where the scenery, changing rooms and cells for storing the wild animals prior to shows (*venationes*) were located. The long cavity in the centre was for hoisting up scenery. Unlike the chambers underneath, which were buried in mud and land-slides, the stands were exposed and thus were stripped of their masonry through the ages (visitors are not allowed on to them). The amphitheatre was built under Vespasian who renamed the city **Colonia Flavia Augusta Puteoli**, in thanks to Puteoli for its aid in the civil war that made him emperor. This was the second amphitheatre in Pozzuoli. Only a few broken arches of the older one survive, 100m to the north. It was probably used for gladiatorial combats.

Pozzuoli's other important ruin is a little embarrassment to the town; for centuries people here were showing off the ancient **Serapeum**—temple to the popular Egyptian god Serapis—until some killjoy archaeologist proved the thing to be an unusually lavish *macellum*, or market. Only the foundations remain, in a park near Pozzuoli's small harbour.

For all ancient Puteoli's size and wealth, little else remains. There is a reason, and Pozzuoli would like to introduce a new word to your vocabulary to explain it. *Bradyseism* is a rare seismic phenomenon that afflicts this town and other spots around the bay. It manifests itself in the form of 'slow' earthquakes. The level of the land fell nearly 20ft since Roman times only to begin rising in the 15th century. Most recently falling, all of Puteoli that hasn't been gently shaken to pieces over the centuries is now underwater. Roman moles and docks can still sometimes be made out beneath the surface.

Solfatara and the Phlegraean Fields

What's troubling Pozzuoli can be seen more clearly just outside the town at Solfatara, the storm centre of what the Greeks called the **Phlegraean** (fiery) **Fields**, in Italian the *Campi Flegrei*. To the Romans, it was the *Forum Vulcani*, and a major attraction of the Campanian coast. It hasn't changed much since. Solfatara (*open daily 8.30–one hour before sunset; adm*) is another crater of a collapsed volcano, but one that just can't be still; sulphur gas vents, bubbling mud pits and whistling superheated steam fumaroles decorate the eerie landscape. Guides are around to keep you away from the dangerous spots. Their favourite trick is to hold a smoking torch to one of the fumaroles—making a dozen others nearby go off at the same time. The effect is produced by the steam condensing around smoke particles. Solfatara is perfectly safe, even though the ground underneath feels hot and sounds strangely hollow. It is; scientists keep a close watch on the huge plug of cooled lava that underlies the whole of the area about Pozzuoli, and they say the pressure on it from below is only one-third as much as it was under Vesuvius in AD 79.

We promised you a baby volcano, and you'll see it near the coast to the west of Pozzuoli. **Monte Nuovo** has been quiet for some time (inexplicably passing up the opportunity to celebrate its 450th birthday, on 29 September 1988). The same earthquake in 1538 that wrecked much of Pozzuoli gave birth to this little cone. It's only about 460ft tall, and an easy climb up to the crater (you can have a picnic inside it). Its percolation from the bowels of

Campania filled up half of the **Lago di Lucrino**, separated from the sea by a narrow strip of land. Since antiquity, it has been renowned for its oysters. About 90 BC, a sharp Roman named C. Sergius Orata first had the idea of farming oysters here, and selling them to the rich owners of the villas around the bay; from this business he made one of the biggest killings of classical antiquity.

Capo Miseno

Baia, the next town along the coast, was nothing less than the greatest pleasure dome of classical antiquity (*see* **Snapshots**, pp.46–7). Anybody who was anybody in the Roman world had a villa here, with a view of the sea, beach access, and a few hundred slaves to dust the statues and clean up after the orgies. You'll find little hint of that today: Goths, malaria and earthquakes have done a thorough job of wrecking the place. Most of ancient Baiae is now underwater, a victim of the same bradyseism that afflicts Pozzuoli. In summer, a glass-bottomed boat departs from Baia harbour to see this Roman Atlantis (✆ 081 526 57 80; *Sat 12 and 4, Sun 10.30, 12 and 4; tour lasts 70 mins*). Modern Baia is a pleasant small town, but its lovely bay has been consigned to use as a graveyard for dead freighters. Nevertheless, the extensive but humble remains of the imperial villa can be visited at the **Parco Archeologico** (*open daily 9–one hour before sunset; adm*). Not much is labelled or explained, but the ruins include a part of the famous baths, a thermal spa for wealthy Romans that was probably the largest and poshest such establishment in the ancient world, and an inspiration for the great public baths of Rome and other cities.

At Baia, the coast curves southwards towards Bacoli and **Capo Miseno** (*Cape Misenum*), a beautiful spot that for centuries was the greatest naval base of the Roman Empire, home to 10,000 sailors (mostly Greeks and Syrians). As at Baia, foundations and bits of columns and cornices are everywhere, though nothing of any real interest has survived intact. Nearby Lake Miseno, also called the 'Dead Sea', was once a part of the base, joined to the sea by a canal dug by Augustus' right-hand man Cornelius Agrippa in 37 BC. A memorable event of antiquity took place when Caligula ordered a double row of boats to be made across the bay, all the way from Bacoli to Pozzuoli. Suetonius wrote that the purpose was to fulfil a prophecy that Caligula would never become emperor until he rode across the bay on his horse (which he proceeded to do); it's more likely, though, that he did it to impress the Persian ambassador with the strength of the Roman navy.

That same distance was covered by the famous 'boy on a dolphin', a story that inspired many classical works of art. Many reliable witnesses attested to Pliny that they had seen it—a little boy of the peninsula who had befriended a dolphin which gave him a ride every day to lessons with his tutor in Puteoli. Pliny records that the boy died after an illness, and that the dolphin, after waiting faithfully for his friend for several days, beached himself and died too. The two were burned together.

The pleasant village of **Bacoli**, nearby, has two sights: a covered Roman reservoir called the **Piscina Mirabile**, a vaulted chamber like the famous one in Istanbul; and the vast ruin of a villa that might have belonged to Julius Caesar, called by the locals **Cento Camarelle**, the 'hundred little rooms'.

Two other lakes, both of which were created as a by-product of volcanic action, lie north of Capo Miseno; one, the **Lago di Fusaro**, is a large, shallow oyster farm, cut off from the sea by a sand bar near the woebegone fishing village of Torregáveta, the terminus of the Circumflegrea and Cumana railways. The decaying rococo palace on an island in the centre is the Casino, built in 1782 by the Bourbon kings' favourite architect, Luigi Vanvitelli. **Lago d'Averno**—Lake Avernus—may ring a bell from your school days; it's the mouth of Hell, according to the ancient Greeks, who believed any passing bird would be suffocated by the infernal fumes rising from it. Cornelius Agrippa didn't have much respect for mythology, and he turned the lake into a part of the naval base by cutting another canal. Among the ruins that surround it are the remains of a domed building, perhaps a temple or a sort of spa, originally as big as the Pantheon in Rome. Emperor Nero was fond of this area, and he built a covered canal lined with colonnades from the lake all the way to Pozzuoli; no trace remains of this now.

Cumae

As the story has it, King Tarquin of Rome came here, to the most venerable and respected oracle in all the western Mediterranean, with the intention of purchasing nine prophetic books from the Cumaean Sibyl. Unwisely, he said they were too dear, whereupon the Sibyl threw three of the books into the fire and offered him the remaining six at the same price. Again he complained, and the Sibyl put three more in the flames; finally Tarquin gave up, and took the last three at the original price. It was a good bargain. The Sibylline Books guided Rome's destiny until they too were burned up in the great fire of 82 BC.

Cumae had other distinctions. As one of the first Greek foundations in Italy the city was the mother colony for Naples and many other cities of Magna Graecia. In 421 BC Cumae lost its independence to the Samnites, and declined steadily from then on; Arab raiders, who did much damage everywhere else around Campania, finally wiped the city off the map in the 9th century AD.

They did a good job of it, and there is little to see at the site (*open daily 9–one hour before sunset; adm*), only the foundations of a few temples on the high **acropolis**, worth the climb for the views around Capo Miseno. One of the ruins was a famous Temple of Apollo, rebuilt by Augustus in thanks to the god after his victory at Actium.

Just below the summit, you may visit the **Cave of the Cumaean Sibyl** itself, discovered by accident in 1932. This was the setting of Aeneas' famous encounter with the Sibyl who leads him into the underworld, described in Book 6 of Virgil's *Aeneid*. It is a place of mystery, a long series of strange, trapezoidal galleries cut out of solid rock—impressive enough, even stripped of the sumptuous decoration they must once have had (all ancient oracles were marvellously profitable).

Nobody has a clear idea how old it is. By classical times, it took the form of an oracle quite like the one at Delphi. At the far end of the cave a plain alcove with two benches marks the spot where the Sibyls would inhale fumes over the sacred tripod, chew laurel leaves and go into their trance. Serious stuff in Virgil's day, the cult was in decline by the 2nd century when Trimalchio, a character in Petronius' *Satyricon*, claims he saw the ancient Sibyl's remains preserved in a jar hanging in the cave.

Nobody has made the western side of the bay a base for their holiday since the 4th century AD. If you are travelling in specially to visit the classical sites you may prefer to grab a sandwich. The mini-market in the Solfatara is a good place to pick up a *panino* for a picnic on the sunny acropolis at Cuma (modern Cumae). At Baia there is another mini-market opposite the station. If you're in need of a proper sit-down, there are a few good places to have lunch.

Pozzuoli

The harbour area of modern Pozzuoli is not particularly scenic, but if you are fresh off the ferry from the islands of Ischia and Procida, or visiting the amphitheatre and Serapeum, there are two recommendations.

On the harbour in Pozzuoli, the **Del Capitano**, Via Lungomare C. Colombo 10, ℗ 081 526 2283 (*moderate*) is a good rendezvous for fish-lovers. *Closed Thurs in low season.* **Il Tempio**, Via Serapide 13, ℗ 081 866 5179 (*moderate*), overlooking the ruined temple in Pozzuoli's main square, is justly famous for its *antipasti*. Leave all the decision-making to the waiter and he will happily bring you plate after plate of mostly fish-based dishes, including octopus, fried squid, baby red mullet, clams and giant prawns, until you tell him to stop. Many people call it a day after this, and few ever get beyond the *primi*. *Closed Wed.*

On the way out of Pozzuoli along the coastal road is **La Granzeola**, Via Cupa Fasane, ℗ 081 524 3430 (*expensive*), where owner-chef Carmine Russo turns fish bought directly off the local boats into a dazzling array of unusual and tasty dishes, especially with pasta. Try the *rigatoni con ragù di cozze*—short pasta with a delicious mussel sauce. *Closed Sun.*

Baia to Cuma

At Baia's **L'Altro Cucchiaro**, Via Lucullo 13, ℗ 081 868 7196 (*expensive*), you can dine on divine concoctions of seafood and pasta, as well as superb fish. The restaurant is just opposite the railway station and perfectly placed to restore your energies for a visit to the archaeological park. *Closed Sun evenings, Mon and three weeks in Aug.*

Back along the road to Pozzuoli at **La Ninfea**, Via Lago Lucrino, ℗ 081 866 1326 (*expensive*), you can bask on the lakeside terrace as you dine on delicious fish and grilled meats.

Along the road from Fusaro to Cuma there are several decent restaurants, all of whom specialize in fish. Leaving Fusaro on the road to Cuma there is the **Villa Chiara**, Via Torre di Cappella 10, ℗ 081 868 7139 (*moderate*). Near the archaeological site at Cuma are the **Giardino degli Aranci**, Via Cuma 75, ℗ 081 854 3120 (*moderate*) and the **Anfiteatro Cumano**, ℗ 081 854 3119 (*cheap*), also on Via Cuma. *Closed Tues.*

Torregáveta

Restaurants in shabbyish Torregáveta are cheaper than in the towns inside the bay. The **Ristorante Al Pontile**, Via Spiaggia Torregáveta, ☏ 081 868 9180 (*cheap*) has full dinners for reasonable prices.

East of Naples: Vesuvius and Around

Getting There and Around

All roads and local rail lines in the area start from the hub of Naples.

by rail

The local lines are the best way to reach Pompei and Herculaneum. The most important of these is the refreshingly efficient **Circumvesuviana**, with its own ultramodern station on Corso Garibaldi just south of the Piazza Garibaldi (☏ 081 772 2444), but all of its trains also make a stop at the Stazione Centrale itself before proceeding east. At Centrale their station is underground, sharing space with that of the Naples Metropolitana; this can be confusing since there are no schedules posted and the ticket windows aren't marked—you need to ask someone to make sure you are heading for the right train.

The main lines run east through **Ercolano** (the stop for Herculaneum) and Torre del Greco, and then diverge near Torre Annunziata, one line heading for Sarno, out in the farm country east of Vesuvius, and the other for Sorrento. For the excavations at **Pompei** take the Sorrento line to the Scavi di Pompei/Villa dei Misteri stop. Circumvesuviana trains usually run every half hour between 5am and 10.45pm. There are several *direttissima* trains daily—locals are much slower. Another Circumvesuviana line has infrequent trains north of Vesuvius to Nola and Baia.

by car

If you are heading towards Pompei and the east bay, use the A3 *autostrada* to get out of Naples if you don't want to spend a long time on the SS18 coast road through the suburbs. Leave the A3 at the Ercolano exit for Herculaneum; south of here, though it's still pretty busy, the SS18 gradually becomes more attractive.

Tourist Information

Pompei town: Via Sacra 1, 80045, ☏ 081 850 7255, ☏ 081 863 2401, with a branch office near the Porta Marina entrance to the old Pompeii site.

Mount Vesuvius

Since Vesuvius' big one of AD 79, over a hundred eruptions have destroyed various towns and villages, some more than once. But, like at Mount Etna in Sicily, people just can't stay away from Vesuvius' slopes. Volcanic soil grows grapes and olives in abundance, though the novelty of it often makes the Italians exaggerate their quality. The AD 79 explosion hasn't been equalled since; it blew the top of the mountain clean off, leaving two peaks, with the main fissure in between. The lower one is called Monte Somma, or *nasone* ('big nose') by the Neapolitans; the higher, parallel peak is Vesuvius proper.

Vesuvius was last heard from in 1944. The final eruption left the lava flows you'll see on the upper slopes; it also sealed the main fissure, putting an end to the permanent plume of smoke that once was such a familiar landmark. You can bet the scientists are watching Vesuvius. Despite the long hiatus, they say there is no reason to expect another eruption soon, though if it were to explode now, they warn, it would cause a catastrophe—the area around the volcano has become one of the most densely populated in all Italy.

To visit the main crater (between the two peaks), take the Vesuvius bus from the Circumvesuviana stop in Ercolano; then you have a stiff half-hour climb up the ash path. Dismiss all hopes of an easy ascent to the top singing 'Funiculi, funicula' from the legendary Thomas Cook cable railway, long since defunct. The white scar up the side of the crater— left by a second funicular which was due to replace the 1970s chairlift—continues a running saga. Work halted after argument for control over it between the two *comunes* of Torre del Greco and Ercolano. Whilst they argued the money 'disappeared'. Now the environmentalists have got a headache campaigning for colouring the concrete back Vesuvius-style (*open daily 9–one hour before sunset; adm*).

Herculaneum

Naples' discouraging industrial sprawl spreads eastwards as far as Torre del Greco without a break. The drab suburb of **Ercolano** is a part of it, built over the mass of rock that imprisons ancient **Herculaneum**, a smaller and less famous sight than Pompeii but just as much worth visiting (*open daily 9–one hour before sunset; adm*). Some people like it even better than its more famous sister site.

Unlike Pompeii, an important commercial centre, Herculaneum seems to have been a wealthy resort, only about one-third the size. Also, Vesuvius destroyed them in different ways. Pompei was buried under layers of ash, while Herculaneum, much closer to the volcano, drowned under a sea of mud. Over time the mud hardened to a soft stone, preserving the city and nearly everything in it as a sort of fossil—furniture, clothing and even some of the goods in the shops have survived.

Like Pompeii, Herculaneum was discovered by accident. In the early 1700s, an Austrian officer named Prince Elbeuf had a well dug here; not too far down, the workmen struck a stone pavement—the stage of the city's theatre. The Bourbon government began some old-fashioned destructive excavation, but serious archaeological work began only under Mussolini. Only about eight blocks of shops and villas, some quite fashionable, have been excavated. The rest is covered not only by tens of metres of rock, but also by a dense modern neighbourhood; bringing more of Herculaneum to light is a fantastically slow and expensive operation, but new digs are still going on.

At any given time, most of the buildings will be locked, but the guards wandering about have all the keys and will show you almost any of them upon request (they are not supposed to accept tips, though you will find they often seem to expect them). Many of the most interesting houses can be found along Cardo IV, the street in the centre of the excavated area.

On the corner of the Decumanus Inferior, the **House of the Wooden Partition** may be the best surviving example of the façade of a Roman house: inside is an amazingly preserved wooden screen (from which the house gets its name) used for separating the *tablinum*—the master's study—from the atrium. Next door, the **Trellis House** was a much more modest dwelling, with a built-in workshop; the **House of the Mosaic Atrium**, down the street, is another luxurious villa built with a mind to the sea view from the bedrooms upstairs.

On the other side of the Decumanus, Cardo IV passes the **Samnite House** (so named because of its early-style atrium), and further up a column with police notices painted on it stands near the **House of the Neptune**, with a lovely mythological mosaic in the atrium.

Other buildings worth a visit are the **House of the Deer**, with its infamous statue of a drunken Hercules relieving himself picturesquely; the well-preserved **Baths**; and the **Palaestra**, or gym, with its unusual serpent fountain and rather elegant, cross-shaped swimming pool.

Beyond Ercolano, the coastal road passes through the unattractive industrial sprawl and modern housing blocks thrown up to rehouse the homeless after the earthquake in 1980. The men of **Torre del Greco** have long been famous for gathering and working coral, a business now threatened by pollution. These days, much of the coral is imported from Asia, though it is still worked locally. Torre del Greco has recently become more famous for organized crime and gangland killings, though the population still turn out *en masse* to express their devotion to the Madonna in the procession for the Immaculate Conception, on 8 December, when the town gives thanks for having been spared in one of the more recent eruptions of Vesuvius.

The Roman Villa at Oplontis

Torre Annunziata, the next town, is another sorry place with a serious drug problem and a penchant for pasta production. The Roman villa excavated here, known as the **Villa Poppaea at Oplontis,** Via Sepolcri (*open daily 9–one hour before sunset; adm*) is well worth a detour. If you are arriving on the Circumvesuviana, exit the station, walk downhill over the crossroads, and it's the open area on the left opposite the military zone.

Two-thirds of the villa have been fully excavated, revealing an extremely opulent pad with its own private bath complex, servants' quarters, monumental reception rooms and ornamental pool. There are beautiful wall paintings (*see* pp.155–6), depicting rich scenes of monumental halls hung with military arms, a magnificent tripod set between a receding colonnade, bowls of figs and fresh fruit and vignettes of pastoral idylls, including one with Hercules under a tree with the apples of the Hesperides which he persuaded Atlas to retrieve for him during his penultimate labour.

The part of the villa near the road is dominated by the great atrium hall and the family quarters. The wing further from the road seems to have been the servants' quarters. Here you can still see amphorae stacked up in a store room. Outside the latrines, partitioned for each sex, it may have been one of the slaves who left his name, scrawled in Greek, 'Remember Beryllos'.

An amphora marked with the name Poppaea has given rise to the suggestion that the villa may have belonged to the wealthy Roman family, the *gens* Poppaea, who also owned the

House of Menander at Pompeii. The most infamous member of this family was Sabina Poppaea, a woman with everything but virtue. She used her charms to captivate the emperor Nero, leaving her second husband Otho—another future emperor—who was dispatched to Lusitania. Spurred on by her, Nero killed off his mother Agrippina and his first wife. Nero eventually killed Sabina by mistake in a fit of rage in AD 65, kicking her in the abdomen while she was pregnant.

Pompeii

Herculaneum may have been better preserved, but to see an entire ancient city come to life, the only place on earth you can go is this magic time capsule, left to us by the good graces of Mount Vesuvius. Pompeii is no mere ruin; walking down the old Roman high street, you can peek into the shops, read the graffiti on the walls, then wander off down the back streets to explore the homes of the inhabitants and appraise their taste in painting—they won't mind a bit if you do. Almost everything we know for sure concerning the daily life of the ancients was learned here, and the huge mass of artefacts and art dug up over 200 years is still helping scholars to re-evaluate the Roman world.

Though a fair-sized city by Roman standards, with a population of some 20,000, Pompeii was probably only the third or fourth city of Campania, a trading and manufacturing centre of no special distinction. Founded perhaps in the 7th century BC, the city came under the Roman sphere of influence around 200; by the fateful year of AD 79 it was still a cosmopolitan place, culturally more Greek than Roman. Vesuvius' rumblings, and the tall, sinister-looking cloud that began to form above it, gave those Pompeiians with any presence of mind a chance to leave. Only about 10 per cent of the population perished.

After the city was buried under the stones and ash of the eruption the upper floors still stuck out; these were looted, and gradually cleared by farmers, and eventually the city was forgotten altogether. Engineers found it while digging an aqueduct in 1600, and the first excavations began in 1748—a four-star attraction for northern Europeans on the Grand Tour. The early digs were far from scientific; archaeologists today sniff that they did more damage than Vesuvius. Resurrected Pompeii has had other problems: theft of artworks, a good dose of bombs in the Second World War, and most recently the earthquake of 1980. The damage from that is still being repaired today, though almost all the buildings are once more open to visitors.

There are two ways to see Pompeii; spend two or three hours on the main sights, or devote the day to scrutinizing details, for a total immersion in the ancient world you won't find anywhere else (the detailed guidebooks sold in the stands outside will help you with this). Your ticket also entitles you to entrance to the Villa of the Mysteries (*see* p.158). This is located five minutes' walk up the Viale Villa dei Misteri, to the left on exiting the Circumvesuviana. This is best left to the end of your sightseeing but remember to keep your ticket (*site open daily 9–one hour before sunset; adm*).

Pompeii isn't quite a perfect time capsule; a little background will help to complete the picture. The site today is all too serene, with a small-town air. Remember that almost every building was two or three storeys high, and that most streets of a Roman town were

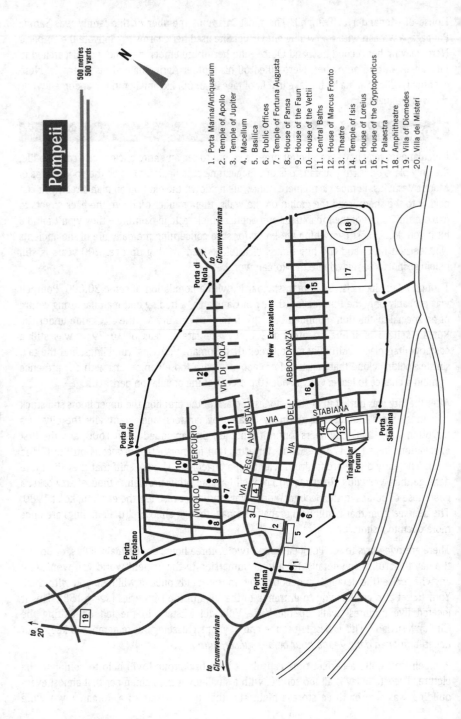

Pompeii

500 metres
500 yards

1. Porta Marina/Antiquarium
2. Temple of Apollo
3. Temple of Jupiter
4. Macellum
5. Basilica
6. Public Offices
7. Temple of Fortuna Augusta
8. House of Pansa
9. House of the Faun
10. House of the Vettii
11. Central Baths
12. House of Marcus Fronto
13. Theatre
14. Temple of Isis
15. House of Loreius
16. House of the Cryptoporticus
17. Palaestra
18. Amphitheatre
19. Villa of Diomedes
20. Villa dei Misteri

Porta di Nola

to *Circumvesuviana*

New Excavations

VIA DI NOLA

Porta di Vesuvio

VICOLO DI MERCURIO

VIA DEGLI AUGUSTALI

VIA DELL' ABBONDANZA

VIA STABIANA

Porta Stabiana

Triangular Forum

Porta Marina

Porta Ercolano

to *Circumvesuviana*

to 20

permanent market-places. When the volcano struck, much of the town was still in the process of being rebuilt after earthquake damage in AD 62.

As long as daylight lasted, Pompeii would have been crowded with improvised *bancarelle*; any wagon-driver who wished to pass would need all manner of creative cursing. At least the streets are well-paved—better than Rome itself in fact; Campania's cities, the richest in western Europe, could well afford such luxuries. All the pavements were much smoother and more even than you see them now. The purpose of the flat stones laid across the streets should not be hard to guess. They were places to cross when it rained—streets here were also drains—and the slots in them allowed wagon wheels to pass through.

The shops, open to the street in the day, would be sealed up behind shutters at night, just as they are in the old parts of Mediterranean cities today. Houses, on the other hand, turn a completely blank wall to the street; they got their light and air from skylights in the *atrium*, the roofed court around which the rooms were arranged.

Later, fancier villas have a second, open court directly behind the first, designed after the Greek *peristyle*. As in Rome, no part of town was necessarily the fashionable district; elegant villas will be found anywhere, often between two simple workmen's flats. Don't take the street names too seriously. They were bestowed by the archaeologists, often, as with the Via di Mercurio (Mercury Street), after mythological subjects depicted on the street fountains.

Roman Frescoes

Not surprisingly, Pompeii and Herculaneum have been of prime importance in the study of Roman painting. It is impossible to know how much of this art was borrowed from the Greeks or the Etruscans, although by the time of Augustus it appears that Rome and Campania were in the vanguard. New fashions set in the palaces of the Palatine Hill were quickly copied in the villas of the Roman California. Or perhaps it was vice versa.

Wealthy Romans tended to regard their homes as domestic shrines rather than a place to kick off their *caligae* and relax after a hard day at the Forum (the public baths served that role—the ancient Italians behaved much like the modern ones, who do everything in groups of ten and can't bear being alone); at home they used as many mosaics and wall paintings as they could afford to lend the place the necessary dignity. In Pompeii and Herculaneum, four styles of painting have been defined by art historians, although as you roam the ruins you'll find that they often overlap.

Style I (2nd century BC) was heavily influenced by Hellenistic models, especially from Alexandria: walls are divided into three sections, often by bands of stucco, with a cornice and frieze along the top and square panels (dados) on the bottom, while the middle sections are skilfully painted to resemble rich marble slabs. The predilection for deep colours, combined with the lack of windows, often makes these small rooms seem somewhat claustrophobic to us (*see* the Samnite House in Herculaneum).

Later Romans must have felt the same lack of air and space for, in about 90 BC, they moved on to the 'architectonic' **Style II**. Columns and architraves were painted around the edges of the wall, an architectural screen designed to provide an illusion of depth and space on the large central panels.

At first the centres were more pseudo-marble, but landscapes and mythological scenes soon became more popular. The Villa of the Mysteries near Pompeii is a prime example; it is also one of the oldest to have portraits of real people, or at least local character types.

Vitruvius, the celebrated writer on architecture, sternly disapproved of **Style III**, which abandoned the pretence and architectural dissimulation in favour of more playful compositions in perspective, still always done with a strict regard for symmetry. A favourite motif was patterns of foliage, fountains and candelabras, decorated with delicate, imaginative figures; these would be called 'grotesques' in the Renaissance, when Raphael and his friends rediscovered some in a Roman 'grotto' that was really a part of Nero's Golden House.

The middle panels are often done in solid colours, with small scenes at the centre to resemble framed paintings. In Pompeii examples include the Houses of Lucretius Fronto and the Priest Amandus, the latter done by a remarkable artist who comes close to scientific perspective, albeit with several vanishing points.

The last fashion to hit Pompeii before Vesuvius did, **Style IV**, combines the architectural elements of Style II and the framed picture effects of Style III, but with a greater degree of elaboration and decoration. Additional small scenes are placed on the sides—landscapes, still lifes, genre scenes from everyday life and architectural *trompe l'œil* windows done with a much more refined use of perspective (*see* the House of the Vettii).

Sometimes an entire stage would be painted, with the curtain pulled aside to show a scene from a play; borders are decorated with flowers, satyrs, grotesques and frolicking Cupids (Italians call these *amoretti*). Humorous vignettes of the gods and incidents from Virgil's *Aeneid* were popular, along with images of Pompeii's divine patroness, Venus. She also inspired the subject matter of the frescoes you have to bribe the guards to see.

Around the Forum

Past the throng of hawkers and refreshment stands, the main entrance to the site takes you through the walls at the **Porta Marina**. Just inside the gate, the **Antiquarium** displays some of the artworks that haven't been spirited off to the museum in Naples, as well as some truly gruesome casts of fossilized victims of the eruption, caught in their death poses.

Two blocks beyond the Antiquarium and you're in the **Forum**, oriented towards a view of Vesuvius. Unfortunately this is the worst-preserved part of town. Here you can see the tribune from which orators addressed public meetings, and the pedestals that held statues of heroes and civic benefactors, as well as the once-imposing **Basilica** (the law courts), temples to Apollo and Jupiter, and, among other buildings, a public latrine and a **Macellum**, or market, decorated with frescoes.

Down Mercury Street

Heading for Pompeii's old East End, there are several interesting houses along the Via di Mercurio, and the **Temple of Fortuna Augusta** on the corner of Via di Nola. The real attractions in this part of town, though, are a few lavish villas off on the side streets: the enormous **House of Pansa**; the **House of the Faun**, with the oldest-known welcome mat (set in the pavement, really); and the wonderful **House of the Vettii**, owned by a pair of wealthy brothers who were oil and wine merchants.

In the latter you can see several rooms that contain excellent, well-preserved paintings of mythological scenes, but the guards will be whispering in your ear (if you are male) to show you the little niche off the entrance with the picture of Priapus. This over-endowed sport, in legend the son of Venus and Adonis, together with a couple of wall paintings along the lines of the Kamasutra, has managed to make Pompeii something more than a respectable tourist trap. There are quite a few paintings of Priapus showing it off in the houses of Pompeii, besides the phallic images that adorn bakers' ovens, wine shops and almost every other establishment in town.

The Pompeiians would be terribly embarrassed, however, if they knew what you are thinking. They were a libidinous lot, like anyone else fortunate enough to live on the Campanian coast during recorded history, but the omnipresent phalluses were never meant simply to serve as decoration. Almost always they are found close to the entrances, where their job was to ward off the evil eye. This use of phallic symbols against evil probably dates from the earliest times in southern Italy; the horn-shaped amulets that millions of people wear around their necks today are their direct descendants. Even so, not so long ago, women visiting Pompeii were not allowed to set eyes on the various erotic images around the site, and were obliged by the guides to wait chastely outside while their spouses or male companions went in for a peek.

The nearby Via di Nola, one of Pompeii's main streets, leads to the north. It passes the **Central Baths**, a new construction that was not yet completed when Vesuvius went off, and the **House of Marcus Fronto**, with more good paintings and a reconstructed roof.

The 'New Excavations'

Beginning in 1911, the archaeologists cleared a vast area of western Pompeii, around what was probably the city's most important thoroughfare, now called the Via dell'Abbondanza. Three blocks west of the Forum, this street leads to the Via dei Teatri and the **Triangular Forum**, bordering the southern walls. Two **Theatres** here are worth a visit, a large open one seating 5000, and a smaller, covered one for concerts.

The big quadrangle, originally a lobby for the theatres, seems to have been converted at one point into a gladiators' barracks. This is only one of the disconcerting things you will find on the streets of Pompeii. The ruined temple in the Triangular Forum was already long ruined in AD 79, and scholars who study the art of the city find the last (fourth) period to betray a growing lack of skill and coarseness of spirit—altogether, there are plenty of clues that 1st-century Pompeii had its share of urban problems and cultural malaise.

The Via dell'Abbondanza

Next to the theatres, a small **Temple of Isis** testifies to the religious diversity of Pompeii; elsewhere around town there is graffiti satirizing that new and troublesome cult, the Christians. Three blocks north, there is a stretch of Via dell'Abbondanza that is one of the most fascinating corners of Pompeii. Among its shops are a smith's, a grocer's, a weaver's, a laundry and a typical Roman tavern with its modest walk-up brothel. The most common are those with built-in tubs facing the street—shops that sold wine, and oil for cooking and for lamps. Notices painted on the walls announce forthcoming games at the town's amphi-theatre, or recommend candidates for public office.

Some of the best-decorated villas in this neighbourhood are to be found along the side streets: the **House of Loreius**, the **House of Amandus**, and an odd underground chamber called the **Cryptoporticus**. Pompeii's two most impressive structures occupy a corner just within the walls: the **Palaestra**, a big colonnaded exercise yard, and the **Amphitheatre**, the best-preserved in Italy, with seating for about 20,000. Tacitus records that a fight broke out here between the Pompeiians and rival supporters from Nocera in a match staged in AD 59. Nero exiled those responsible for the games and forbade further spectacles for ten years.

Not all of Pompeii's attractions are within the walls. If you have the time, it would be worth visiting the tombs around the **Via delle Tombe**. The Romans buried their dead outside their cities. The manner of burial naturally depended on wealth and status, but here you can see several of the more impressive funerary monuments to local dignitaries and their families.

Finally, the famous **Villa dei Misteri**, a surburban villa located close to the same road out of Pompeii, may have been used as a place of initiation in the forbidden Bacchic (or Dionysiac) Mysteries, one of the cults most feared by the Roman Senate, and later by the emperors. Scenes from the myth of Dionysus and of the rituals are painted on the villa's walls.

Modern Pompei

The town of Pompei (the modern town has one 'i'), an important pilgrimage centre, is also worth a visit, if nothing else for a look at the wonderfully overdone church, dedicated to the **Madonna di Pompei** (*open daily 6–2 and 3–6.30*). For a good view over the town and the excavations take the lift up the tower (*open daily 9–1 and 3–5; adm*). The Madonna of the church holds a special place in the affections of Neapolitan women. You'll probably see some of them, busily saying their rosaries, asking for the Madonna's intercession to help sort out their problems. If they have bare feet, this is not poverty, but devotion—usually the fulfilment of a personal pledge to the Madonna in thanks for a favour received. Neapolitans who ask for the Madonna's help often promise to walk there barefoot from Naples (26km) if their prayers are answered.

It is only justice that Pompei should play host to the **Vesuvian Museum** on Via Colle San Bartolomeo (*open Mon–Sat 8–2; closed Sun*), a couple of minutes' walk from Piazza B. Longo in front of the church. This has more than enough to satisfy most basic volcano questions: prints of the volcano erupting, exhibits on the various materials produced in eruptions and much more that is explosive, if you like that kind of thing.

On leaving Pompei the road leads to the beginning of the Sorrentine peninsula. At the foot of the peninsula lies **Castellammare di Stabia**, which little suggests the beauty further on. Roman *Stabiae* was the port of Pompeii, and the other big town destroyed by Vesuvius. Most famously it was where Pliny the Elder, who was in command of the fleet at Misenum during the AD 79 eruption, met his death as he tried to bring help to those fleeing the catastrophe. The description of the eruption and these events are recorded for posterity in his nephew's letter to Tacitus. Here, beneath a 12th-century Hohenstaufen castle, are the modern shipyards of the Italian navy. From Castellammare, you can take a short ride in the cable car up to **Monte Faito**, a broad, heavily forested mountain that may well be the last really tranquil spot on the bay—though a few hotels have already appeared—and a pleasant place for walks (*open April–Oct*).

Where to Stay

The proximity of the picturesque Sorrentine peninsula, with its excellent selection of hotels between Vico Equense and Sorrento, means you would be unwise to base yourself in this built-up semi-industrial area. Sorrento itself is only 40 minutes away on the Circumvesuviana railway in one direction. Naples is about the same in the other.

Eating Out

At Ercolano there are no on-site facilities apart from toilets. The **Bar degli Amorini**, opposite the entrance, has a deceptively small front, but upstairs is a reasonable dining area if you are hunting for a snack or pizza. If you are spending the whole day in Pompeii (which is only too easy) there is a restaurant on site just beyond the ancient forum area through the Arch of Tiberius. The food from the self-service is nothing special, but if you wish to escape the crowds opt for the waiter service and sit out under the colonnade adjoining the ancient baths.

Otherwise, restaurants in modern Pompei have a captive market in visitors to the ruins, and it is true that some of them see the tourists as easy targets. You can choose for yourself among the ubiquitous multilingual menus, or try one of the following if you're in the mood for a treat.

Zi Caterina, Via Roma 20, © 081 850 7447 (*moderate*), with live lobsters in the tank and other noteworthy seafood dishes, is also a good place to try Lacrima Christi wine from the nearby slopes of Vesuvius. At **Al Gamberone**, Via Piave 36, © 081 863 8322 (*moderate*), close to Pompei's main church, you can feast on prawns doused in cognac and other good fish dishes. In summer you may dine outside under the lemons and oranges. If you do not want fish there is an array of other dishes including a good cannelloni. *Closed Fri.*

Immediately outside the excavations' exit, next to the amphitheatre, is **Anfiteatro**, Via Plinio 9, © 081 863 1245. Here the seafood is more modest—it's one of the few places in Pompei you'll see *baccalà* (salt cod) on the menu, along with truly good *spaghetti alle vongole. Closed Fri.*

In **Castellamare di Stabia**, the sprawl of Portakabins in the harbour is much favoured by locals who come to dine *al fresco* in the hot summer evenings.

Sorrento, Capri and the Amalfi Drive

Naples' hinterlands share fully in the peculiarities and sharp contrasts of the big city. Creation left nothing half-done or poorly done; against any other part of the monotonous Italian coastline, the Campanian shore seems almost indecently blessed, possessing the kind of irresistibly distracting beauty that seduces history off the path of duty and virtue. Today, for all the troubles that come seeping out of Naples, this coast is still one of the capitals of Mediterranean languor.

Getting There and Around

Naples, of course, is the hub for all transport throughout the area; buses, ferries and local commuter rail lines lead out from the city to all points (*see* pp.111–2).

by rail

Regular FS trains aren't much help here, except for a fast trip between Naples and Salerno. Fortunately, there are the local lines, of which the **Circumvesuviana** is the best way to reach Sorrento. This line has its own ultramodern station, on Corso Garibaldi just south of the Piazza Garibaldi (© 081 772 2444), but all of its trains also make a stop at the Stazione Centrale itself before proceeding east. At Centrale their station is underground, sharing space with that of the Naples Metropolitana; this can be confusing since there are no schedules posted and the ticket windows aren't marked—it's as well to ask someone to make sure you are heading for the right train.

The main lines run east through Ercolano and Torre del Greco, and then diverge near Torre Annunziata, one line heading for Sarno and the other for Sorrento.

The Circumvesuviana terminal in **Sorrento** is two streets east from Piazza Tasso, the town centre. Circumvesuviana trains usually run every half-hour between 5am and 10.45pm. On a *direttissima*, of which there are several daily, the Naples–Sorrento trip takes 1hr 10mins—locals are considerably slower.

by bus

The Circumvesuviana makes buses unnecessary for most of the east bay. Departing from the airport there is a bus to Sorrento three times a day. The express bus from Naples to Salerno, which usually runs every half-hour, leaves from the **SITA** office on Via Pisanelli, just off the Piazza Municipio, © 081 552 2176, and arrives in Salerno at the terminal at Corso Garibaldi 117, © 089 226 604.

SITA also runs the buses from Salerno for the Amalfi coast, with regular departures for Sorrento (in front of the Circumvesuviana station), or stopping short at Amalfi, Ravello or other towns *en route*; they are usually so frequent that it is easy to see all the main coast towns on a day-trip, hopping from one to the next. Buses are definitely the best way to do it; driving yourself can be a hair-raising experience when it's busy.

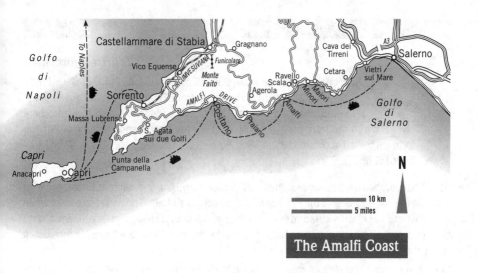

The Amalfi Coast

by road

If you are heading towards the east bay—where the distances are much greater, and so a car is much more useful—use the A3 *autostrada* to get out of Naples. At Pompei the SS145 turns off to the right for the Sorrento peninsula; beyond Sorrento it becomes the famous, or infamous, **Amalfi drive**. This spectacular road—at its most extreme no more than a winding ledge of hairpins halfway up a sheer cliff—is unquestionably worth seeing, but drivers should be aware of what is ahead of them, and avoid it in bad weather. The road was resurfaced and widened (!) as part of the works for the 1990 football World Cup. For some idea of the difficulties of the road, consider that it takes the express bus almost three hours to navigate the 66km from Salerno to Sorrento.

As Sorrento is so well connected by ferries, coach and the Circumvesuviana, car hire is hardly essential. **Avis** have an office on Viale Nizza 53, © 081 878 24059/© 081 807 1143. Do not be tempted into hiring a moped. The small roads are always busy with tour coaches and natives impatient to overtake.

by ferry and hydrofoil

Sorrento is well connected in summer by ferries and hydrofoils which ply from the Marina Piccola to Capri, Amalfi, Positano and Naples. This is only an option during daylight hours since few crossings run later than 7.30pm. In winter only reduced services to Capri and Naples operate.

Alilauro, © 081 878 1430, offer a fast alternative to the Circumvesuviana to Naples, a hydrofoil service which takes only 30 minutes. These run to both Molo Beverello near the Castel Nuovo and to the berths at Mergellina. For the return trip to Sorrento it is important to check from which station the hydrofoil is leaving.

Tourist Information

Sorrento: Via L. de Maio 35, 80067, ✆ 081 807 4033, ✆ 081 877 3397. It is a little difficult to find: from Piazza Tasso walk towards the sea into Piazza S. Antonino; the office is just off the road from here down to the ferry port (signposted). They are very friendly and helpful if you have yet to find accommodation. **Vico Equense**: Via S. Ciro 16, 80069, ✆ 081 879 8826, ✆ 081 879 9351.

After Pompei, the coastline swings outwards to meet Capri. At first, there is little intimation that you are entering one of the most beautiful corners of all Italy. The first clue comes when the coast road begins to climb into a corniche at **Vico Equense**, a pretty village that is becoming a small resort, absorbing some of the overflow from Sorrento; there is a nice beach under the cliffs at the back of the town.

Sorrento began its career as a resort in the early 19th century, when Naples began to grow too piquant for English tastes. The English, especially, have never forsaken it; Sorrento's secret is a certain perfect cosiness, comfortable like old shoes. Visitors get the reassuring sense that nothing distressing is going to happen to them, and sure enough, nothing ever does. It helps that Sorrento is a lovely, civilized old town. Not many resorts can trace their ancestry back to the Etruscans, or claim a native son like the poet Torquato Tasso. (Today, the Sorrentines are more proud of a songwriter named De Curtio, whose *Come Back to Sorrento*, according to a local brochure, ranks with *O Sole Mio* as one of the 'two most familiar songs in the world'. There's a bust of him in front of the Circumvesuviana station.)

Sorrento doesn't flagrantly chase after your money, unlike many other places in Italy, and it lacks the high-density garishness of, say, Rimini. However, its one big drawback is its lack of a decent beach—though at some of the fancier hotels you may enjoy taking a lift down to the sea. There are also several *stabilimenti*—piers jutting out into the sea, which are kitted out with loungers and beach umbrellas, for the use of which you have to pay a hire charge.

Sorrento is built on a long cliff that follows the shore. A narrow ravine cuts the town in half, between a suburban area of quiet, mostly expensive hotels, around Via Correale, and the old town itself, which still preserves its grid of narrow Roman streets. There isn't much of artistic or historical interest; Sorrento was never a large town, though in the Middle Ages it was for a while an important trading post. The Sorrentini still recall with pride that their fleet once beat Amalfi's fleet in a sea battle (even though it was in 897). Today the population is only 15,000.

Sorrento comes alive at dusk. Its major draw is the pleasant walk through the old streets, the *passeggiata*, which goes on till late in the evening. The old town around the tiny Via San Cesareo draws Italians and visitors alike. The sizeable community of British expats call it 'The Drain'. Half the shop windows seem to be displaying *intarsia*—surprisingly fine pictures done in inlaid woods, a local craft for centuries. Look out too for the laboratories, open to the street, producing perfume and *limoncello*, the distinctive lemon liqueur made from the lemons grown throughout the peninsula.

On Via S. Cesareo, look out for the Sedil Dominova: built in 1349, it used to be the seat where the local nobility discussed the city's matters. Now a working men's club, old men gather here to play cards under its 16th-century *trompe-l'œil* cupola. In Piazza S. Francesco stands the church of the same name adjoining a small 14th-century arched cloister with arabesques. In summer there are art exhibitions (*free*) and impromptu concerts. Nearby, the Public Gardens offers the classic Sorrentine view along the cliff tops, with the sea and Vesuvius in the distance. You can get down to the *stabilimenti* by taking the lift from here.

If you are stuck on a rainy day, you can visit the **Correale Museum,** on Via Correale, a grab-bag of Neapolitan bric-a-brac, art and curiosities (*open Mon and Wed–Fri 9.30–12.30 and 3–5, Sat and Sun 9.30–12.30; closed Tues; adm*).

Around Sorrento, as far as the mountains permit, stretches one of the great garden spots of Campania, a lush plain full of vines and lemon groves. From the town, to the west you can follow the winding path to the **Bagni Regina Giovanna,** a natural triangular seapool where you can see the scanty ruins of the Roman **Villa di Pollio**. You can also take the short trip to **Massa Lubrense**, an uncrowded fishing village with more fine views as far as Campanella Point, the tip of the peninsula, opposite the rugged outline of Capri. In the old days, a permanent watch was kept on Campanella Point, and it takes its name from the big bell that was hung here and rung to warn the towns around the bay when pirates were sighted. These days Massa Lubrense absorbs some of Sorrento's overflow of tourists.

For a picnic, the delicatessen **Apreda**, Via Tasso 6, © 081 878 2351, has a mouthwatering range of breads, hams, salami and cheeses, including the best Sorrentine *treccia* (the local variety of *mozzarella*).

Sorrento ✉ *80067*   ***Where to Stay***

Beyond Vico Equense to Sorrento you can easily find hotels of most categories from which to launch your explorations into Campania, even without a car. The excellent Circumvesuviana connects you to the entire Bay of Naples. The Amalfi coast has an efficient bus network linking Sorrento and Salerno. In Sorrento alone some 90 hotels compete for your attention, the best of which are converted villas by the sea—almost indecently elegant, even when they're a bit frayed at the edges.

expensive

Sorrento isn't the status resort it once was, but it still seems to have more four-star places than anywhere in Italy; most of them are good bargains too, compared to equivalent spots in the north. For a plunge into a Grand Tour atmosphere the ★★★★**Grand Hotel Excelsior Vittoria**, Piazza T. Tasso 34, © 081 807 1044, ✆ 081 877 1206, *exvitt@exvitt.it*, is the place to stay. Built at the turn of the century and owned by the same family for four generations, it's set in its own plush park complete with orange and olive groves, overlooking the sea. Wagner, Alexandre Dumas, Nietzche, Princess Margaret, Sophia Loren and the omnipresent Pavarotti have all stopped by.

The Manniello family chain offers good-value quality hotels. The ★★★★**Grand Hotel Ambasciatori**, Via Califano 18, © 081 878 2025, ✆ 081 807 1021, is a bit removed from the centre, but with a palatial interior, pool, sea-bathing platform and gardens overlooking the sea. In the same area they also own the beautifully remodelled ★★★★**Grand Hotel Royal**, ✆ 081 807 3434, ✉ 081 877 2905, also with a pool and beach access. Both hotels perch atop the the the cliffs above the Riviera Massa, west of the old centre. Most rooms have good balconies, so opt for the sea view.

In a more central location, set in incredible tropical gardens on Via Vittorio Veneto, the ★★★★**Imperial Tramontana**, ✆ 081 878 1940, ✉ 081 807 2344, is one of the places long favoured by British travellers, as is evident from the club-like décor. There is a lift down to the private beach, and also a pool. Another villa-hotel, just around the corner on Via Marina Grande, is the ★★★★**Bellevue-Syrene**, ✆ 081 878 1024, ✉ 081 878 3963. This one has lush gardens and beautifully restored rooms as well as a lift to the beach. The cliff-top colonnade is a lovely spot for a drink even if you are not staying at the hotel. Do not be put off by the pompous staff.

If you have a car, beyond Sorrento where the dark cliff rises above the town you can follow the coastal road past the Marina Grande, turning left up SS145 until you reach the ★★★★**President**, Via Nastro Verde, Colle Parise, ✆ 081 878 2262, ✉ 081 878 5411. It is set in its own park, with lovely views and a good-sized pool.

moderate

Not all the hotels in Sorrento are luxury villas; one of its charms is that it manages to cater for every budget. A real bargain, in a villa with a private beach, and a good restaurant to boot, is the ★★**Pensione La Tonnarella**, Via Capo 31, ✆ 081 878 1153, ✉ 081 878 2169; it's advisable to make reservations here early. On the road east out of Sorrento, the ★★★**Minerva**, Via Capo 30, ✆ 081 878 1011, ✉ 081 878 1949, has 50 nice rooms, some with stunning views over the sea. *Closed Nov–Mar.*

In Vico Equense, the best places to stay are a little outside the town centre, notably the ★★★★**Capo La Gala**, ✆ 081 801 5758, ✉ 081 879 8747, on the beach at nearby Scrajo (where there are sulphur springs)—a beautiful modern resort hotel where every room has its own private terrace overlooking the beach. There's plenty of sea, and a swimming pool too, but note that full board is usually required, especially in high season.

cheap

A *pensione* with lovely sea views is the ★★**Loreley et Londres**, Via Califano 2, ✆ 081 807 3187. The friendly staff make up for the somewhat dreary décor (there are neon lights everywhere), and the terrace overlooking the sea provides the most romantic sunsets anywhere in town. In summer they insist you stay on half-board if you want one of the rooms overlooking the sea—and away from the noisy road. There is also a lift down to a private sea-bathing platform, reserved for guests.

Several simple hotels can be found around the town centre, of which the ★**City**, Corso d'Italia 217, ✆ 081 877 221, ✉ 081 877 2210, is one of the nicest, close to the centre but not too noisy. The ★**Nice**, Corso Italia 257, ✆ 081 807 2530, ✉ 081 807 1154, conveniently located on the corner of the main road just in front of the Circumvesuviana station, is also a surprisingly good find, again conveniently close to the town centre. Rooms are clean and pleasant, and have small but well-appointed bathrooms. They will be happy to give you a key if you plan to stay out late in the bars and clubs, or catch the last train back from Naples.

If you have a car, a good deal is to stay up on the hill at the *azienda agrituristica* **Il Giardino di Vigliano**, Località Villazzano, Massa Lubrense, © 081 533 9823. Look out for the nameplate on the wall marking the turn-off from the main road. Then after driving through an olive grove and under a lemon pergola, you'll find the 17th-century building complete with a Saracen tower. The view of Capri from the roof terrace is breathtaking. Half-board and apartment rental are also available. They sell their own organic oil and produce.

Sorrento ✉ *80067*   **Eating Out**

very expensive–expensive

At Nerano, on the road from Sorrento to Massa Lubrense, **Da Pappone**, © 081 808 1209, specializes in fish fresh out of the sea, and elaborate (but pricey!) *antipasto* surprises.

Sorrento has every kind of restaurant, including the grand and gloriously decorated **O' Parrucchiano**, Corso Italia 67, © 081 878 1321, by tradition one of Italy's best, with a choice of anything you could imagine. On Piazza Tasso, **Caruso** © 081 807 3156, also has a vast and inventive menu, from rich melty *crocchette ai fiori di zucca* to fresh delicate *polpetti al pomodoro*. It all comes with attentive service and an extensive wine list. The wintry atmosphere and lack of outside tables doesn't seem to deter customers—booking for dinner is essential. Try to leave room for the dessert trolley, if you can. *Closed Mon, Oct–April.*

If you are celebrating a special occasion, or just in the mood for a memorable experience, the place to go nowadays is **Don Alfonso**, Piazza Sant'Agata, © 081 878 0026, in Sant'Agata sui Due Golfi, a Michelin-starred restaurant that some food critics reckon to be the best in southern Italy. Food here is an art form, beautifully cooked, and presented on fine china with wine served in delicate crystal glasses. The restaurant, run by husband-and-wife team Alfonso and Livia Iaccarino, is actually 9km outside Sorrento, but the trip is well worth it. *Closed Sun evenings Sept–May and Mon all year.*

moderate–cheap

In Sorrento, **La Lanterna**, Via S. Cesareo 23–25, © 081 878 1355, is right in the middle of it all, with outside tables in the alley area which are a little quieter. It has tasteful décor, friendly and efficient service and, most important, impeccable *risotto ai frutti di mare*. For one of the best deals in town, try the **Trattoria da Emilia**, Via Marina Grande 62, © 081 807 2720, a family-run *trattoria* with tables on a terrace overlooking the sea, and an excellent-value fixed menu based on fresh local ingredients and classic Sorrento recipes. *Closed Tues.*

In the basement of an old Roman villa, the **Taverna Artis Domus**, Via San Nicola 56, © 081 877 2073, is a lively place for a snack or a drink in the evening. In summer there is live music every night. *The inflated cost of your first drink includes* *admission.* For a very cheap meal, or a take-away, try the **Panetteria-Pizzeria Franco**, Corso Italia 265, ✆ 081 877 2066, where you sit at long wooden tables and watch as your pizza is prepared in front of you. A popular place with locals.

In Nerano, **Maria Grazia**, Via Marina del Cantone 65, ✆ 081 808 1011, is renowned for her *spaghetti con le zucchine*. People come from all over the coast to savour it.

bars and ice-cream

There is no shortage of variety in Sorrento as far as bars are concerned, like the honestly named **Boozer Pub**, Via P.R. Giuliani 65, ✆ 081 878 3617, with light dinners, English beer and music. The place to be seen, though, is most definitely the **Fauno Bar**, Piazza Tasso 1, ✆ 081 878 1021, where you can watch young and old alike gather in the piazza in the evening.

In a land where ice cream is culture you can hardly go wrong, but **Davide**, Via P.R. Giuliani 39, ✆ 081 878 1337, is exceptional. At least fifty flavours are on offer at any one time, usually supplemented by others from yet another fifty-long list 'elaborated in about 40 years of ice cream tradition'.

Capri

Without a doubt, the islands in the Bay of Naples are the holiday queens of the Italian islands. Every schoolchild has heard of Capri, the notorious playground of Emperor Tiberius and Norman Douglas' 'gentlemanly freaks'. Still, the smart set can't get there fast enough; Capri is connected to Naples' Capodichino Airport by helicopter.

Capri is pure enchantment, and can lay fair claim to being the most beautiful island in the Mediterranean, a delicious garden of Eden with over 800 species of flowers and plants cascading over a sheer chunk of limestone. An Eden, but one where the angels have definitely let down their guard.

Unlike Ischia and other, more recent, tourist haunts, Capri has the relaxed worldly air of having seen it all. No room remains for property speculators. Everything has been built and planted; the tourists come and go every day and night, almost invisible to the Capriots and other residents who have learned to turn a blind eye to them, since the space they occupy will be filled next day by other anonymous camera-clutching tourists. Between June and September you begin to understand why the word 'trash' is inscribed on the bins in 30 different languages. However, if you don't mind all the trendy shops being closed, try going in November or February, when you may be lucky to arrive for a few brilliant days between the rains, and feel like Adam or Eve (well, almost). It's worth the risk of a soaking or two.

There are various capricious schools of thought on the etymology of the island's name. The belief that it came from the Latin word for goat (*capra*) is now in disfavour; those who think it derived from the Greek *kapros* (boar) have fossils to back them up. Yet another group maintains that it comes from an ancient Etruscan word meaning 'rocky' (*capr—*), similar to Caprera (an island off Sardinia), Cabrera (off Majorca) and Caprara in the Tremiti Islands, to name just a few. Make sure you pronounce it CAPri, not CapRI, like the Ford.

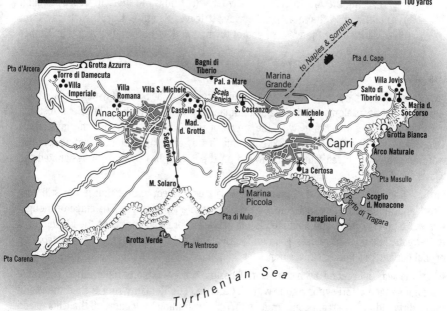

Capri

Pta d'Arcera · Grotta Azzurra · Torre di Damecuta · Villa Imperiale · Villa Romana · Villa S. Michele · Bagni di Tiberio · Pal. a Mare · Scala Fenicia · Marina Grande · to Naples & Sorrento · Pta d. Capo · Villa Jovis · Salto di Tiberio · S. Maria d. Soccorso · Castello · Anacapri · Mad. d. Grotta · S. Costanzo · S. Michele · Capri · Grotta Bianca · Arco Naturale · Seggiovia · M. Solaro · La Certosa · Pta Masullo · Marina Piccola · Scoglio d. Monacone · Pta di Mulo · Faraglioni · Porto di Tragara · Grotta Verde · Pta Ventroso · Pta Carena

Tyrrhenian Sea

Getting There

In summer, there are as many as six ferries and 20 hydrofoils a day from Naples to Capri. In addition, there are a frequent ferries and hydrofoils daily from Sorrento to Capri: a very short ride. For more information on long-distance ferry services from Naples, *see* p.111.

from Naples

Ferries and hydrofoils from Naples to Capri leave from two points along the harbourside—**Molo Beverello**, in the centre of the port, and **Mergellina**, further to the west. Check which is the right dock for your ticket and destination. Listed here are the main ferry and hydrofoil operators; check with them for timetables, or look in the newspaper *Il Mattino*. In summer there are up to six ferries and 20 hydrofoils a day.

From **Molo Beverello**: **Caremar** (ferries and hydrofoils), ✆ 081 551 3882; **Navigazione Libera del Golfo** (hydrofoils), ✆ 081 552 7209; **Alilauro** (hydrofoils), ✆ 081 552 2838.

From **Mergellina** (hydrofoils only): **SNAV**, ✆ 081 761 2348.

from Sorrento

Caremar, ✆ 081 807 3077, ✉ 081 807 2479, run five ferries daily to Capri and back (45mins). **Linea Jet**, ✆ 081 878 1861, run hydrofoils to Capri eight times a day, taking 20 minutes. **Alilauro**, ✆ 081 878 1430, run 17 daily hydrofoil crossings.

In addition, from Salerno there is a boat called the *Faraglione* that offers a different way of seeing the Amalfi coast, a daily ferry that hugs the shore to Capri, stopping at Amalfi and Positano along the way. It leaves Salerno at 7.30 each day from Molo Manfredi, at the western end of town, and does not run between 15 October and 6 January.

History

Back in the Quaternary period when Capri broke away from the Sorrentine peninsula, it took elephants and tigers along with it. The first humans appeared in the Palaeolithic era. A strong tradition associates the island with the sirens of the *Odyssey*, and with the mysterious Teleboeans from the Greek island of Kephalonia, led by their king Telon. Neolithic ceramic-ware decorated with red bands, first found on the island, has since been designated the 'Capri style'.

Little is known of Capri at the time when Augustus arrived, except that it was still very Greek and that a dying ilex suddenly revived and sprouted new leaves. The emperor thought this was a good portent, and he traded Ischia to Naples for Capri and made the island one of his retreats. Life must have been good on Capri; at one point Augustus called it *Apragopolis*, or 'Lubberland', as Robert Graves translates Suetonius' 'land of layabouts'.

Augustus was succeeded by his stepson Tiberius, whose exploits reported by the same Suetonius made Capri synonymous with decadence. The Roman writer turned the island into a dirty old man's dream come true, with Tiberius hurling his victims off the cliffs to add a touch of reality (*see* pp.173–4). Tabloid journalism or not, his images of sexual acrobats dressing up as nymphs and frolicking in Tiberius' gardens, along with the anthropophagous Sirens singing seductive songs on the seashore, are an intrinsic part of the Capri myth.

Under Tiberius, Capri was the capital of the Roman Empire between AD 27 and 37. The sheer cliffs made it into a natural citadel from where the ageing emperor conducted (or neglected) the affairs of state as he pleased, and nurtured the future Emperor Caligula.

After the death of Tiberius, Capri lost its lustre and is occasionally mentioned only as a place of exile. Then the Benedictine friars arrived and built chapels on the island, and it suffered the usual ravages of Saracens and pirates. In 1371 a Carthusian monastery (La Certosa) was founded on land granted by the Angevins. A plague in 1656 left the island all but abandoned; only the Carthusians stayed behind, safe inside the walls of La Certosa, picking up the titles to land that had no owners and becoming quite wealthy (and unpopular) in the process.

In 1806 Hudson Lowe was commander of the English garrison on Capri. Napoleon's life was full of strange coincidences. Lowe, for example, was quartered in Napoleon's house in Ajaccio when the English occupied Corsica, and he later became Napoleon's jailer on St Helena. He took his job on Capri seriously indeed, fortifying the island until it became 'a little Gibraltar', but for all that still managed to lose it to the French in 1808—a 'discreditable Lowe business' according to Norman Douglas, longtime resident and writer on things Capricious.

The last chapter of the island's history began with the 'discovery' of the Blue Grotto by a German artist called Kopisch in 1826; he swam into it 'by accident'. Perhaps it was just a coincidence that Kopisch's discovery followed the landslide that had covered the entrance of another, even lovelier cave. Anyway, the magic of the name, Blue Grotto of Capri, proved irresistible, and the Capriots converted their fishing boats into excursion boats to take tourists to the cave while farmers sold their land and built hotels.

Getting Around

Arriving in Marina Grande, you can ascend to either Capri or Anacapri by **bus** (*daily 8am–10pm every 15 mins, 10pm–midnight every half-hour*). There is also a **funicular** that runs up to Capri town (*summer daily 6.30am–12.30am every 15 mins; Oct–April daily until 9pm*).

The **chairlift** from Anacapri to Monte Solaro (a 12-minute ride) runs continuously (*summer 9.30–sunset; Nov–Feb 10.30–3; closed Tues*). Buses run from Capri town to Anacapri, Marina Piccola and Damecuta. There are also buses from Anacapri to the Blue Grotto, Faro and Marina Piccola. Daily **tours** of Capri by motor launch leave from Marina Grande (*June–Sept; first tour 9am*). Otherwise you can walk to most places; the beautiful trails across the island are major attractions, but pack a mac out of season, just in case.

Tourist Information

Capri town: Piazza Umberto 1, 80073, ✆ 081 837 0686.
Marina Grande: at Banchina del Porto, ✆ 081 837 0634.
Anacapri: Via G. Orlandi 59/a, 80071, ✆ 089 837 1524.
The tourist office in Marina Grande will help to find accommodation.

Marina Grande and the Grotta Azzurra

All the ferries and hydrofoils from the mainland call at **Marina Grande** (most pleasure boats anchor in the Marina Piccola on the other side of the island). Here, Capri's dependence on tourism is at its most evident. Marina Grande is little more than a commercialized station platform, but as such does its best to get you off to your destination: the *funicolare* (cable railway) will lift you to the town of Capri, buses will wind you up to Anacapri, glorious old bath-tub convertible taxis hope to trundle you off to your hotel, boats for the Grotta Azzurra and other excursions around the island bob up and down at their landings. There is even a genuine yellow submarine waiting to take you down for an underwater tour around the island.

The **Blue Grotto** is well named if nothing else—its shimmering, iridescent blueness is caused by the reflection of light on the water in the morning. Similar caverns are fairly common in the Mediterranean, but Capri's is the yardstick by which they are measured. In summer (*1 June–30 Sept*), boats for the Blue Grotto leave at 9am—when the sea is calm. The entrance to the cave is quite low, and if there's any swell on the sea at all someone is sure to get a nasty knock on the head.

The **sea excursion around the island** is a rare experience, but again possible only in good weather. Besides visiting other lovely grottoes, such as the **Grotta Bianca** and the **Grotta Verde** (the White Cave and the Green Cave), it provides breathtaking views of the cliffs and Capri's uncanny rock formations.

Capri Town

Haunted by the smiling shade of Gracie Fields, the charming white town of Capri is daily worn down by the tread of thousands of her less ectoplasmic followers. The **megalithic walls** supporting some of the houses have seen at least three millennia of similar comings and goings, although on a much smaller scale than the tourist crowds you'll find in August. Capri's architecture complements the island's natural beauty—much of what is typical and 'home-made' in Mediterranean building can be seen here in the older quarters: the moulded arches and domes, the narrow streets and stairways crossed by buttresses supporting the buildings, the ubiquitous whitewashed walls, the play of light and shadow, and the sudden little squares, just large enough for a few children to improvise a game of football.

Most of the island's hotels are scattered throughout the town, generally very tasteful and surrounded by gardens. The supreme example is the famous Quisisana, a hotel whose register over the years is like a veritable *Who's Who* of the famous and pampered.

If you go up to Capri by *funicolare*, you'll surface next to Piazza Umberto and the much photographed **cathedral**, with its joyful campanile and clock. Built in the 17th century in the local baroque style, the cathedral has a charming buttressed roof. In a little square in the church's shadow, known as **La Piazzetta**, are the outdoor cafés frequented by such a variety of past eccentrics, dilettantes and celebrities that each chair should have a historical plaque on it. The other side of the piazza is a sheer drop down to Marina Grande.

Walks from the Town

For the post office and for buses to Anacapri, take the Via Roma from the piazza; for the exclusive boutiques, head towards the Via Vittoria Emanuele to Via Camarelle and Via Tragara. The latter eventually leads to the **Faraglioni**, the three enormous limestone pinnacles towering straight up in the ever blue-green sea. These rocks are home to the rare blue lizard (*Lacerta caerulea Faraglionensis*) and a rare species of seagull that supposedly guffaws. From Via Tragara a stairway descends to the point and the **Porto di Tragara**, where you can take a swim from the platforms beneath the vertical rocks.

Nearby is the **Tragara Terrace**, with magnificent views, and the tall skinny rock called **Pizzolungo**. Follow the main track along the coast and up the stairway to the **Grotta di Matromania**, centre of the cult of the goddess Cybele (*Mater Magna*) whose worship was banned in Rome itself. Part of Capri's reputation as an island of orgies may derive from this ancient eastern cult's noisy hypnotic rituals, which culminated abruptly with the self-castration of the priest for a day. Only vestiges remain of the cave's elaborate décor.

From the Grotta di Matromania a stepped path leads down to yet another famous eroded rock, the **Arco Naturale**, where dark pines—as everywhere else on Capri—cling to every tiny ledge they can sink their roots into. On the way back to town you'll pass some of the island's vineyards that produce the rare and famous *Lacrimae Tiberii*, and, in the Piazza Cerio next to the cathedral, the **Centro Caprense Ignazio Cerio**, with fossils and archaeological finds from Capri (*open Mon–Fri 10–12*). Ignazio Cerio was not the first person on the island to take an interest in such things. Emperor Augustus had founded a museum for the 'weapons of ancient heroes' and the collection of what he called his old 'Big Bones', then popularly believed to be the remains of monsters.

The Old Goat of Capri

London has its tabloids, and ancient Rome had Gaius Suetonius Tranquillus, born *c*. AD 60. All of Suetonius's other books are lost, including such titles as the *Lives of Famous Whores* and the *Physical Defects of Mankind*, but enough copies of his celebrated scandalmongering classic, *The Twelve Caesars*, were written out to ensure that the whole juicy text has survived. Modern historians have always argued over Suetonius's reliability, but the nature of his subjects has been confirmed by enough other sources to suggest that Suetonius couldn't have exaggerated that much. And his book was written with full access to the imperial archives; the author was chief secretary to Emperor Trajan.

One of the most entertaining chapters deals with the man who put Capri on the map, the Emperor Tiberius, adopted son of Augustus. A good general and, at first, a capable ruler, Tiberius had an unusual habit of declining honours and titles. Suetonius hints that the Emperor suspected that he would eventually go a bit mad, and wanted no pointless flattery left behind for his enemies to mock later. Mad or not, Tiberius did have a mania for privacy. He left Rome in AD 26 for Capri, which he admired for its beauty and for the fact that it had only one landing port, and he never went back to the capital again. The entire island became his pleasure garden, and while imperial decrees went out prohibiting 'promiscuous kissing' and ordering a clampdown on loose women, the Emperor himself was whooping it up. According to Suetonius:

> *Bevies of young girls and men, whom he had collected from all over the Empire as adepts in unnatural practices, and known as* spintriae, *would perform before him in groups of three, to excite his waning passions. A number of small rooms were furnished with the most indecent pictures and statuary imaginable, also certain erotic manuals from Elephantis in Egypt; the inmates of the establishment would know from these exactly what was expected of them.*

Once aroused, apparently, the imperial pervert would bore in on anything that caught his fancy, and the smaller the better. Suetonius pictures him rushing through a religious sacrifice to get at the little boy who was carrying the incense casket, and training other little boys, his 'minnows', to 'chase him while he went swimming and get between his legs to lick and and nibble him...such a filthy old man he had become!' Even Suetonius is shocked. Distracted by such pleasures, Tiberius let the Empire go to pot; the Persians invaded from the east, while Germanic bands roamed unchecked in Gaul. The generals and the civil service managed to see that no serious harm was done, but they could not stop the ageing Tiberius, in his island isolation, from turning into a murderous paranoid, torturing and killing anyone who opposed him, or seemed to. Suetonius names all the names and tells all the tales; nobody was ever better at capturing the essential vileness of imperial Rome.

One of the stories related by Suetonius of Tiberius' time on Capri is that of a fisherman who decided to surprise Tiberius, bringing him the gift of an enormous mullet. Tiberius was so scared that he ordered his guards to rub the poor man's face raw with it. In agony the fisherman shrieked, 'Thank Heavens I didn't bring that huge crab I caught!' Tiberius sent for the crab and had it used the same way.

La Certosa and the Gardens of Augustus

A shorter but equally enjoyable walk starting from the Piazza Umberto (take Via Vittorio Emanuele, which becomes Via F. Serena, then Via Matteotti) leads you to **La Certosa** (*open daily 9–2; closed Mon*), the Carthusian charterhouse founded in 1371 by Giacomo Arcucci, member of a famous Capri family, and suppressed in 1808. Built over one of Tiberius' villas and topped by a 17th-century baroque tower, the charming golden-hued church and cloisters contain a collection of mediocre paintings from the 17th to the 19th centuries.

A few minutes away from La Certosa are the **Gardens of Augustus**, founded by Caesar himself. A wide variety of trees and plants grow on the fertile terraces and belvederes over-looking one of the most striking views in the world. A narrow road (*currently closed for reinforcement work*)—Via Krupp, built by the German arms manufacturer, who spent his leisure hours studying lamprey larvae off the Salto di Tiberio—takes you down the cliffs in a hundred hairpin turns to the **Marina Piccola**, the charming little port with most of Capri's bathing establishments: Da Maria, La Canzione del Mare, Le Sirene and Internazionale (all but the last connected to restaurants). On one side are the ruins of a Saracen tower; on the other is the **Scoglio delle Sirene** (Sirens' Rock); if you read the books of Norman Douglas and Edwin Cerio, son of Ignazio Cerio the archaeologist, they will convince you that this really was the home of the Sirens. There is a bus, fortunately, that makes the steep climb back up the cliffs to Capri town.

A much longer but equally rewarding walk (Via Botteghe to Via Tiberio) is to the **Villa Jovis** (*open 9–one hour before sunset; adm*) passing the church of **Monte San Michele**, a fine example of local architecture, built in the 14th century. The Villa Jovis on Punta Lo Capo (1017ft) was the most important of the twelve imperial villas on Capri: from here Tiberius governed the Roman Empire for his last ten years. Although much has been sacked through the centuries, the extent of the remaining walls and foundations gives a fair idea on what scale an imperial pervert lived. The centre of the villa was occupied by vast cisterns for supplying the private baths, scene of so many naughty capers.

Close by, the **Faro** (lighthouse) was believed to have been part of a system for sending messages to the mainland. The great sheer cliff beside the villa, the **Salto di Tiberio**, is always pointed out as the precipice from which the emperor hurled his victims. It had already become a tourist attraction in Suetonius' day. Its view of both the Bay of Salerno and Naples is as spec-tacular as any, even if it's not altogether what the Neapolitans mean by 'see Naples and die'!

Towards Anacapri

On the north coast between Capri and Anacapri, the only other town on the island, are the so-called **Baths of Tiberius** and the meagre remains of Augustus' sea palace, the **Palazzo a Mare**. You can swim here at the establishment of Bagni di Tiberio. Above here, carved into the escarpment of Anacapri, is the **Scala Fenicia** ('the Phoenician Stair'), in truth Greco-Roman in origin and until the 19th century the only way to reach the upper part of the island. Originally 800 in number, the steps have now crumbled and are impassable today. Near here, on the road from Marina Grande to Anacapri, lies the first Christian church on the island, dedicated to its patron saint, **San Costanzo**. According to legend Costanzo was a bishop of Constantinople whose body, packed in a barrel, floated to Capri during the Iconoclasm in Greece. A church, which came with a reputation for defending the island from Saracens, was built for him in the 11th century over one of the Roman villas. In the form of a Greek cross, four ancient columns support the Byzantine dome.

Anacapri

On top of the green plateau spreads the town of Anacapri, once a fierce rival to Capri, each town regarding the other as barbaric and uncouth. The building of the roads in 1874 has slowly taught them to reconcile their differences. Although it has its share of hotels, Anacapri retains a rustic air, with its many olive trees and surrounding vineyards, and its simple style of architecture, rather Moorish in style with cubic, flat-roofed houses.

In Anacapri's Piazza San Nicola, the 18th-century church of **San Michele** (*open April–Oct daily 9–7; Nov–Mar daily 10–3*) contains a magnificent mosaic floor of majolica tiles by the Abruzzese artist Leonardo Chiaiese, based on a design by D.A. Vaccano of Adam and Eve in the Garden of Eden and their expulsion. The church of **Santa Sofia**, very near it on the Piazza Diaz, was built in the Middle Ages, but later baroqued.

From Piazza Vittoria a chairlift travels to the summit of **Monte Solaro**, the highest point on the island at 1,919ft. Also from Piazza Vittoria, take Via Orlandi to Via Capodimonte and the **Villa San Michele** of Axel Munthe (1857–1949), one of the greatest physicians of his day, and a leader in the field of psychiatry who spent most of his career in Paris. Extremely generous, donating his services to the victims of plagues, earthquakes and the First World War, he also found time to establish bird sanctuaries on Capri and elsewhere; in 1929 he wrote his best-selling autobiography, *The Story of San Michele*, to which his villa owes most of its fame. One of Munthe's hobbies was collecting stray animals and Roman artefacts; the latter are still on display (*open daily 9–sunset; adm*).

Near here is the ruined 8th–9th-century **Castello di Barbarossa**, after the Turkish pirate captain who plagued the Mediterranean for so many years. Via Capodimonte continues through the valley of **Santa Maria a Cetrella**, another white church of local design. From the church the road goes to the top of Monte Solaro.

Another path from Piazza Vittoria (Via Caposcuro to Via Maigliara) skirts Monte Solaro, passing through the vineyards to the **Belvedere della Migliara**, from where you can see the Faraglioni and the entrance of the **Green Grotto**. A bus leaves Anacapri every hour in the summer for Punta Carena and its lighthouse at the southernmost tip of the island. The unusual arched doorways on the left belonged to the **Torre di Materita**; further on, overlooking the **Cala del Tombosiello**, is a ruined watchtower. **Punta Carena** is the most out-of-the-way place on the island for a quiet swim.

Another bus leaves from the piazza for the Grotta Azzurra and its bathing area, passing the old windmill and the **Villa Imperiale**, another of the summer residences built by Augustus, known also as the 'Damecuta'. After the Villa Jovis, this villa is the best preserved on Capri, and has recently been further excavated (*open 9–one hour before sunset; closed Mon*).

Capri ✉ *80073*   ***Where to Stay***

Not surprisingly, hotel prices on Capri are well above average for the surrounding area on-shore, and rooms for the summer months are often booked up months in advance. When looking for a hotel on Capri consider the following: exclusivity, space, a central position, the view and the extent of facilities available count for most here.

very expensive

If money is no object, the ★★★★★**Grand Hotel Quisisana**, Via Camerelle 2, ✆ 081 837 0788, ✉ 081 837 6080, is the place to stay in Capri town, a luxurious palace of a hotel set in its own grounds and equipped with pool, gym, tennis courts and just about everything else needed for a smart holiday on the island. The building was originally a sanatorium built by an Englishman, George Clark. With acres of white tiled floors, plush white sofas and lamps borne by carved ebony figures, it is not merely the luxury but the sheer size that impresses (especially on an island where space is at a premium).

For more of the same, but with the focus on privacy, ★★★★**La Scalinatella**, Via Tragara 8, ✆ 081 837 06 33, ✉ 081 837 8291, is a jewel of a hotel, with 31 beautifully decorated rooms and stunning views. There is a pool and good restaurant but there are no large public areas; the hotel doesn't take tour groups.

Outside Capri town at Punta Tragara, the ★★★★**Hotel Punta Tragara**, Via Tragara 57, ✆ 081 837 0844, ✉ 081 837 7790, is a de luxe resort hotel, offering pool, gym, restaurants and more in a building designed by Le Corbusier. The architect's distinctive modern style and the predominance of strong reds, oranges and dark wood fittings come at a price, but then the views from the rooms are spectacular.

expensive

★★★★**La Palma**, Via V. Emanuele, ✆ 081 837 0133, ✉ 081 837 6966, is good value by Capri standards. Just above the Quisisana in Capri town, it is set in its own gardens, with lovely majolica-tiled floors in the rooms and a pleasant airy feel. Established as a hotel in 1822, it's older than the Quisisana; the staff are charming and the whole atmosphere is more comfortable than that of many of the more expensive hotels.

Further up on the way to the panoramic Punta Tragara, the ★★★★**Villa Brunella**, Via Tragara 24, ✆ 081 837 0122, ✉ 081 837 0430, is a pretty hotel with rooms on terraces that overlook Monte Solaro. There is a good restaurant and pool for lazing away hot afternoons. The emphasis is on villa-style accommodation and privacy, suiting those who are looking for a retreat.

The **★★★Floridiana**, Via Campo di Teste, ✆ 081 837 0101, 🖷 081 837 0434, in Capri town, also has fine panoramas of the sea. Below the Quisisana and thus a little outside the limelight, the management are upgrading many of its rooms in unashamed pursuit of another star from the tourist board. Until prices go up this is a fair value hotel. Single travellers do not pay outrageous supplements, but merely half the cost of a double room. *Open all year.*

moderate

You'll need to book well ahead to stay at the **★★Villa Krupp**, Viale Matteotti 12, ✆ 081 837 0362, 🖷 081 837 6489, one of the loveliest and most historic lower-priced hotels in Capri. Situated above the path up to the Gardens of Augustus, the hotel has enviable views, antique furniture and a relaxed, welcoming ambience where one can sit and compose letters all day. Trotsky stayed here and even left a samovar.

cheap

Clean and well-run, the centrally located **★Stella Maris**, Via Roma 10–19, ✆ 081 837 0452, 🖷 081 837 8662, close to the bus station, is a cosy family-run affair. They have been here for generations and are proud of their hospitality, so you will not want for towels. Most rooms look down to the Marina Grande below and distant Ischia. **★La Tosca**, Via D. Birago, ✆/🖷 081 837 0989, still in Capri town, but overlooking the opposite coast, has clean tiled rooms with high ceilings. Ask for one with a view.

Capri ✉ *80073*

Eating Out

expensive

Capri's best restaurant has long been **La Capannina**, Via delle Botteghe 12–14, ✆ 081 837 0732, set in a secluded garden in Capri town, with delicately prepared shellfish, pasta and fish, and good desserts. **I Faraglioni**, Via Camerelle 75, ✆ 081 837 0320, has delectable house specialities like *crêpes al formaggio*, paper-thin pancakes filled with cheese, and *risotto ai frutti di mare*.

moderate

At **Da Paolino**, on Via Palazzo a Mare 11, ✆ 081 837 6102, on the way down from Capri town to Marina Grande, you'll eat in an arbour of lemon trees, tasting dishes mainly inspired by the fruit—as in the pasta, fish and dessert courses, all heavily lemon-influenced. Up the stairs past the cathedral and down the tunnel to the right in Capri town, is another island institution, **Da Gemma**, Via Madre Serafina 6, ✆ 081 837 0461, 🖷 081 837 8947. It's as nice in winter as it is in summer, a welcoming trattoria with walls decked with brass pans and ceramic plates, and superbly cooked local dishes including a fine *risotto alla pescatore* and delicious mozzarella grilled on a lemon leaf. It also serves very good pizza.

In Anacapri, about a half-hour's walk from the Piazzetta, **Da Gelsomina la Migliara**, Via La Migliara 72, ✆ 081 837 1499, offers not only home-made wine, but true home-cooked island specialities, including mushrooms collected on Monte Solaro. The risotto here is a real treat in all its forms.

The Amalfi Drive

> ...*the only delectable part of Italy,*
> *which the inhabitants there dwelling do call the coast of Malfie,*
> *full of towns, gardens, springs and wealthy men.*

Boccaccio

When confronted with something generally acclaimed to be the most beautiful stretch of scenery in the entire Mediterranean, the honest writer is at a loss. Few who have been there would argue the point, but describing it properly is another matter. Along this coast, where one mountain after another plunges sheer into the sea, there is a string of towns that not long ago were accessible only by boat.

Today, a spectacular corniche road of 'a thousand bends' covers the route, climbing in places to a thousand feet above the sea; necessity makes it so narrow that every encounter with an oncoming vehicle is an adventure, but everyone except the driver will have the treat of a lifetime. Nature here has created an amazing vertical landscape, a mix of sharp crags and deep green forests; in doing so she inspired the Italians to add three of their most beautiful towns.

This coast has always attracted foreigners, but only relatively recently has it become a major resort area. Places like Positano have become reserves for the wealthy, and swarms of day trippers are likely to descend at any moment. Rumour has it that the boutiques here are so fashionable that the Romans come to Positano to shop for their summer wardrobe (though you would never guess it from the baskets of frilly bikinis piled up in the street). But tourism will never spoil this area; all the engineers in Italy couldn't widen the Amalfi road, and the impossible terrain leaves no room at all for new development.

Tourist Information

Positano: Via Saracino 4, ✆ 089 875 067, ✆ 089 875 760.

Amalfi: Corso Roma 19, ✆ 089 871 107, ✆ 089 872 619.

Ravello: Piazza Duomo, ✆ 089 857 096, ✆ 089 857 977.

Maiori: Corso Regina, ✆ 089 877 452, ✆ 089 853 672.

Salerno: Piazza V. Veneto (outside the railway station), ✆/✆ 089 231 432 (very helpful). Their excellent *Annuario Alberghi* has a list of hotels located throughout the province.

Getting Around

Buses are the only form of public transport on the Amalfi coast. **SITA** services travel regularly between Sorrento and Salerno (about every 50min; *see* p.162).

Positano

To complement the vertical landscape, here is Italy's most nearly vertical town. Positano spills down from the corniche like a waterfall of pink, cream and yellow villas. The day trippers may walk down to the sea; only the alpinists among them make it back up (fortunately, there is a regular bus service along the one main street).

After the Second World War, Positano became a well-known hideaway for artists and writers—many of them American, following John Steinbeck's lead—and fashion was not slow to follow. Now, even though infested with coach parties, Positano reverts to the Positanesi in the off-season, and quietens down considerably. However, do be aware that parking here, as with most of the Amalfi coast, is extremely tricky and you may be forced to hand over a fat wad of lira if you bring your car. Off the main thoroughfare, the road spirals down to the town centre—avoid bringing your car this far if you can. There are usually more spaces as you approach along the drive, and even when it looks to be a fair hike into town, steps often provide a short cut down the hillside. When you get to the bottom, there is a pebbly, grey beach and the town's church, decorated with a pretty tiled dome like so many others along this coast. A highlight of the town's year is its spectacular *festa* on the Feast of the Assumption, 15 August—the main holiday of the summer throughout Italy—when the local people take their town back in order to stage a performance recreating the Amalfi coast's centuries-long battles with the Saracens (*see* 'Festivals', p.16).

If you have time, take a trip further up to **Montepertuso**, a village perched 3km above Positano, which takes its name (meaning 'hole in the mountain') from an old legend—the devil challenged the Virgin Mary to blow a hole in the mountain, saying the winner could have control of the village. The devil tried, but failed miserably, while the Virgin coolly walked through the mountainside, leaving a hole still visible today. The locals re-enact the scene each 2 July, with much merriment and fireworks. On the last Saturday in August, the village stages another of the best festas in all Italy, the *sagra del fagiolo*—the feast of the bean. The streets are decked out with stalls selling beans cooked in every possible way, plus a great many other home-cooked dishes, washed down with local wine served from oak barrels by waiters dressed in traditional costume.

The next town east along the drive from Positano, **Praiano**, could be Positano's little sister, with a similar beach and church, but not quite as scenic and perpendicular, or as beleaguered by tourism. Her natural attractions, however, leave her ripe for creeping exploitation.

After Praiano, keep an eye out for the most impressive natural feature along the drive, the steep, impenetrable

Furore Gorge. On either side are tiny isolated villages along the shore, with beaches—if only you can find a way to get to them. Further down the road you'll notice the lift leading down to the **Grotta Smeralda** (*open April–Oct daily 9–5; Nov–Mar daily 10–6; adm*). The strange green light that is diffused throughout this sea-level cavern gives it its name. Beyond this, **Conca dei Marini** is another vertical village, with a beach and a Norman lookout tower to climb.

Positano ✉ *84017*

luxury

With Positano's high-fashion status come some of the highest hotel prices in Italy. If you're feeling self-indulgent—and very rich—you may care to stay at a place many believe to be the finest resort hotel in the country. The ★★★★★**San Pietro**, ✆ 089 875 455, ✉ 089 811 449, lies 1½km outside Positano *en route* to Amalfi. The entrance is hidden behind an old chapel, with only a discreet sign to alert you to the intimate paradise which spills down the cliff face beneath you. It's all part of the management's plan to maintain the privacy and tranquillity of its celebrity clientele. Amid the richly coloured gardens, 58 individual rooms are immaculately maintained, each offering a private terrace and spectacular views round every corner—even when you're soaking in a hot tub. It also offers a private beach, tennis courts and its own excursion boat. Given its position outside Positano, it's worth bearing in mind that a car is vital if you wish to explore further afield—unless you bring your helicopter that is, for which there is a landing pad. Still, shopping *is* available in the form of branded T-shirts and towels, and given the extraordinary range of facilities, you may never want to leave. *Closed Nov–Mar.*

★★★★★**Le Sirenuse**, Via Cristoforo Colombo 30, ✆ 089 875 066, ✉ 089 811 798, is the former home of a noble Neapolitan family to whom it still belongs. It became a hotel in 1951 and takes its name from the islands of the Sirens which it overlooks. Everything is done with style, from the beautifully decorated drawing room to the swimming pool with its mosaic tiles. Cool and sophisticated, it lies close to the shops and restaurant, and offers a private pool, jacuzzi and fitness area.

very expensive–expensive

The ★★★★**Palazzo Murat**, Via dei Mulini 23, ✆ 089 875 177, ✉ 089 811 419, in the heart of Positano, is an 18th-century palazzo which once belonged to Napoleon's brother-in-law Joachim Murat, briefly King of Naples. It has plenty of old-world charm, with antiques in many rooms and a beautiful courtyard shaded by lofty palm trees, where classical concerts are sometimes staged in summer. An elegant hotel with oodles of atmosphere. The ★★★★**Covo dei Saraceni**, Via Regina Giovanna 5, ✆ 089 875 400, ✉ 089 875 878, is a comfortable hotel in one of the best locations in town, at the bottom of the hill right on the edge of the harbour, with wonderful views up through town and out to sea. The rooms are simple and spacious, and tastefully furnished with antique furniture. Relax, and let the sound of the sea lull you to sleep at night.

On a more modest level, the ★★★**Casa Albertina**, Via Favolozza 4, ✆ 089 875 143, 🖷 089 811 540, is furnished in a lovely, understated manner, the better to accentuate the views over Positano and the sea. It's a family-run place, with a nice restaurant on the rooftop terrace, a few minutes from the beach, and in the busy season its quietness can be an advantage. Be aware that half-board is compulsory during high season. A little closer to the water is ★★★**L'Ancora**, on Via Columbo, ✆ 089 875 318, 🖷 089 811 784. A small and professionally run place, it offers sea views and much-needed parking in the centre of town.

With a car, you can expand your horizons to include some of the more secluded spots along the coast. Tourism has yet to infiltrate the heart of Praiano and if you climb up behind the road, you will find a sleepy fishing village, undisturbed by the whirr of cameras or the rumble of coaches. Still, there is some pleasant accommodation running along the coast, much of it just outside the village at Vettica Maggiore—a little way back towards Positano along the Amalfi drive.

One exceptional bargain here is the ★★★**Tramonto d'Oro**, ✆ 089 874 008, 🖷 089 874 670, which offers tennis courts, a pool, beach access and great views. The management is friendly and helpful. Forty recently renovated rooms are tastefully decorated with attractive tiling and bright materials. The high number of return clients speaks for itself. Further towards Amalfi at Conca dei Marini, the ★★★★**Belvedere**, ✆ 089 831 282, 🖷 089 831 439, is an airy and modern resort hotel in a delightful setting, with a nice beach and an old Norman tower in the grounds. The sea-water pool offers a refreshing dip to those not averse to salt.

In Positano, a good bargain is the ★★**California**, Via Colombo 141, ✆/🖷 089 875 382, with 15 very pleasant rooms and a lovely terrace for breakfast and other meals. Set slightly back from the sea, it is nonetheless well located and charmingly run. Still in Positano, the ★**Maria Luisa**, Via Fornillo 40, ✆/🖷 089 875 023, has 10 rooms and a friendly family atmosphere. A few very cheap *pensioni* can also be found along Via Fornillo and on the other streets leading down to the beach.

In Praiano, similarly, there are some cheaper old pensions by the port, but they are usually full to bursting in the summer. For a clean and reliable option, look out for ★★★**Le Terrazze**, ✆ 089 831 290, under the same management as Tramonto D'Oro and situated right on the sea. A more individual choice, also in Praiano, is ★★**La Tranquillità**, ✆ 089 874 084, a holiday village offering small wooden bungalows with windows on to the sea and a private terrace for that evening tipple. Steps built out of the rocks offer access to the water and plenty of opportunity to tone your calf muscles on the way back up. Breakfast can be taken on the restaurant terrace and evening meals are also available. Not luxurious, but clean, thoughtfully managed and a cheap alternative for the more independent traveller. For young groovers, it is so close to the Amalfi coast's hottest dance floor, the Africana nightclub, you can dance to the music in your own bedroom.

In the high season at least, most of the resort hotels along the coast will expect you to take half-board, which means having either lunch or dinner in their restaurant. Not that that's always bad—some of the better hotels have gourmet restaurants and are often extremely good value. However, there are also some equally good places elsewhere to enjoy—if you can escape! Like many of the restaurants on the Costiera, a good number of Positano's eateries close from November till Easter.

expensive

La Cambusa, Spiaggia Grande, ✆ 089 875 432, in a lovely position with a terrace looking out on to the beach, is a Positano favourite. The chef serves excellently cooked fresh fish and seafood in as many ways as you can think of, and more. A house speciality is *penne con gamberetti, rucola e pomodoro* (penne with prawns, rocket and fresh tomatoes). Across the road, the **Buca Di Bacco**, Via Rampa Teglia 8, ✆ 089 875 699, is another Positano institution and *the* place to stop off for a drink on the way back from the beach. The fish is always well-cooked here, and you'd be crazy to go for anything else. It also has a few rooms.

Situated right on the beach in Positano, the centre of the action in the summer is **Chez Black**, Via Brigantino, ✆ 089 875 036, a slick and sophisticated joint run by local entrepreneur Salvatore Russo. As with all the restaurants along the Spiaggia Grande, it's not what you eat, but who sees you eating, that matters. Those privileged enough to be seated in a director's chair, close to the water's edge, will know they have really arrived. However, good Neapolitan favourites like *spaghetti alle vongole* are also done well here; try a banana split with *liquore Strega* for dessert.

moderate

O'Caporale, just off the beach on Via Regina Giovanna, ✆ 089 811 188, offers simple and well-cooked seafood. The swordfish and *zuppa di pesce* are come particularly recommended. **Lo Guarracino**, Via Positanesi d'America 12, ✆ 089 875 794, is situated in one of Positano's most lovely spots, on a terrace perched over the sea, reached by a short walk along the cliff path towards Fornillo beach. This pizzeria-cum-trattoria is pleasantly informal after the fashionable Spiaggia Grande, and as such it is a favourite with the Positanesi.

Further uptown, the **Grottino Azzurro**, Via Chiesa Nuova, ✆ 089 875 466, is a family-run trattoria, where the *signora* comes to the table to advise you on the catch of the day, and how best you should sample it.

In summer, for a memorable experience, watch out for boats marked **Da Laurito** leaving the jetty at Positano beach. This is a free ferry service to a delightful trattoria (✆ 089 875 022) around the next bay, set on a small beach, with makeshift tables under a straw canopy. The speciality here is good old-fashioned recipes such as *totani con patate* (squid cooked with potatoes in a wonderful sauce of oil and garlic), all washed down with white wine spiked with fresh peaches. At the end of your meal, they'll ferry you back again as part of the service.

Just east of Praiano, a sharp turn down to the beach brings you to the **Petit Ristorante**, Via Praia 15, ℗ 089 874 706, tucked away in a tiny bay at the foot of Il Furore. This informal eaterie's tempting smells beckon in the hungry bather. Dine at tables outside, surrounded by gaily painted fishing boats, choosing from a menu that features mainly simple dishes such as fresh grilled fish and salad. *Closed Oct–Easter.*

cheap

Given Positano's fashionable standing, genuinely cheap places to eat are hard to find, though there are some pizzerias around Via Fornillo, and some of the restaurants listed above, such as Chez Black, provide pizzas at less than their main-menu prices.

Those with a car could try **Taverna del Leone**, Via Laurito 43, ℗ 089 875 474, just outside Positano heading towards Amalfi. This busy pizzeria, bustling with young Positanesi, serves tasty nosh in relaxed surroundings and at very reasonable prices. For those looking for something more sophisticated, the adjoining restaurant is more formal, though equally popular. At Montepertuso, above Positano, **Il Ritrovo**, Via Monte 53, ℗ 089 811 336, is a pretty trattoria, with tomatoes strung from beams and good local dishes including, a rarity in these parts, grilled meats. A pleasantly rustic experience for anyone wishing to escape the crowds (if only for a night).

Entertainment and Nightlife

If you fancy a night on the town, two bright firmaments stand out along the Amalfi coast. The **Africana**, Via Torre a Mare, Praiano, ℗ 089 874 042, is *the* place to be seen. It is built into a man-made cave at sea level, so you can dance with the fish as they swim in brightly lit pools beneath your feet, or strut like a tribal chief amid the African bric-a-brac. Watch out for the parrot, he's vicious! For those looking to arrive in style, there is a boat service available from Positano. Alternatively you can park your car at the tiny bay at Furore and walk along the cliff path (about 5 mins). *Open May–Oct.*

For cabaret-style entertainment, try the recently opened **Music on the Rocks**, Grotte dell'Incanto 51, ℗ 089 875 874, owned by the proprietor of Chez Black, and a short stroll to the left of the Spiaggia Grande.

Amalfi

Sometimes history seems to be kidding us. Can it be true, can this minuscule village once have had a population of 80,000? There is no room among these jagged rocks for even a fraction of that—but then we remember that in Campania anything is possible, and we read how most of the old town simply slid into the sea during a storm and earthquake in 1343. Until that moment, Amalfi was a glorious place, the first Italian city to regain its balance after the Dark Ages, the first to recreate its civic pride and its mercantile daring, showing the way to Venice, Pisa and Genoa, though she kept few of the prizes for herself.

History

It is only natural that the Amalfitani would try to embroider their history a bit to match such an exquisite setting. Legends tell of a nymph named Amalphi who haunted this shore and became the lover of Hercules. As for their city's founding, they'll tell you about a party of Roman noblemen, fleeing the barbarians after the fall of the Empire, who found the site a safe haven to carry on the old Roman spirit and culture.

Amalfi first appears in the 6th century; by the 9th it had achieved its independence from the dukes of Naples and was probably the most important trading port of southern Italy, with a large colony of merchants at Constantinople and connections with all the Muslim lands. In 849 the chroniclers record the Amalfitano fleet chasing off an Arab raid on Rome. At the beginning, the Amalfitano Republic was ruled by officers called *giudici*, or judges; the year 958 brought a change in constitutions, and Amalfi elected its first doge, in imitation of Venice. At about the same time, the city's merchants developed the famous *Tavola Amalfitana*, a book of maritime laws that was widely adopted around the Mediterranean.

All of this came at a time for which historical records are scarce, but Amalfi's merchant adventurers must have had as romantically exciting a time as those of Venice. Their luck turned sour in the 11th century. The first disaster was a sacking by Robert Guiscard in 1073. Amalfi regained its freedom with a revolt in 1096, but the Normans of the new Kingdom of Sicily came back to stay in 1131.

These, unfortunately, proved unable to protect it against two more terrible sackings at the hands of its arch-enemy, Pisa, in 1135 and 1137. Today Amalfi only gets a chance to recapture its glory days once every four years, when it hosts the Pisans, Genoese and Venetians in the antique boat race of the Four Maritime Republics. Amalfi next hosts the race on the first Sunday in June 2001.

The Cathedral and the Cloister of Paradise

The disaster of 1343 ensured that Amalfi's decline would be complete, but what's left of the place today—with its 5,000 or so people—is beautiful almost to excess. Over the little square around the harbour, a conspicuous inscription brags: 'Judgement Day, for the Amalfitani who go to heaven, will be a day like any other day.' The square is called **Piazza Flavio Gioia**, after Amalfi's most famous merchant adventurer (his statue looks as if he's offering you a cup of tea); he's probably another fictitious character—more Amalfitano embroidery—but they claim he invented the compass in the 12th century.

From here, an arch under the buildings leads to the centre of the town, the **Piazza del Duomo**, with a long flight of steps up to what may be the loveliest **cathedral** in all the south of Italy (9th–12th centuries). Not even in Sicily was the Arab-Norman style ever carried to such a flight of fancy as in this delicate façade, with four levels of interlaced arches in stripes of different-coloured stone (much restored a century ago). The lace-like open arches on the porch are unique in Italy, though common enough in Muslim Spain, one of the countries with which Amalfi had regular trade relations.

The cathedral's greatest treasure is its set of bronze doors, cast with portraits of Christ, Mary, St Peter and Amalfi's patron, St Andrew; the first of such bronze doors in Italy, they were made in Constantinople in 1066 by an artist named Simon of Syria (he signed them), commissioned by the leader of the Amalfitan colony there. The cathedral's interior, unfortunately, was restored in the 18th-century baroque *à la* Napoletana, with plenty of frills in inlaid marble. The red porphyry baptismal font, in the first chapel on the left, is believed to have come from the ruins of Paestum. Down in the crypt you can see more coloured marble work and frescoes, a gift of Philip II of Spain, and also the head of St Andrew; this relic was a part of Amalfi's share of the loot in the sack of Constantinople in 1204.

One of the oldest parts of the cathedral to survive is the **Chiostro del Paradiso** (*open daily 9–6.45; adm*), a whitewashed quadrangle of interlaced arches with a decidedly African air (*unfortunately still under restoration*). To the side of the cloister is the **Basilica del Crocifisso**, the original cathedral, where amidst the surviving frescoes many of the bits and pieces of old Amalfi that have endured its calamities have been assembled: there are classical sarcophagi, medieval sculptures and coats of arms. Best of all are the fragments of Cosmatesque work, brightly coloured geometric mosaics that once were parts of pulpits and pillars, a speciality of this part of Campania. Don't miss the lovely 16th-century *Madonna col Bambino* by the stairs down to the Crypt.

From the centre of Amalfi, you can walk in a few minutes out to the northern edge of the city, the narrow 'Valley of the Mills', set along a streambed between steep cliffs; some of the mills that made medieval Amalfi famous for paper-making are still in operation, and there is a small **Paper Museum** (*open 9–1; closed Mon and Fri; adm*) in the town. You can also watch paper being made and buy paper products at **Armatruda**, Via Fiume, ✆ 089 871 315, in central Amalfi, near the museum.

If you'll be staying some time in this area, one of the best ways to spend it is walking the many lovely paths that navigate the steep hills into the interior of the peninsula, passing through groves of chestnut and ash; these, such as they are, were the main roads in the days of the Republic. One particularly nice one is the Amalfi–Pontone path, passing the ruins of the old monastery of Sant'Eustacchio, and there are many others around Ravello and Scala; ask the locals to point them out.

Amalfi ✉ *84011*　　　　　　　　　　　　　　　　　　　*Where to Stay*

Unlike Positano, Amalfi has been a resort for a long time, and some of its older establishments are among the most distinctive on the Mediterranean coast.

very expensive

The ★★★★★**Santa Caterina**, ✆ 089 871 012, ✆ 089 871 351, just outside Amalfi, has perhaps the loveliest gardens of all. A converted villa, it sits on a cliff-top providing wonderful sea views from most rooms. Its staff are courteous and discreet and its atmosphere cool and elegant. One refreshing slip—family snapshots with Hillary Clinton are on display in the reception.

St Francis himself is said to have founded the ★★★★**Luna,** ✆ 089 871 002, 🖨 089 871 333, though the lifts and Hollywood-style pool are a little more recent. This former monastery, above the drive on Amalfi's eastern edge, was already a hotel in the waning days of the Grand Tour—Wagner stayed here while searching for his Garden of Klingsor, and they can show you the room where Ibsen wrote *A Doll's House*. Among other famous guests, the owners claim the Luna to have been a favourite of both Mussolini and Otto von Bismarck. Deftly modernized, it provides comfortable rooms and attentive service.

On the opposite side of town, along the drive between Positano and Amalfi, the efficient ★★★★**Miramalfi,** ✆ 089 871 588, 🖨 089 871 287, is a sixties-style hotel with pool, beach and private parking.

To get away from it at all, your best bet is the 12th-century ★★★★**Cappuccini Convento,** Via Annunziatella 46, ✆ 089 871 877, 🖨 089 871 886, built by Emperor Frederick II on a mountainside over the town, with a suitably ancient lift running down through the cliffs to the beach. The converted cells, now hotel bedrooms, are dark and unsophisticated, in keeping with the closed monastic order that once prevailed here. You eat in the original refectory and there is a 12th-century chapel and cloister which seems to ensure a spiritual hush throughout. Set high above the tourist-infested streets, its colonnade bedecked with flowers offers the best view in Amalfi. Meals, like the hotel, are a treat to be savoured. Indulge!

Right in the centre of town, through a series of warren-like streets, the ★★★**Amalfi** on Via dei Pastai, ✆ 089 872 440, 🖨 089 872 250, is popular with package tours, and is a valuable alternative for those without transport.

Further along the Corso Roma, the ★★**Sole,** Largo della Zecca, ✆ 089 871 147, is located in a quiet piazza, behind the beach front and next to the Highland Pub—should you be in need of a spot of eclectic refreshment. It's clean and airy, with private parking. There is also a fair collection of inexpensive places around the cathedral; two of the best are the tiny and elaborately furnished ★★**Sant'Andrea**, Via Santolo Camera 1, ✆ 089 871 145, with good views of the cathedral and an effusive welcome from your proprietress; and the ★★**Fontana**, Piazza Duomo 7, ✆ 089 871 530, which has 16 spotless rooms offering plenty of space and a prime location at bargain prices. Both are perfect for night owls, with the main piazza humming away until the early hours. There's no need to bring an alarm clock either: the cathedral bells should do the job nicely. Consider ear plugs.

Amalfi ✉ *84011*   **Eating Out**

Amalfi has several fine restaurants, including those in the luxury hotels mentioned above. But for a sense of this exuberant little city, try one of the many attractive restaurants listed below. Amalfi lacks the pretensions of her sister, Positano, but what you lose in finery, you make up for in the fundamentals—good, honest grub!

Da Gemma, Via Fra Gerardo Sasso 9, ✆ 089 871 345, established in 1872, is one of Amalfi's oldest restaurants, with an attractive dining terrace and an excellent fish-based menu. Their *zuppa di pesce* is a wonderfully rich mixture of all sorts of different fish and seafood, although at L100,000 for two, this is no poor man's gruel. Leave room for the *melanzane al cioccolato* (grilled aubergines in chocolate sauce), an unexpected but heavenly combination. *Closed Wed.* **La Caravella**, Via Matteo Camera 12, ✆ 089 871 029, near the tunnel by the beach, is a busy restaurant which serves generous helpings of home-made pasta, including delicious ravioli stuffed with seafood, and a good range of home-made desserts. *Closed Tues.*

Antico Hostaria Bacco, Via G.B. Lama 9, Furore, ✆ 089 830 360, ✆ 089 830 352, up in the hills on the road to Agerola, is a wonderful detour if you have a car; the drive alone is spectacular. The delightful Ferraioli family serve delicious seafood *antipasti* and pasta—*ferrazzuoli* with sword fish and rocket—and, for dessert, their own *melanzane al cioccolato* (*see* above). They also offer the local white wine, Costa d'Amalfi Furore (available for sale across the road). There are a few charming rooms (*moderate*), with views to the sea below.

Almost directly under the cathedral is the cosy **Taverna degli Apostoli**, Via Sant'Anna 5, ✆ 089 872 991, with a warm and informal atmosphere which when we last visited echoed with the ribald laughter of local festivities. Highly recommended. *Closed Tues.* At **Lo Smeraldino**, Piazzale dei Protontini 1, ✆ 089 871 070, at the far end of the port on the water's edge, you'll be offered the area speciality, *scialatielli ai frutti di mare*—fresh pasta with mixed seafood—and a range of good *secondi*, most notably an excellent *fritto misto*. Good food and bustling waiters are the order of the day in this popular eaterie.

Heading up the main street towards the Valley of the Mills, you could do worse than stop at **La Taverna del Duca**, Largo Spirito Santo 26, ✆ 089 872 755. Tables lie scattered around a small piazza and diners eat off hand-painted plates. A relaxing midday stop, offering pizza, pasta and traditional Amalfi cooking. *Closed Thurs.*

North of the cathedral, the **Tarì**, Via P. Capuano, ✆ 089 871 832, is a pretty, welcoming trattoria with traditional checked tablecloths and service with a smile. It's cool, cavernous surroundings beckon in the hot and weary traveller and there are no unpleasant surprises when it's time for the bill.

Da Baracca, Piazza dei Dogi, ✆ 089 871 285, is everything an Italian trattoria should be. Tables and chairs spill out on to this tranquil piazza just west of the cathedral, where diners are shielded from the midday sun by a shady awning and leafy plants. Friendly waiters proffer tasty snacks and plates of steaming pasta—and there are no hidden costs to leave you with a sour taste in your mouth.

At the **San Giuseppe**, Via Ruggiero II 4, ☎ 089 872 640, a family-run hostelry, the pizza is sublime—it should be: the owner is a baker. Homely bowls of pasta are also available, brought to you by a trio of portly brothers, and consumed amid the noise of television and shrieking children. *Closed Thurs.* Near the cathedral, **Da Maria**, Via Lorenzo d'Amalfi 14, ☎ 089 871 880, displays a highly embellished—and multi-lingual—menu to entice the traveller off the streets and into this lively trattoria and pizzeria. Allow yourselves to be tempted: the waiters are cheerful and helpful, and the food a cut above some of the other less expensive places.

Villages Inland: Ravello and Scala

As important as it was in its day, the Amalfitan Republic never grew very big. At its greatest extent, it could only claim a small part of this coast, including these two towns up in the mountains; like Amalfi they were once much larger and more prosperous than you see them today. **Ravello** is another beauty, a balcony overlooking the Amalfi coast and a treasure house of exotic medieval art and tropical botany. The sinuous climb can be made by bus or car, but be aware that parking here is a nightmare—and expect to pay through the nose if you bring your car. Ravello seems to have been a resort even in Roman times; numerous remains of villas have been found. As the second city of the Amalfitan Republic, medieval Ravello had a population of 30,000 (at least that's what they claim); now it provides an example of that typically Italian phenomenon—a village of 2,000 with a first-rate cathedral.

Ravello's chief glories are two wonderful gardens. The **Villa Cimbrone** (*open daily 9–7; adm*) was laid out by Lord Grimthorpe, the Englishman responsible for the design of Big Ben. The priceless view over the Amalfi coast is now owned by the Swiss Vuillemier family who also run the Hotel Palumbo (*see* below) and it is, without doubt, one of the most beautiful properties in all Italy. The **Villa Rùfolo** (*open daily 9–8 ; adm*), as fans of Wagner will be interested to know, is none other than Klingsor's magic garden. Wagner says so himself, in a note scribbled in the villa's guest book. He came here looking for the proper setting in which to imagine the worldly, Faustian enchanter of *Parsifal*, and thus his imagination was fired. The villa itself is a remarkable 11th-century pleasure palace, a temporary abode of Charles of Anjou, various Norman kings and Adrian IV, the only English pope (1154–9), who came here when fleeing a rebellion in Rome. Even in its present, half-ruined state, it is worth a visit; inside there is a small collection of architectural fragments, including a Moorish cloister and two crumbling towers, one of which can still be climbed. The garden, with more fine views, is a semi-tropical paradise; in summer it reverberates with 'sounds and sweet airs' as the setting for various open-air concerts.

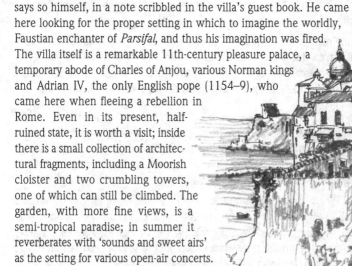

The **cathedral** is named after Ravello's patron, San Pantaleone, an obscure early martyr; they have a phial of his blood in one of the side chapels, and it 'boils' like the blood of San Gennaro in Naples whenever the saint is in the mood. Lately he hasn't been, which worries the Ravellans. The cathedral has two particular treasures: a pair of bronze doors by Barisano of Trani (1179), inspired by the Greek ones at Amalfi, and an exquisite pair of marble *ambones*, or pulpits, that rank among the outstanding examples of 12th–13th-century sculptural and mosaic work; the more elaborate one, its columns resting on six curious lions, dates from 1272. The sacristy contains two paintings by the southern Renaissance artist Andrea da Salerno, including an unusual subject, the *Assumption of the Magdalen*. Downstairs there is a small **museum** (*open daily 9.30–1 and 3–7; adm*) containing more bits of the original Cosmatesque interior and an intriguing bust of Sigilgaida Rufolo by Bartolomeo di Nicola, the sculptor of the lions' *ambone*. In this cathedral in 1149, the English pope, Adrian IV, crowned William the Bad as King of Sicily. Two other Ravello churches where you can see decorative work similar to the cathedral's are **Santa Maria a Gradello** and **San Giovanni del Toro**.

From Ravello, it is a lovely 1½km walk to **Scala**, smallest and oldest of the three Amalfitan towns and a genteel option for the traveller seeking peace and parsimony in the refreshing mountain air. Perched on the hillside across from Ravello, this is a timeless gem, which offers a rural escape, unfettered by the glitz of other resorts. Scala has another interesting old cathedral, **San Lorenzo**; inside, over the main altar is a 13th-century wooden crucifix.

Gerardo da Sasso, a citizen of Scala, started out running a small hostel for pilgrims in Jerusalem and ended up founding the Knights Hospitallers, or Knights of St John (1118); his family's ruined palace can be seen near the village. After the fall of Jerusalem, the order moved to Rhodes and subsequently Malta. The Sovereign Order of the Knights of Malta still share the distinctive swallow-tail cross which you see throughout Amalfi. Above Scala, the chapel of **San Pietro in Campoleone** has medieval carvings of St Michael and St Catherine inside, if you can find someone with the key.

Between Amalfi and Ravello, before reaching the turn-off inland, the Amalfi drive passes through **Atrani**, an old village whose church of San Salvatore has another tiled dome, and yet another set of bronze doors from Constantinople; inside it, note the lovely Byzantine relief of a pair of peacocks (peacock flesh was believed to be incorruptible back then, and therefore a symbol of immortality; but why the birds are standing, respectively, on a man and a rabbit is anybody's guess). In the days of the Republic this church was called San Salvatore della Biretta; the Amalfitan doges wore cloth caps like those of Venice, and they would come here for their ceremonies of investiture. Atrani and Amalfi don't much care for each other. Such Lilliputian rivalries are common on this coast (it's the same with Ravello and Scala); in Amalfi they'll tell you how Atrani was ruined after the Pisan raids, and how Emperor Manfred repopulated it with Muslims from Sicily. Such neighbours!

Beyond the Ravello turn, next along the way towards Salerno, come **Minori** and **Maiori**. Minori is a typical *Costiera* hill-town which, despite encroaching tourism, maintains considerable charm. Its bigger sister is somewhat less enticing, mainly due to a major flood in 1954 which washed away most of the seafront; today most of the buildings and hotels along the shore are depressingly modern. **Erchie**, a tiny hamlet on the shore far below the road, seems a lovely spot—if you can figure out a way to get down to it. Then, near the end of the drive, the real world comes back into view as the busy port of Salerno stretches before you. Here you find the tiny resort of **Cetara**, with a fine beach behind a newly constructed fishing port, and, just before Salerno, **Vietri sul Mare**, another steep and pretty town, famous throughout Italy for its beautiful *maiolica* ware. There are ceramics shops everywhere, where you can watch craftsmen hand-painting jugs, vases and tiles, and pick up souvenirs at surprisingly good prices.

Ravello ✉ *84010*   **Where to Stay**

Ravello also has its share of dream hotels, offering no beaches, but unforgettable gardens and views down over the coast. In the shadow of Amalfi and Ravello, the two pleasant beach lidos of Minori and Maiori may seem a little dull, but they can be useful bases, especially if hotels in the better-known resorts are full.

luxury

One of Ravello's finest, with an incredible guest book full of the names of the famous over the last 120 years, is the ★★★★★**Palumbo**, Via S. Giovanni del Toro 28, ✆ 089 857 244, ✉ 089 857 347, *palumbo@amalfinet.it*. The entrance opens on to an elegant Arabic-style courtyard which only hints at the 12 rooms, each individually decorated with antiques. The restaurant is highly renowned, and the excellent Episcopio wine really is house wine—made on the premises. It's certainly elitist and your absolute privacy is guaranteed, but if you are searching for a taste of the real Italy, the smart, international atmosphere might just disappoint. There is also a simpler *dipendenza* (a cheaper alternative) with seven rooms. Transport, pool share (with Hotel Giordano), and private parking all available.

The other top establishment in Ravello is the recently renovated ★★★★★**Palazzo Sasso**, Via S. Giovanni del Toro 58, ✆ 089 818 181, ✉ 089 858 900, *info@palazzosasso.com*. Originally a 12th-century villa belonging to the Sasso family, it was first owned by Fra Gerardo, the founder of the Sovereign Military Order of Malta. It's to here that Wagner rushed back in order to fix on paper the vision he caught in Villa Rufolo. These days you're likely to bump into Gore Vidal having dinner in their famed Rossellinis restaurant. Now run by an all-female management, it's recently been awarded the American *Five Star Diamond Award*. Refreshingly, the plush décor and astonishing views come with a very friendly staff.

very expensive

With the lushest gardens on the coast, the ★★★**Villa Cimbrone**, Via Santa Chiara 26, ✆ 089 857 459, ✉ 089 858 072, is a very special place to stay: another elegant old villa, once the property of an English duke, set in its own parkland perched dizzyingly high on the cliffs. The 10 rooms are beautifully decorated (half with sea views) and the view from the terrace where breakfast is served is a feast all of its own. There are drawbacks, however, such as the lack of a restaurant and the 10-minute walk needed to get there (cars have to be parked further down in the village). Nonetheless, it does have a swimming pool.

In Ravello, the ★★★★**Caruso Belvedere**, Via S. Giovanni del Toro 2, ✆ 089 857 111, @ 089 857 372, was once popular with the Bloomsbury set and with Greta Garbo (she had room 21). Behind its sun-bleached façade, this hotel encapsulates the quiet elegance of the old patrician villa it once was—even the laundry room holds a fading fresco. The present owner's grandfather, a cousin of the famous Neapolitan tenor Enrico Caruso, opened it as a hotel 100 years ago. In the beautifully laid out gardens, there is a belvedere over the sea and mountains, and the well-tended vegetable garden and vineyard on another level provide fresh produce and the hotel's own wine. Guests are encouraged to take half-board, which is no real hardship since the food is superb, and meals are taken on one of the loveliest terraces in Ravello.

One of the prettiest hotels, and perhaps the most welcoming place to stay in Ravello, is the delightful ★★★★**Villa Maria**, Via Santa Chiara 2, ✆ 089 857 255, @ 089 857 071. A light, airy charm prevails in this gracious and tastefully converted villa. First choice among such leading lights as Rudolf Nureyev, Tim Robbins and Susan Sarandon, and the disgraced Andreotti (whose visit is barely acknowledged!), it is made all the more attractive by the helpful and friendly owner, Vincenzo Palumbo, known to everyone as *Il Professore* or 'Prof'. The vast suite (more expensive than the normal rooms) has one of the most breathtaking terraces in Ravello and there is a beautiful eating area in the garden, sheltered by vines and graced with yet another astonishing view. Even if you don't stay here, it's worth coming to eat. The restaurant recently won an award in the highly reputed '*gambero rosso*' scheme, and is acknowledged throughout the region.

Further along the coast in the small suburb of Raito, just outside Vietri sul Mare, is the ★★★★★**Raito**, ✆ 089 210 033, @ 089 211 434, a grandiose hotel in a formidable position and recently restored from top to bottom. It is popular with business conferences, as is apparent from the smart, functional interiors and impeccable service.

moderate

Under the same obliging ownership as the Villa Maria, and only a few minutes walk away, is the ★★★**Hotel Giordano**, Via Trinità 14, ✆ 089 857 255, @ 089 857 071. A modern hotel, with the added advantage of a heated outdoor swimming pool and solarium, the Giordano is a comfortable alternative, reasonably priced and well stocked up with useful information on the area. Villa Maria guests have equal access to the facilities, and parking for both hotels is available here.

Along the coast in Minori, certainly the best of the hotels in the less elegant resorts of Maiori and Minori, is the ★★★★**Villa Romana**, ✆ 089 877 237, @ 089 877 302, a stylish and comfortable modern hotel. The management is eager to please, and the hotel is well situated in the heart of the town (although unfortunately not on the sea). The rooftop pool is well away from crowds and car fumes, and the rooms are clean and pleasant. Parking, however, is difficult. In Maiori the ★★★★**San Pietro**, ✆ 089 877 220, @ 089 877 025, is a modern hotel popular with Italian holidaymakers. Don't expect a beauty spot. Besides being situated at the far end of town, and well away from the beach, it's square, grey and characterless. However, for a longer stay on the coast, its sports facilities are good, and there are private family-sized bungalows in the grounds.

Heading out to Salerno, the tiny resort of Cetara is based around a fine sandy bay and ancient village. The ★★★★**Cetus**, ✆/🖷 089 261388, clings precariously to the cliffs between the devilish drive and the deep blue sea. Attractively redecorated with a hint of Art Deco, its isolated position and undisturbed bay make the Cetus a rising star among the hotels on this coastline, the only disadvantage being the long journeys back and forth along the often packed Amalfi drive. Parking available.

Should you find yourself in Vietri sul Mare, or prefer to stay here instead of Salerno, you could try the ★★★**Hotel Bristol**, Via C. Colombo 2, ✆ 089 210 216, 🖷 089 761 170, just above the beach. It's clean and characterless, but useful for a stopover. A swimming pool and beach are available, but if you're planning a night on the town, it's a long walk uphill!

cheap

For a five-star view at a third of the price in Ravello, why not check into the ★★**Villa Amore,** ✆/🖷 089 857 135, a delightful small hotel with 12 clean simple rooms, and a lovely terrace where you can take cappuccino with the canaries. It retains a warm, homely atmosphere not common to most of the larger hotels in this area.

Another gem in this price category can be found in unspoilt Scala. The **Villa Giuseppina**, ✆/🖷 089 857 106, offers comfort and charm at affordable prices. Good food and great views from the swimming pool make this a tranquil spot to while away those hazy days of summer. If you prefer you can stay at the older-style **Margherita** which shares the facilities. Parking is easy and you can enjoy some lovely walks down to Amalfi. Just be sure to catch the bus back.

In Maiori, there are several simple hotels near the beaches, such as the ★★**Baia Verde**, ✆ 089 877 276, and the ★★**Vittoria**, ✆ 089 877 652, that offer some of the most convenient budget accommodation on the Amalfi coast. These clean but unglamorous *pensione* will suit those hoping to explore the Amalfi coastline without paying the price. Typically, both are situated at the top of modern blocks of flats and Baia Verde in particular offers a great view from its terrace. If you can cope with the cranky lifts and strict noise restrictions ('no clogs!'), this might be the place for you. Parking available.

Located on one of the main roads in Minori, the ★★★**Santa Lucia,** ✆/🖷 089 877 142, is a convenient and inexpensive option, not far from the beach and almost next door to the archaeological park, though just why it was awarded three stars is hard to imagine. The nylon furnishings will delight those with fond memories of the sixties.

Ravello ✉ *84010*   **Eating Out**

Unusually, most of the best dining in Ravello is in the hotels, most notably at **Villa Maria**, at the **Caruso** and at **Palazzo Sasso** (*see* above); non-residents are welcome at any of them, either for lunch or dinner.

By comparison the rest of the restaurants pale into insignificance, but one exception is **Cumpà Cosimo**, Via Roma 44–46, ✆ 089 857 156 (*moderate*), where owner-cook Signora Netta Bottone is always happy to advise diners on her latest concoctions and try out her school English on visitors. She's something of an earth mother, and swears by the fresh produce grown on the family farm in Scala. Framed recommendations, lovingly cut from both national and international papers, line the walls enthusing over recipes handed down by Grandma and the warm, homely atmosphere of this traditional restaurant. A holiday high spot, where any meal feels like a family affair. If you make the trip up to Scala, alongside Ravello, try **Zi'Ntonio**, ✆ 089 857 118 (*moderate*), which serves well-cooked local dishes out on a beautiful covered terrace.

At Maiori, you'll get good fresh fish at **Mammato**, Via Arsenale 6, ✆ 089 877 036 (*moderate*). A glass-fronted restaurant appropriately located overlooking the sea, Mammato is a popular and relaxed venue for beach bums and locals alike. *Closed Wed*. As you leave Maiori, you'll see the **Torre Normanna**, Via D. Taiani, ✆ 089 877 033 (*moderate*), a Saracen tower jutting into the sea, only worth stopping at if you can eat on the outside terrace (*open summer only*) since the acoustics inside are way above any acceptable decibel limit (even by Italian standards). The beautiful setting is accompanied by very good food at reasonable prices.

On a side street in sleepy Minori, is the pretty and floral **Il Giardinello**, Corso V. Emanuele 17 ✆ 089 877 050 (*cheap*). Pass under the leafy archway, and you find yourself in an elegant restaurant, humming with appreciative diners. The menu is varied and interesting, with plenty of fish, but also pasta and the house speciality— pizza for four!

Even if it's not on the agenda, one delightful reason for stopping in Vietri sul Mare is **Ristorante La Locanda**, Corso Umberto 1, ✆ 089 761 070 (*cheap*). Despite the electronic doorbell, the atmosphere is mellow and welcoming. Guests eat upstairs in a stone-walled dining room that flickers with candlelight, so it's probably more suited to dinner *à deux* than a rowdy party. The food is inventive, tasty and plentiful, and served on the attractive hand-painted plates which have made the town famous. Finishing touches, rarely found in an area now consumed by tourism, make this a truly memorable experience— and if you're really good, you might even take home some pottery of your own. *Closed Mon*.

Salerno

Getting There

Unlike some of its neighbours, Salerno is easily accessible by car, and has well organised supervised parking lots, including one by the harbour.

Anywhere else in the south of Italy, a city like Salerno would be an attraction in itself; here it gets lost among the wonders of the Campanian coast—just the big town at the end of the Amalfi drive—and few people ever stop for more than a very brief visit. Nevertheless,

Salerno has its modest charms, not least of which is that it is a clean and orderly place; that should endear it to people who hate Naples. Its setting under a backdrop of mountains is memorable. The Italian highway engineers, showing off as usual, have brought a highway to Salerno on a chain of viaducts, one lofty span after another, an unusual and pleasing ornament for the city; at night the road lights hang on the mountain slopes like strings of fairy lights on a Christmas tree.

Salerno's ancient distinction was its medical school, the oldest and finest of medieval Europe. Traditionally founded by the legendary 'Four Doctors'—an Italian, a Greek, a Jew and an Arab—the school was of the greatest importance in the transmission of Greek and Muslim science into Europe. Most of us, however, may recognize Salerno better as the site of the Allied invasion in September 1943, one of the biggest and most successful such operations of the Second World War. Seven months later Salerno was to become capital of Italy until the liberation was completed.

Salerno's port is on the outskirts of town, and the shore all through the city centre is graced with a pretty park, the Lungomare Trieste. Parallel with it, and two streets back, the Corso Vittorio Emanuele leads into the old town. Here it changes its name to Via dei Mercanti, most colourful of Salerno's old streets. The **cathedral**, a block to the north on Via del Duomo, is set with its façade behind a courtyard, or *quadroporticos* (*currently under restoration*), with a fountain at the centre, and a detached campanile—as if it were not a church at all, but a mosque. It was begun by Robert Guiscard in 1085 and is one of the most ambitious buildings of the early Middle Ages, an idiosyncratic work that shows a faithfulness to early Christian fashions (like the exterior *quadroporticus*). The Corinthian columns around it come from the ancient city of Paestum, not far down the coast. The cathedral's treasures are of the same order as those of the Amalfi coast: another pair of bronze doors from Constantinople, and another beautiful pair of Cosmatesque pulpits, though a surprise comes with the overwhelming mosaic floor, a 1968ft^2 expanse of marble and polychrome tiles of Byzantine inspiration. The building itself has been much restored, and many of the best original details have been preserved in the adjacent **Museo del Duomo** (*open April–Oct daily 9–7; Nov–Mar daily 9–4.30*).

Robert the Cunning and his Blushing Bride

On the inscription across the cathedral façade you can read how the cathedral was built by 'Duke Robert, greatest of conquerors, with his own money'. This was Robert Guiscard, 'the Cunning', one of the first and greatest of the Norman warriors who came to plunder southern Italy in the 11th century. Robert de Hauteville came to Italy in 1046, one of the younger brothers of the Norman family that would one day found a dynasty in Sicily. His elder brother, Drogo, chief of the clan, had no lands to give him, so Robert was on his own, hiring his sword out first to the Lombard Count Pandulf of Capua, later to his brothers or anyone else who could pay for it.

Contemporary accounts describe Robert as a fair-haired, blue-eyed giant. The Byzantine Anna Comnena wrote of him as 'in temper tyrannical, in mind most clever, brave in action, very clever in attacking the wealth and substance of magnates...'. He earned his soubriquet Guiscard for tricks like the taking of Malvita, a fortified monastery in Calabria. A party of unarmed Normans came up to the gate with a coffin, and asked to have a funeral Mass said for one of their comrades. The monks let them in, whereupon the coffin burst open to reveal a very live knight lying on a pile of swords. Combined with cleverness, Robert's formidable strength and skill in battle soon earned him an important position in the south. In 1058 he found a fitting bride, Princess Sichelgaita of the ruling Lombard house of Salerno. Nearly as tall and strong as Robert himself, she loved nothing better than accompanying him into battle, her long blond hair pouring out from her helmet. The pair went from success to success, and capped it all with Robert's papal investiture as Duke of Puglia and Calabria.

But Robert's greatest exploit would not come until 1084, a year before his death. That year there were two popes in Rome, a common occurrence, one supported by the German emperor Henry and the other, Gregory VII, by Robert. When the Normans brought up a big army to force the issue, Rome resisted, and Robert's men (along with Saracen mercenaries from Sicily) took the city and treated it to the worst sacking in its history, far more destructive than anything the 5th-century barbarians ever dared. Gregory—the great reformer Hildebrand before becoming pope—had worked unceasingly for decades to build the power of the papacy; now he had his victory, but the Romans hated him so thoroughly he could not stay in the city. He was forced to accompany Robert to Salerno, where he died soon after. Robert buried him in this cathedral, which he had begun, perhaps in expiation, the same year.

From Salerno you can make an easy excursion up into the mountains to the town of **Cava de' Tirreni**. Near it, perched precariously on the slopes of the Val di Bonea, is a little-visited Benedictine monastery called **La Trinità di Cava**—rebuilt, as usual, in tiresome baroque, but preserving a wealth of 12th–14th-century frescoes, stone-carving and Cosmati work.

Salerno ✉ *84100*   ### Where to Stay

Salerno's hotels are fairly modest and utilitarian. Though the cathedral is well worth a visit, this is not a good base for a holiday. The beach is elbow-room only and covered with litter. Instead head up to Paestum where beaches are cleaner and less crowded. If you just want to stay a couple of nights, the hotels and restaurants should satisfy most explorers' needs.

expensive

At the top end the ★★★★**Jolly Hotel delle Palme**, Lungomare Trieste 1, ☎ 089 225 222, ✆ 089 237 571, is pleasant and reliable, and right on the seafront.

moderate

More than acceptable for an overnight stay is the ★★★**Plaza**, Piazza Ferrovia 42, ☎ 089 224 477, ✆ 089 237 311, right across from the station offering modern and comfortable rooms. Close by, in the pedestrian area, is the ★★★**Montestella**, Corso

Vittorio Emanuele 156, ✆ 089 225 122, 🖷 089 229 167. Convenient for the beach is the ★★★**Fiorenza**, Via Trento 145, ✆/🖷 089 338 800, a clean, well-run hotel with 30 rooms.

cheap

Several cheaper hotels are to be found on or around the Corso Vittorio Emanuele. Try the ★★**Salerno**, Via G. Vicinanza 42, ✆ 089 224 211, 🖷 089 224 432—simple but comfortable. Lastly Salerno also has a youth hostel, **Ostello per la Gioventu' Irno**, Via Luigi Guercio 112, ✆ 089 790 251, 🖷 089 252 649. *Closed daily 10.30–5; curfew 1am.*

Salerno ✉ *84100*

Eating Out

expensive

Nicola dei Principati, Corso Garibaldi 201, ✆ 089 225 435, in the old centre of Salerno, serves mainly fish dishes, including an excellent *linguine con astice* (long pasta with lobster). At **Il Timone**, Via Generale Clark 29, ✆ 089 335 111, the speciality is *tubetti alla pescatrice* (short pasta served with a delicious fish sauce). The second courses, almost all fish, are equally good. *Closed Mon.*

moderate

One of the liveliest restaurants in town, right in the *centro storico*, is the **Vicolo della Neve**, Vicolo della Neve 24, ✆ 089 225 705, an attractive place decorated with wall paintings by some of the many artists who have established it as their local. The chef turns out good Campanian favourites such as *melanzane alla parmigiana*, aubergines cooked in layers with mozzarella, parmesan, tomato and basil, and the classic *pasta e fagioli*. You can also order excellent pizza. *Open evenings only; closed Wed.*

At **Alla Brace**, Lungomare Trieste 11–13, ✆ 089 221 733, as well as the usual fish dishes, you will be offered a host of delicious local specialities such as stuffed peppers, ravioli filled with ricotta, and a remarkable potato soufflé. There is also a wide range of homemade desserts. **Al Cenacolo**, Piazza Alfano I, ✆ 089 228 818, in front of the cathedral, serves excellent seafood and is recommended by the locals.

cheap

Da Sasa, Via Diaz 42, ✆ 089 220 330, is a good cheap trattoria, with traditional home-cooking and especially tasty pasta courses. For good pizza and seafood, **Ristorante Pinocchio**, Lungomare Trieste 56–58, ✆ 089 229 964, is also great value. Head here to dine shoulder to shoulder with Salernitani. *Closed Fri.*

For something sweet, visit the oldest pastry shop in town, the **Pantaleo**.

ambulatory: an aisle around the apse of a church.

atrium: entrance court of a Roman house or early church.

badia: *abbazia*, an abbey or abbey church.

baldacchino: baldachin, a columned stone canopy above the altar of a church.

basilica: a rectangular building, usually divided into three aisles by rows of columns. In Rome this was the common form for law courts and other public buildings, and Roman Christians adapted it for their early churches.

campanile: a bell tower.

campo santo: a cemetery.

cardo: transverse street of a Roman castrum-shaped city.

cartoon: the preliminary sketch for a fresco or tapestry.

caryatid: supporting pillar or column carved into a standing female form; male versions are called telamons.

castrum: a Roman military camp, always nearly rectangular, with straight streets and gates at the cardinal points. Later the Romans founded or refounded cities in this form.

cavea: the semicircle of seats in a classical theatre.

centro storico: historic centre.

ciborium: a tabernacle; the word is often used for large, free-standing tabernacles, or in the sense of a baldacchino.

chiaroscuro: the arrangement or treatment of light and dark in a painting.

comune: commune, or commonwealth, referring to the governments of the free cities of the Middle Ages. Today it denotes any local government, form the Comune di Roma down to the smallest village.

condottiere: the leader of a band of mercenaries in late medieval and Renaissance times.

confraternity: a religious lay brotherhood, often serving as a neighbourhood mutual aid and burial society, or following some specific charitable work (Michelangelo, for example, belonged to one that cared for condemned prisoners in Rome).

contrapposto: a dramatic but rather unnatural twist in a statue, especially in a Mannerist or baroque work, derived from Hellenistic and Roman art.

Architectural, Artistic & Historic Terms

Cosmati work: or *Cosmatesque*; referring to a distinctive style of inlaid marble or enamel chips used in architectural decoration (pavements, pulpits, paschal candlesticks, etc.) in medieval Italy. The Cosmati family were its greatest practitioners.

cupola: a dome.

decumanus: street of a Roman castrum-shaped city parallel to the longer axis, the central, main avenue called the Decumanus Major.

duomo: cathedral.

forum: the central square of a Roman town, with its most important temples and public buildings. 'Forum' means 'outside', as the original Forum was outside the city walls.

fresco: wall painting, the most important Italian medium of art since Etruscan times. The artist draws the sinopia (q.v.) on the wall. This is covered with plaster, only a little at a time, as the paint must be on the plaster before it dries. Leonardo da Vinci's endless attempts to find clever shortcuts ensured that little of his work would survive.

Ghibellines: one of the two great medieval parties, supporting the Holy Roman Emperors.

grotesques: carved or painted faces used in Etruscan and later Roman decoration; Raphael and other artist rediscovered them in the 'grotto' of Nero's Golden House in Rome.

Guelphs (*see* Ghibellines): a great political faction of medieval Italy, supporters of the Pope.

intarsia: work in inlaid wood or marble.

narthex: the enclosed porch of a church.

palazzo: not just a palace, but any large, important building (though the word comes from the Imperial palatium on Rome's Palatine Hill).

Pantocrator: Christ 'ruler of all', a common subject for apse paintings and mosaics in areas influenced by Byzantine art.

piano: upper floor or story in a building; piano nobile, the first floor.

pieve: a parish church, especially in the north.

podestà: mayor or governor from outside a *comune*, usually chosen by the emperor or over-lord; sometimes a factionalized city would invite in a *podestà* for a time to sort it out.

polyptych: an altarpiece composed of more than three panels.

predella: smaller paintings on panels below the main subject of a painted altarpiece.

presepio: a Christmas crib.

putti: flocks of plaster cherubs with rosy cheeks and bums that infested Baroque Italy.

quadriga: chariot pulled by four horses.

quattrocento: the 1400s—the Italian way of referring to centuries (duecento, trecento, quattrocento, cinquecento, etc.).

rocca: a citadel.

Sacra Conversazione: Madonna enthroned with saints.

scuola: the headquarters of a confraternity or guild, usually adjacent to a church.

sinopia: the layout of a fresco (q.v.), etched by the artist on the wall before the plaster is applied. Often these are works of art in their own right.

thermae: Roman baths.

tondo: round relief, painting or terracotta.

transenna: marble screen separating the altar area from the rest of an early Christian church.

triptych: a painting, especially an altarpiece, in three sections.

trompe l'œil: art that uses perspective effects to deceive the eye—for example, to create the illusion of depth on a flat surface, or to make columns and arches painted on a wall see real.

tympanum: the semicircular space, often bearing a painting or relief, above a portal.

The fathers of modern Italian were Dante, Manzoni and television. Each played its part in creating a national language from an infinity of regional and local dialects; the Florentine Dante, the first to write in the vernacular, did much to put the Tuscan dialect into the foreground of Italian literature. Manzoni's revolutionary novel, *I Promessi Sposi*, heightened national consciousness by using an everyday language all could understand in the 19th century. Television in the last few decades has performed an even more spectacular linguistic unification; although many Italians still speak a dialect at home, school and work, their TV idols insist on proper Italian.

Italians are not especially apt at learning other languages. English lessons, however, have been the rage for years, and at most hotels and restaurants there will be someone who speaks some English. In small towns and out-of-the-way places, finding an Anglophone may prove more difficult. The words and phrases below should help you out in most situations, but the ideal way to come to Italy is with some Italian under your belt; your visit will be richer, and you're much more likely to make some Italian friends.

Pronunciation

Italian words are pronounced phonetically. Every vowel and consonant is sounded. Most consonants are the same as in English, exceptions are the c which, when followed by an 'e' or 'i', is pronounced like the English 'ch' (*cinque* thus becomes cheenquay). Italian g is also soft before 'i' or 'e' as in *giro*, or jee-roh. H is never sounded; r is trilled, like the Scottish r; z is pronounced like 'ts' or 'ds'. The consonants sc before the vowels 'i' or 'e' become like the English 'sh'; ch is pronouced like a 'k' as in Chianti; gn as 'nya' (thus *bagno* is pronounced ban-yo); while gli is pronounced like the middle of the word million (Castiglione, pronounced Ca-stil-yohn-ay).

Vowel pronunciation is as follows: a is as in English father; e when unstressed is pronounced like 'a' in fate as in *padre*, when stressed it can be the same or like the 'e' in pet (*bello*); i is like the 'i' in machine, o like 'e', has two sounds, 'o' as in hope when unstressed (*tacchino*), and usually 'o' as in rock when stressed (*morte*); u is pronounced like the 'u' in June.

The stress usually (but not always!) falls on the penultimate syllable.

Language

Useful Words and Phrases

yes/no/maybe	*sì/no/forse*	Speak slowly	*Parla lentamente*
I don't know	*Non lo so*	Could you assist me?	*Potrebbe aiutarmi?*
I don't understand	*Non capisco*	Help!	*Aiuto!*
(Italian)	(*italiano*)	Please	*Per favore*
Does someone here	*C'è qualcuno qui che*	Thanks (very much)	(*Molto*) *grazie*
speak English?	*parla inglese?*	You're welcome	*Prego*

It doesn't matter	Non importa	Why?	Perché?
All right	Va bene	How?	Come?
Excuse me	Mi scusi	How much?	Quanto?
Be careful!	Attenzione!	I am lost	Mi sono smarrito
Nothing	Niente	I am hungry	Ho fame
I; is urgent!	E urgente!	I am thirsty	Ho sete
How are you?	Come stai? (informal)	I am sorry	Mi dispiace
	sta (formal)	I am tired	Sono stanco
Well, and you?	Bene, e lei?	I am sleepy	Ho sonno
What is your name?	Come si chiama lei?	I am ill	Mi sento male
Hello	Salve or ciao	Leave me alone	Lasciami in pace
	(both informal)	good	buono/bravo
Good morning	Buon giorno	bad	male/cattivo
	(formal hello)	It's all the same	Fa lo stesso
Good afternoon,	Buona sera (also	slow	lento/piano
evening	formal hello)	fast	rapido
Good night	Buona notte	big	grande
Goodbye	Arrivederla (formal)	small	piccolo
	Arrivederci (informal)	hot	caldo
What do you call	Come si chiama	cold	freddo
this in Italian?	questo in italiano?	up	su
What?	Che cosa?	down	giù
Who?	Chi?	here	qui
Where?	Dove?	there	lì
When?	Quando?		

Shopping, Service, Sightseeing

I would like ...	Vorrei ...	money	soldi
Where is/are?. . .	Dov'è/Dove sono?...	museum	museo
How much is it?	Quanto via questo?	newspaper (foreign)	giornale (straniero)
open	aperto	chemist	farmacia
closed	chiuso	police station	commissariato
cheap	a buon mercato	policeman	poliziotto
expensive	caro	post office	ufficio postale
bank	banca	sea	mare
beach	spiaggia	shop	negozio
bed	letto	telephone	telefono
church	chiesa	tobacco shop	tabacchaio
entrance	entrata	WC	toilette/bagno
exit	uscita	men	Signori/Uomini
hospital	ospedale	women	Signore/Donne

Time

What time is it?	Che ore sono?	today	oggi
month	mese	yesterday	ieri
week	settimana	tomorrow	domani
day	giorno	soon	fra poco
morning	mattina	later	più tardi
afternoon	pomeriggio	It is too early	E troppo presto
evening	sera	It is too late	E troppo tardi

Days

Monday	*lunedì*	Friday	*venerdì*
Tuesday	*martedì*	Saturday	*sabato*
Wednesday	*mercoledì*	Sunday	*domenica*
Thursday	*giovedì*		

Numbers

one	*uno/una*	twenty	*venti*
two	*due*	twenty-one	*ventuno*
three	*tre*	twenty-two	*ventidue*
four	*quattro*	thirty	*trenta*
five	*cinque*	thirty-one	*trentuno*
six	*sei*	forty	*quaranta*
seven	*sette*	fifty	*cinquanta*
eight	*otto*	sixty	*sessanta*
nine	*nove*	seventy	*settanta*
ten	*dieci*	eighty	*ottanta*
eleven	*undici*	ninety	*novanta*
twelve	*dodici*	hundred	*cento*
thirteen	*tredici*	one hundred and one	*cent'uno*
fourteen	*quattordici*	two hundred	*due cento*
fifteen	*quindici*	thousand	*mille*
sixteen	*sedici*	two thousand	*due mila*
seventeen	*diciasette*	million	*milione*
eighteen	*diciotto*	billion	*miliardo*
nineteen	*diciannove*		

Transport

airport	*aeroporto*	port station	*stazione marittima*
bus stop	*fermata*	ship	*nave*
bus/coach	*autobus/pulmino*	automobile	*macchina*
railway station	*stazione(ferroviaria)*	taxi	*tassi*
train	*treno*	ticket	*biglietto*
train/platform	*binario*	customs	*dogana*
port	*porto*	seat (reserved)	*posto (prenotato)*

Travel Directions

I want to go to . . .	*Voglio andare a ...*	When does the next train leave?	*Quando parte il prossimo treno?*
How can I get to...?	*Come posso arrivare a ...?*	From where does it leave?	*Da dove parte?*
The next stop, please	*La prossima fermata, per favore*	How long does the trip take?	*Quanto tempo dura il viaggio?*
Where is ... / where is it?	*Dove ... /Dov'è?*	How much is the fare?	*Quant'è il biglietto?*
How far is it to ...?	*Quanto siamo lontani da ... ?*	Have a good trip!	*Buon viaggio!*
What is the name of this station?	*Come si chiama questa stazione?*	near	*vicino*
		far	*lontano*

left	*sinistra*	south	*sud/mezzogiorno* (the South of Italy)
right	*destra*		
straight ahead	*sempre diritto*	east	*est/oriente*
forward	*avanti*	west	*ovest/occidentale*
back	*indietro*	around the corner	*dietro l'angolo*
north	*nord/settentrionale* (the North of Italy)	crossroads	*bivio*
		street/road	*strada*
		square	*piazza*

Driving

car hire	*noleggio macchina*	breakdown	*panna*
motorbike/scooter	*motocicletta/Vespa*	driver's licence	*patente di guida*
bicycle	*bicicletta*	driver	*guidatore*
petrol/diesel	*benzina/gasolio*	speed	*velocità*
garage	*garage*	danger	*pericolo*
This doesn't work	*Questo non funziona*	parking	*parcheggio*
		no parking	*divieto di sosta*
mechanic	*meccanico*	narrow	*stretto*
map/town plan	*carta/pianta*	bridge	*ponte*
Where is the road to . . . ?	*Dov'è la strada per. . . ?*	toll	*pedaggio*
		to slow down	*rallentare*

Italian Menu Vocabulary

Antipasti

These appetizers can include almost anything, among the most common are:

antipasto misto	mixed antipasto	*gamberi ai fagioli*	prawns with beans
bruschetta	toast with garlic and tomatoes	*mozzarella (in carrozza)*	cow or buffalo cheese (fried with bread in batter)
carciofi (sott'olio)	artichokes (in oil)		
crostini	liver pâté on toast	*olive*	olives
frutti di mare	seafood	*prosciutto (con melone)*	raw ham (with melon)
funghi (trifolati)	mushrooms (with anchovies, garlic and lemon)	*salame*	cured pork
		salsiccia	sausage

Minestre e Pasta

These dishes are the principal first courses (*primi piatti*) served throughout Italy.

agnolotti	meat-filled pasta	*minestrone*	soup with meat, vegetables and pasta
cacciucco	spiced fish soup		
cappelletti	small ravioli, often in broth	*orecchiette*	ear-shaped pasta, often served with turnip greens
crespelle	crêpes		
fettuccine	long strips of pasta	*panzerotti*	ravioli filled with mozzarella, anchovies and egg
frittata	omelette		
gnocchi	potato dumplings		
minestra di verdura	thick vegetable soup	*pappardelle alla lepre*	flat pasta ribbons with hare sauce

pasta e fagioli	soup with beans, bacon and tomatoes	spaghetti alla carbonara	with bacon, eggs and black pepper
pastina in brodo	tiny pasta in broth	al pomodoro	with tomato sauce
penne all'arrabbiata	pasta tubes in spicy tomato sauce	al sugo/ragù	with meat sauce
polenta	cake or pudding of corn semolina, fried, baked or grilled	alle vongole	with clam sauce
		stracciatella	broth with eggs and cheese
risotto (alla Milanese)	rice cooked with stock, saffron and wine	tagliatelle	flat egg noodles
		tortellini al pomodoro/ panna/ in brodo	stuffed rings of pasta filled with meat and cheese, served with tomato sauce, cream, or in broth
spaghetti all' Amatriciana	with tomatoes, bacon and garlic, plus pecorino cheese		
		vermicelli	very thin spaghetti

Second Courses—*Carne* (Meat)

abbacchio	milk-fed lamb	lepre (in salmi)	hare (marinated in wine, herbs etc)
agnello	lamb		
anatra	duck	lombo di maiale	pork loin
animelle	sweetbreads	lumache	snails
arista	pork loin	maiale (al latte)	pork (cooked in milk)
arrosto misto	mixed roast meats	manzo	beef
bistecca alla Fiorentina	Florentine beef steak	osso buco	braised veal knuckle with herbs
bocconcini	veal mixed with ham and cheese and fried		
		pancetta	bacon
bollito misto	stew of boiled meats	pernice	partridge
braciola	pork chop	petto di pollo	boned chicken breast
brasato di manzo	braised beef	(alla Fiorentina/ Bolognese/ Sorpresa)	(fried in butter/ with ham and stuffed and deep fried)
bresaola	dried salt beef served with lemon, olive oil and parsley		
		piccione	pigeon
capretto	kid	pizzaiola	beef steak with tomato and oregano sauce
capriolo	roe buck		
carne di castrato/suino	mutton/pork	pollo	chicken
carpaccio	thin slices of raw beef served like bresaola	(alla cacciatora/ alla diavola/ al Marengo)	(with tomatoes and mushrooms cooked in wine/grilled/fried with tomatoes, garlic & wine)
cassoeula	winter stew with pork and cabbage		
Cervello (al burro nero)	brains (in black butter sauce)	polpette	meatballs
		quaglie	quails
cervo	venison	rane	frogs
cinghiale	boar	rognoni	kidneys
coniglio	rabbit	saltimbocca	veal scallop with prosciutto and sage, cooked in pieces of beef or veal, usually stewed
cotoletta (alla Milanese/ alla Bolognese)	veal cutlet (fried in breadcrumbs/with ham and cheese)		
fagiano	pheasant		
faraona (alla creta)	guinea fowl (in earthenware pot)	stufato	beef braised in white wine with vegetables
		tacchino	turkey
fegato alla veneziana	liver and onions	trippa	tripe
involtini	rolled slices of veal with filling	vitello	veal

Pesce (Fish)

acciughe or alici	anchovies	merluzzo	cod
anguilla	eel	nasello	hake
aragosta	lobster	orata/dorata	gilthead
aringhe	herrings	ostrice	oysters
baccalà	salt cod	pesce azzuro	various small fish
bonito	small tuna	pesce S. Pietro	John Dory
branzino	sea bass	pesce spada	swordfish
calamari	squid	polipi	octopus
conchiglie	scallops	rombo	turbot
cefalo	grey mullet	sarde	sardines
cozze	mussels	seppie	cuttlefish
datteri di mare	razor (or date) mussels	sgombro	mackerel
		sogliola	sole
dentice	dentex (perch-like fish)	squadro	monkfish
		tonno	tuna
fritto misto	mixed fish fry, with squid and shrimp	triglia	red mullet (rouget)
		trota	trout
gamberetto	shrimp	trota salmonata	salmon trout
gamberi (di fiume)	prawns (crayfish)	vongole	small clams
granchio	crab	zuppa di pesce	mixed fish in sauce or stew
insalata di mare	seafood salad		
lampre	lamprey		

Contorni (Side Dishes, Vegetables)

asparagi	asparagus	lattuga	lettuce
(alla Fiorentina)	(with fried eggs)	lenticchie	lentils
broccoli	broccoli	melanzane	aubergine/eggplant
(calabrese, romana)	(green, spiral)	(al forno)	(filled and baked)
carciofi (alla giudia)	artichokes (deep fried)	patate (fritte)	potatoes (fried)
		peperonata	stewed peppers, onions and tomatoes
cardi	cardoons, thistles		
carote	carrots	peperoni	sweet peppers
cavolfiore	cauliflower	piselli (al prosciutto)	peas (with ham)
cavolo	cabbage	pomodoro	tomato
ceci	chickpeas	porri	leeks
cetriolo	cucumber	radicchio	red chicory
cipolla	onion	radiche	radishes
fagioli	white beans	rapa	turnip
fagiolini	French (green) beans	sedano	celery
fave	broad beans	spinaci	spinach
finocchio	fennel	verdure	greens
funghi (porcini)	mushroom (boletus)	zucca	pumpkin
insalata	salad	zucchini	courgettes

Formaggio (Cheese)

Bel Paese	soft, white cow's cheese	fontina	rich cow's milk cheese
cascio/ casciocavallo	pale yellow, often sharp cheese	groviera	mild cheese
		Gorgonzola	soft blue cheese

Parmigiano	Parmesan cheese	*provolone*	sharp, tangy cheese; *dolce* is more mild
pecorino	sharp sheep's cheese	*stracchino*	soft white cheese

Frutta (Fruit, Nuts)

albicocche	apricots	*mandorle*	almonds
ananas	pineapple	*melograna*	pomegranate
arance	oranges	*mele*	apples
banane	bananas	*melone*	melon
cachi	persimmon	*more*	blackberries
ciliege	cherries	*nespola*	medlar fruit
cocomero	watermelon	*nocciole*	hazelnuts
composta di frutta	stewed fruit	*noci*	walnuts
dattero	date	*pera*	pear
fichi	figs	*pesca*	peach
fragole (con panna)	strawberries (with cream)	*pesca noce*	nectarine
frutta di stagione	fruit in season	*pompelmo*	grapefruit
lamponi	raspberries	*pignoli*	pine nuts
macedonia di frutta	fruit salad	*susina*	plum
mandarino	tangerine	*prugna secca*	prune
		uve	grapes

Dolci (Desserts)

Amaretti	macaroons	*panforte*	dense cake of chocolate, almonds and preserved fruit
cannoli	crisp pastry tube filled with ricotta, cream, chocolate or fruit	*Saint Honoré*	meringue cake
		semifreddo	refrigerated cake
coppa	assorted ice cream	*sorbetto*	sorbet
crema caramella	crème caramel	*spumone*	a soft ice cream or mousse
crostata	fruit flan		
gelato (produzione propria)	ice cream (homemade)	*tiramisù*	mascarpone, coffee, chocolate and sponge fingers
granita	flavoured ice, usually lemon or coffee	*torrone*	nougat
		torta	tart
Monte Bianco	chestnut pudding with whipped cream	*torta millefoglie*	layered custard tart
panettone	sponge cake with candied fruit and raisins	*zabaglione*	whipped eggs, sugar and Marsala wine, served hot
		Zuppa Inglese	trifle

Drinks

acqua minerale con/senza gas	mineral water with/without fizz	*latte*	milk
aranciata	orange soda	*(magro)*	(skimmed)
birra (alla spina)	beer (draught)	*limonata*	lemon soda
caffè (freddo)	coffee (iced)	*sugo di frutta*	fruit juice
cioccolata	hot chocolate	*tè*	tea
(con panna)	(with cream)	*vino (rosso, bianco, rosato)*	wine (red, white, rosé)

Cooking Terms, Miscellaneous

aceto (balsamico)	vinegar (balsamic)	mostarda	sweet mustard sauce, served with meat
affumicato	smoked		
aglio	garlic	olio	oil
ai ferri	grilled	pane (tostato)	bread (toasted)
al forno	baked	panini	sandwiches
alla brace	braised	panna	fresh cream
arrosto	roasted	pepe	pepper
bicchiere	glass	peperoncini	hot chilli peppers
burro	butter	piatto	plate
cacciagione	game	prezzemolo	parsley
conto	bill	rosmarino	rosemary
costoletta/cotoletta	chop	sale	salt
coltello	knife	salmi	wine marinade
cucchiaio	spoon	salsa	sauce
filetto	fillet	salvia	sage
forchetta	fork	senape	mustard
forno	oven	tartufi	truffles
fritto	fried	tazza	cup
ghiaccio	ice	tavola	table
limone	lemon	tovagliolo	napkin
magro	lean meat/or pasta without meat	tramezzini	finger sandwiches
		in umido	stewed
marmellata	jam	uovo	egg
miele	honey	zucchero	sugar

General and Travel

Barzini, Luigi, *The Italians* (Hamish Hamilton, 1964). A perhaps too clever account of the Italians by an Italian journalist living in London, but one of the classics.

Douglas, Norman, *Old Calabria* (Century, 1983). Reprint of a rascally travel classic.

Goethe, J.W., *Italian Journey* (Penguin Classics, 1982). An excellent example of a genius turned to mush by Italy; brilliant insights and big, big mistakes.

Haycraft, John, *Italian Labyrinth* (Penguin, 1987). One of the latest attempts to unravel the Italian mess.

Hutton, Edward, *Naples and Campania Revisited* (Hollis & Carter).

Morton, H.V., *A Traveller in Southern Italy* (Methuen, 1957, 1969). Among the most readable and delightful accounts of the region in print. Morton is a sincere scholar, and a true gentleman. Also a good friend to cats.

Nichols, Peter, *Italia, Italia* (Macmillan, 1973). An account of modern Italy by an old Italy hand.

History

Acton, Harold, *The Bourbons of Naples* (Methuen, 1956).

Burckhardt, Jacob, *The Civilization of the Renaissance in Italy* (Harper & Row, 1975). The classic on the subject (first published 1860), the mark against which scholars still level their poison arrows of revisionism.

Carcopino, Jérome, *Daily Life in Ancient Rome* (Penguin, 1981). A thorough and lively account of Rome at the height of Empire—guaranteed to evoke empathy from modern city dwellers.

Ginsborg, Paul, A *History of Contemporary Italy: Society and Politics 1943–1988* (Penguin, 1990). A good modern account of events up to the fall of Rome.

Hale, J.R., (ed.), *A Concise Encyclopaedia of the Italian Renaissance* (Thames and Hudson, 1981). An excellent reference guide, with many concise, well-written essays.

Hibbert, Christopher, *Benito Mussolini* and *Rise and Fall of the House of Medici* and *Rome* (Penguin, 1965, 1979, 1985).

Further Reading

Joll, James, *Gramsci* (Fontana, 1977). A look at the father of modern Italian communism, someone we all should get to know better.

Masson, Georgina, *Frederick II of Hohenstaufen* (London, 1957).

Norwich, John Julius, *The Normans in the South* (Thames and Hudson, 1967).

Procacci, Giuliano, *History of the Italian People* (Penguin, 1973). An in-depth view from the year 1000 to the present—also an introduction to the wit and subtlety of the best Italian scholarship.

Rand, Edward Kennard, *Founders of the Middle Ages* (Dover reprint, New York), a little-known but incandescently brilliant work that can explain Jerome, Augustine, Boethius and other intellectual currents of the decaying classical world.

Art and Literature

Boccaccio, Giovanni, *The Decameron* (Penguin, 1972). The ever-young classic by one of the fathers of Italian literature. Its irreverent worldliness still provides a salutary antidote to whatever dubious ideas persist in your mental baggage.

Calvino, Italo, *Invisible Cities*, *If Upon a Winter's Night a Traveller* (Picador). Provocative fantasies that could only have been written by an Italian. Something even better is his recent compilation of Italian folktales, a little bit Brothers Grimm and a little bit Fellini.

Cellini, *Autobiography of Benvenuto Cellini* (Penguin, trans. George Bull). Fun reading by a swashbuckling braggart and world-class liar.

Clark, Kenneth, *Leonardo da Vinci* (Penguin).

Dante Alighieri, *The Divine Comedy* (plenty of equally good translations). Few poems have ever had such a mythical significance for a nation. Anyone serious about understanding Italy and the Italian world view will need more than a passing acquaintance with Dante.

Gadda, Carlo Emilio, *That Awful Mess on Via Merulana* (Quartet Books, 1980). Italy during the Fascist era.

Henig, Martin (ed.), *A Handbook of Roman Art* (Phaidon, 1983). Essays on all aspects of ancient Roman art.

Lawrence, D.H., *Etruscan Places* (Olive Press).

Levi, Carlo, *Christ Stopped at Eboli* (Penguin, 1982). Disturbing post-war realism.

Murray, Linda, *The High Renaissance* and *The Late Renaissance and Mannerism* (Thames and Hudson, 1977). Excellent introduction to the period; also Peter and Linda Murray, *The Art of the Renaissance* (Thames and Hudson, 1963).

Pavese, Cesare, *The Moon and the Bonfire* (Quartet, 1979). Postwar classic.

Petrarch, Francesco, *Canzoniere and Other Works* (Oxford, 1985). The most famous poems by the 'First Modern Man'.

Vasari, Giorgio, *Lives of the Artists* (Penguin, 1985). Readable, anecdotal accounts of the Renaissance greats by the father of art history, also the first professional Philistine.

Wittkower, Rudolf, *Art and Architecture in Italy 1600–1750* (Pelican, 1986). The Bible on baroque, erudite and full of wit.

Main page references are in **bold**. Page references to maps are in *italics*

Index

Also Available from Cadogan Guides...

Country Guides

Antarctica
Belize
Central Asia
China: The Silk Routes
Egypt
France: Southwest France;
    Dordogne, Lot & Bordeaux
France: Southwest France;
    Gascony & the Pyrenees
France: Brittany
France: The Loire
France: The South of France
France: Provence
France: The Côte d'Azur
Germany: Bavaria
India
India: South India
India: Goa
Ireland
Ireland: Southwest Ireland
Ireland: Northern Ireland
Italy
Italy: The Bay of Naples and Southern Italy
Italy: Italian Riviera
Italy: Lombardy, Milan and the Italian Lakes
Italy: Tuscany and Umbria
Italy: Venetia and the Dolomites
Japan
Morocco
Portugal
Portugal: The Algarve
Scotland
Scotland's Highlands and Islands
South Africa, Swaziland and Lesotho
Spain
Spain: Southern Spain
Spain: Northern Spain
Syria & Lebanon
Tunisia
Turkey
Western Turkey
Yucatán and Southern Mexico

City Guides

Amsterdam
Brussels, Bruges, Ghent & Antwerp
Edinburgh
Florence, Siena, Pisa & Lucca
Italy: Three Cities—Rome, Florence, Venice
Italy: Three Cities—Rome, Naples, Capri
Italy: Three Cities—Venice, Padua, Verona
Japan: Three Cities—Tokyo, Kyoto, Ancient
    Nara
Spain: Three Cities—Granada, Seville,
    Cordoba
London
London, Paris
Madrid
Manhattan
Moscow & St Petersburg
Paris
Prague
Rome
Venice

Island Guides

Caribbean and Bahamas
NE Caribbean; The Leeward Is.
SE Caribbean; The Windward Is.
Jamaica & the Caymans

Greek Islands
Crete
Mykonos, Santorini & the Cyclades
Rhodes & the Dodecanese
Corfu & the Ionian Islands

Madeira & Porto Santo
Malta
Sicily

Plus...

Southern Africa on the Wild Side
Bugs, Bites & Bowels
Travel by Cargo Ship
London Markets

Available from good bookshops or via, in the UK, **Grantham Book Services**, Isaac Newton Way,
Alma Park Industrial Estate, Grantham NG31 9SD, ✆ (01476) 541 080, ⊕ 541 061;
and in North America from **The Globe Pequot Press**, 6, Business Park Road, Old Saybrook,
Connecticut 06475-0833, ✆ (800) 243 0495, ⊕ 820 2329.